FORWARD

In a year with high-profile rider changes, exciting rookies and a new manufacturer joining the premier-class, the 2017 FIM MotoGP™ World Championship started with an extra special air of anticipation under the floodlights in Qatar.

The big question on everybody's lips was whether anyone would be able to take the championship fight to Repsol Honda's Marc Marquez, and stop him charging towards a fourth title in five years. Would Jorge Lorenzo bring Ducati back to title glory? Would Maverick Viñales start off where Lorenzo left off on the Yamaha? Would one of the four rookies, including then Moto2™ Champion Johann Zarco, make life difficult for the regular top finishers? Or would it be the established guard like Valentino Rossi, Dani Pedrosa or Andrea Dovizioso that would dethrone Marquez?

If the first two races were anything to go by, it seemed as if the championship had been set, as Maverick Viñales adapted to the Yamaha with ease taking two victories in his maiden races with the Japanese manufacturer. Marquez on the other hand struggled in the early stages of the season, and it looked like 2017 was not going to be his year. On top of that, Jorge Lorenzo's adaptation to the Ducati was not quite going to plan, as the change in aerodynamic regulations affected him more than other riders on the grid. Yet the racing was nonetheless close with the battles as fierce as ever as the world's top 23 riders put on a fantastic show for fans.

By the halfway point the championship already painted a significantly different picture. Dovizioso showed that the Ducati was a winning package, Marquez had bounced back, and the Yamahas had begun to encounter difficulties. Add to that the ever-improving KTMs with Pol Espargaro and Bradley Smith, the competitive Aprilias with Aleix Espargaro, as well as the Suzukis, and the title hunt was still wide open. An untimely injury before his home race in Misano for Valentino Rossi significantly hindered his championship aspirations, though this also coincided with an upswing in form from his ex-teammate Lorenzo.

At the same time, it was often the independent team riders that were the stars on Sunday. Podiums and front rows from Danilo Petrucci, Johann Zarco and Jonas Folger, coupled with fantastic rides from the likes of Cal Crutchlow and Jack Miller meant that fans were always left sitting at the edge of their seats, never quite sure what to expect in the title hunt. Phillip Island being the prime example: races do not get better than that!

The title hunt, I'm glad to say, did come right down to the very last race in Valencia once again; for the third time in five years we enjoyed an astonishing victory from Dani Pedrosa, his second of the 2017 season. MotoGP fans enjoyed stunning performances and amazing on-track battles from both Andrea Dovizioso and Marc Marquez, with the pair lining up on the final grid of the season with a chance at taking home the most coveted motorcycle racing trophy in the world. Dovizioso had to work harder for the crown, but it was Marquez's to lose. Come the big day, there was more drama than you could have asked for. Without giving too much away: this is the first time I have ever seen a title saved by an elbow and a knee in such spectacular style!

Of course none of this would be possible without the continuous stream of incredible talent coming up through the ranks. The intermediate Moto2™ Championship saw Italian Franco Morbidelli crowned World Champion in Sepang this year, after Swiss rider Tom Lüthi pushed him all the way until injury cut his season short. Battles raged on track in every round, as resurgent veterans like Mattia Pasini were joined by fast rookies such as Pecco Bagnaia to delight crowds with what was one of the best Moto2™ seasons since it started in 2010.

Those remaining in Moto2™ might be touch wary after watching the lightweight-class Moto3™ World Championship and triumphant Spaniard Joan Mir. Mir, who will step up a class next year, had a record braking year, where he showed not only speed, but also race-craft and maturity. Though Mir's 10 victories don't necessarily paint the full picture of the other talents that the class has unearthed, with great rides by the likes of Romano Fenati, Jorge Martin, Aron Canet, John McPhee and many more that graced the podiums and front rows throughout the season.

Just thinking about all the on-track action that we have seen this year, is already making me eager to see the red lights go out in Qatar to start what will no doubt be another fantastic season of racing in MotoGP in 2018. But until then, I hope you enjoy reliving the 2017 season as much as I do.

CERMELO | *EZPELETA*

DORNA SPORTS CEO
NOVEMBER 2017

Published in November 2017

A catalogue record for this book is available from the British Library

ISBN 978-1-527214-36-1

PUBLISHED BY | Motocom Limited, Liscombe Park, Liscombe East, Soulbury, Bucks, LU7 0JL, UK www.motocom.co.uk

PRINTED & BOUND BY | Gomer Press, Llandysul Enterprise Park, Llandysul, Ceredigion SA44 4JL

This product is officially licensed by Dorna SL, owners of the MotoGP trademark (© Dorna 2017)

EDITORIAL DIRECTOR | Julian Ryder

DESIGN & ARTWORK | Peter Neal

SPECIAL SALES & ADVERTISING MANAGER | David Dew (david@motocom.co.uk)

PHOTOGRAPHY | Front cover and race action by Andrew Northcott / AJRN Sports Photography; studio technical images of bikes (pp21-33) and studio rider images (pp36-43) by Dorna; other technical images (pp14–18) by Neil Spalding

AUTHOR'S ACKNOWLEDGEMENTS | Thanks to photographer Andrew Northcott, contributors Mat Oxley, Neil Spanding, Mat Birt, Neil Morrison and Barry Coleman, and official MotoGP statistician Martin Raines. Couldn't have done it without you!

I would also like to acknowledge the support of my colleagues at BT Sport: Keith Huewen, Neil Hodgson, Colin Edwards, James Toseland, Gavin Emmett, Suzi Perry, and the entire crew.

CONTENTS

IT KEEPS GETTING BETTER

MOTOGP'S 69TH SEASON WAS ANOTHER CLASSIC – THE BATTLE RAGED UP FRONT ALL YEAR AND THE RACING WAS AS THRILLING AND UNPREDICTABLE AS EVER.

MotoGP 2016 broke a few records: never had there been so many different race winners in a season and never had there been so many crashes. The two numbers were linked, of course. Riders and teams were working their way into a new technical era, so results were up and down, just as the riders were up and down. It was thrilling and unpredictable season. Some dared called it the best-ever. But 2017 was even better.

Tension was high from round one to round 18, four riders and three factories were in the hunt for much of the season and the title went down to the last race. That's a proper championship.

In the end, the panache of Marc Marquez won the day, again. When he was crowned at Valencia the 24-year-old Spaniard took two new records that highlight his standing in the history of the sport. He became the youngest rider to win four premier-class titles, taking that record from Valentino Rossi. And he became the first rider in 69 years of Grand Prix racing to win at least five races per season, across three or more categories. Previously, Mike Hailwood had achieved at least five victories per season over seven years, between 1961 and 1967. Most people consider either Rossi or Hailwood to be the greatest riders of all time, but for how long?

Marquez's fourth MotoGP title in five seasons was very different

from the previous three. Except in the way he rode: like a rodeo rider, at eight or nine corners out of every ten. His crash rate was as high as ever – 27 tumbles across 18 races – but nearly all of them in practice. And he won the championship, which is all that really matters. His racing philosophy is the you-can't-make-an-omelette-without-breaking-eggs racing philosophy.

No other bike racer has left as much rubber on racetracks as Marquez. And while others lay rubber with the rear tyre, he lays rubber with the rear and the front, most spectacularly during Malaysian GP practice where most of put lane had its jaw on the floor as he laid a five metre smear of rubber with his front, without crashing. Marquez has a greater ability to adapt to different situations and ride around problems than did Casey Stoner, which is saying something. Not many will admit it, but most of his rivals are in awe of his skills, even though they know he's far from unbeatable.

The tale of the 2017 championship is a tale of Marquez riding around problems, while developing a significantly new motorcycle and adapting to two significantly new front tyres. He made a grim start to the championship, scoring just 13 points from the first two races, while Maverick Viñales roared off into the distance, with a full 50 points.

Viñales had also dominated preseason testing, topping each of the three sessions at Sepang, Phillip Island and Qatar, so he looked like he might be unbeatable just about everywhere. Honda meanwhile seemed in trouble, while Ducati were once again there or thereabouts. The title seemed to be going Yamaha's way: Viñales won two of the first three races and Rossi was on the podium at all three.

There was a blip at Jerez, where the new Movistar team-mates struggled their way around a very greasy track, then they were back at it at Le Mans, duelling all the way for victory. Well, nearly all the way. Rossi crashed with three corners to go. The next finisher after Viñales was dazzling rookie Johann Zarco, riding last year's Yamaha. The closest non-Yamaha finisher was Dani Pedrosa, almost eight seconds back and another three ahead of top Ducati, Andrea Dovizioso. As Pedrosa crossed the finish line his Repsol Honda team-mate was already back in his motorhome, licking his wounds after a second crash and DNF in five races. With almost a

third of the season done, Marquez was 27 points behind Viñales, with Rossi and Pedrosa also ahead of him on points.

But what most people didn't know was that the championship tipping point had already happened. The 2017 MotoGP title changed forever on Friday evening at Le Mans, when the riders voted to switch to a different construction front tyre. Only three voted against the harder carcass tyre and Viñales was one of them.

It is significant that Dovizioso won the next race at Mugello and four of the next seven races, thus commencing his title attempt, while Viñales all but disappeared from view. The new tyre gave to Dovizioso and Ducati, while taking away from Viñales and Yamaha. The Ducati brakes deep into turns, so the stiffer tyre worked for the bike, whereas the Yamaha likes to glide into corners, preferring the feel of the softer tyre. Viñales didn't win another race all season.

Plenty of people believed that Dovizioso's Mugello win was a one-off and after his next win at Barcelona the following Sunday they thought that perhaps this was just two one-offs, back to back.

ABOVE | *Marquez and Dovizioso fought a long duel for the title, always smiling and joking together, even after their more vicious encounters*

BELOW, LEFT-RIGHT | *Marquez was a worthy champion, rolling the dice like no one else can and amazing with his jaw-dropping talent; Rossi was still the fan's favourite, even if this was his worst season since his grim sojourn at Ducati; Viñales started the season wearing a big smile, but it didn't last*

In fact, Ducati were on a roll. And from here on in the 2017 season was a straight Honda versus Ducati duel. Gigi Dall'Igna and his Ducati Corse crew had worked almost four years for this – a Desmosedici that generated the right amount of grip from its tyres and worked at most racetracks.

Dovizioso had joined Ducati in 2013, one season before Dall'Igna, so no one knows better how the bike has changed.

"I can't even say the 2013 bike was a bike!" said Dovizioso. "The difference between then and now is huge – I can't compare anything on that bike to this year's bike."

Ducati had logically refined the Desmosedici in every way, but that wasn't all, because Dall'Igna's creativity and keenness for searching out new go-faster technologies makes him different from his rival chief engineers. During the previous two seasons he had been the first with proper wings and in 2017 he was the first to unveil a radical answer to MotoGP's new aero regulations. Rumour had it that the 2017 Desmosedici also used a Formula 1-inspired mass damper, to improve various areas of performance. In August Ducati admitted they had started working with new tyre-modelling software; another F1-derived technology. And Ducati were the only factory to start 2017 with new carbon-fibre forks; although Ohlins had offered this latest upgrade to other factories.

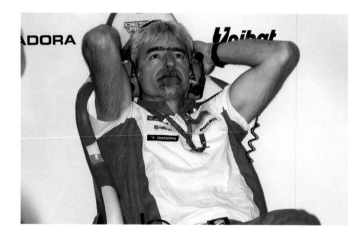

The Bolognese crew certainly deserved their 2017 successes, but there's little doubt that the technical regulations also helped shift the balance of power in their direction. No one in MotoGP has more experience of Magneti Marelli than Ducati, so they almost certainly still have an advantage over the others with Dorna's control software. And the switch to Michelin definitely worked in their favour.

"Maybe our situation would be worse with the Bridgestones," said Dovizioso "The Michelins seem to be positive for us. If you used one or two more degrees of lean angle with the Bridgestones you didn't have any rear grip, so you were slow. With the Michelins you can use a lot of angle and keep the grip." This was a vital factor in fixing some (but not all) of the Ducati's last real negative: mid-corner turning.

Dovizioso also deserves a lot of respect. Last season was his tenth season in MotoGP, and over the years he had gone quietly about learning the skills he would need to challenge for the title, once he had the right bike. A lot of riders now overlay brake and throttle to help load the tyres correctly through corners. Dovizioso does that and more; his GP17 is fitted with two rear-brake levers: one operated by his left thumb, the other by his right foot. He uses both methods through most corners, the thumb brake to slow the bike in the middle of the corner and to get the bike turned, then the foot brake to damp down suspension pump as soon as he touches the throttle.

And yet at the beginning of the season few pit-lane people believed he had the fight within him to match his undoubted riding skills. By season's end, there's was no doubt that he did.

The defining moment of the Dovizioso/Marquez title battle and the abiding memory of the 2017 championship season was the final lap of round ten, at the Red Bull Ring in Austria. The lap should be watched while listening to the theme tune from Jaws. The wild young Spaniard is chasing the wise old Italian, and although it's obvious that Marquez is already on the limit, in fact over the limit, just trying to keep up, you just know that whatever happens he will somehow muster an attack, "otherwise I wouldn't be able to sleep tonight".

The attack comes at the final corner, where Marquez slings his RC213V up the inside. What happens next is fascinating and proves that Dovizioso is different from most MotoGP warriors. Compare his reaction to Marquez's attack with Jorge Lorenzo reaction of to Marquez's attack at the last corner of the 2013 Spanish GP at Jerez. Both Lorenzo and Dovizioso knew the kid was coming through, one way or another.

Lorenzo's instinctive reaction was to slam the door shut, with inevitable consequences: the pair collided. Lorenzo was on the outside, so the impact sent him off the track, while Marquez was

on the inside, so the impact had him wobble around the corner and win the race to the finish line.

Dovizioso was cleverer than that. Instead of trying to block Marquez's attack he left the door wide open. Of course, Marquez was carrying too much speed, so he couldn't make the corner correctly, allowing Dovizioso to simply cut back inside and get it to the chequered flag first. It was a masterful and rare moment of motorcycle racing: a top rider using his brain instead of his ego.

In the end, however, Dovizioso couldn't match the sheer skill of Marquez, who started the season with Honda's first big-bang MotoGP engine and with Michelin's new profile front, which he knew would nullify some of the advantages he had enjoyed in 2016. Twice in the first five races he fell victim to the new tyre, crashing out at Termas del Rio Hondo and again at Le Mans. Then the second front tyre arrived at Mugello, to further confuse matters. It took Marquez and HRC several races to get the hang of the tyre. By Germany Marquez was ready. He won his first race since COTA in April to sneak into the championship lead for the first time. The paddock went off on its summer holiday with the points chase closer than it had ever been in 69 years of GP racing, the top four covered by just ten points: Marquez, Viñales, Rossi and Pedrosa.

Honda made further important set-up changes during their Brno tests during the summer break, adjusting bike balance to better suit the harder front tyre. After that Marquez was in the hunt for victory whenever he needed to be, even when he had to rely on himself to make the difference, as he did in Japan, where the Ducati had a clear advantage in the wet.

"I was going into corners faster, not because I wanted to go in faster, but because I couldn't stop the bike," he said. "I was locking the front, releasing the brake, going in and seeing what happens. You need to release the brakes and believe." Wow.

Marquez was on the edge, rain or shine. "I'm pushing all the time, trying to take all the potential from my bike," he said. "I've had many, many crashes because I'm pushing! It's a very, very tough championship. You need to understand which bike is better at which track. Also, when the temperature changes, the tyres change, so you need to adapt really quick with set-up. Me and the team are both growing up a lot because we've learned so many things this season and because we are pushing so much."

While Marquez and Dovizioso rode along on a confidence high, Viñales slipped downward into a pit of despondency. He lost his way and so did Yamaha. For many years the M1 had been the most balanced machine on the grid – take it to any track and it will work straight out of the truck, more or less. But not anymore. Viñales struggled to find the feeling he needed from the harder front tyre and he had more serious problems exiting the corners, with wheelspin wherever he went, dry and wet. Yamaha tried three slightly different frames during the year and none of them seemed to work as well as the 2015/2016 unit used by Monster Tech 3 riders Zarco and Jonas Folger. But there was no going back, because the latest engine and other parts didn't fit the old frame.

At Assen Viñales suffered "the strangest crash of my life" and by halfway through the season the 22-year-old Spaniard's confidence was shot.

Rossi might have finished the year ahead of his new team-mate if he hadn't fallen off a dirt bike at the end of August, just days after his brilliant third-place finish at Silverstone had reignited his championship chances. The 38-year-old still showed no real signs of ageing. He won in treacherous conditions at Assen and battled

ABOVE, LEFT-RIGHT | *Folger was a rookie revelation, until his season was ended early by a liver disorder; Dall'Igna's four years of work at Ducati turned the Desmosedici into a title challenger*

BELOW, LEFT-RIGHT | *When Yamaha struggled, 2017 became a Honda versus Ducati duel; New Ducati team-mates Dovizioso and Lorenzo helped push the Italian factory forward; Marquez found the midseason pressure so stressful he suffered hair loss! Rookie Zarco was acrobatic, on the bike and off it*

for victory at Silverstone and Phillip Island. If the M1 had been a better bike in 2017, Rossi might have fully challenged for the title, dirt-bike crashes notwithstanding.

Jorge Lorenzo made a better job than Rossi of switching from Yamaha to Ducati, thanks mostly to Dall'Igna. Six years down the line the Desmosedici is a much friendlier machine, so it took rider and factory only two thirds of one season to meet in the middle – by adjusting riding technique and bike set-up – and run up front. Next year Lorenzo will most likely challenge for the title.

Marquez's team-mate Pedrosa had another tough year, the diminutive Spaniard once again hostage to control-tyre regulations. When he could generate heat in his tyres he was fast, when he couldn't he wasn't. And it was more of the latter than the former.

However, Pedrosa's woes – soothed somewhat by a thrilling last-lap win at the Valencia finale – were as nothing compared to those of Suzuki. The factory that won its first dry-weather MotoGP race with Viñales in 2016 had decided to go into the new season with a completely new line-up: they let Aleix Espargaro let go to make way for Andrea Iannone, who had been bumped out of Ducati to make way for Lorenzo, while rookie Alex Rins took the other side of the garage.

Iannone and the GSX-RR weren't a good fit. Through the year the wild Italian complained of a lack of feel going into corners and to much wheelspin on the way out, the Suzuki as always working rather like Yamaha's M1. Not until the final races of the season, after an intensive two days of private testing at Aragon, did the team begin to find the way, with a better bike balance. Iannone

finally got to challenge for a podium finish at Phillip Island, while Rins finally overcame earlier injuries to prove he can get the best out of a MotoGP bike.

Aprilia were another factory who decided to start the year with a completely new look, axing Alvaro Bautista in favour of Espargaro and Stefan Bradl for Moto2 star Sam Lowes. Espargaro was sometimes fast but three engine blow-ups during the first few races – two caused by overring on bumps, just like Yamaha at Mugello in 2016 – blunted their hopes.

MotoGP's newcomers KTM were as impressive as they've been in every other championship they've contested, 125cc, 250cc, Moto3 and Moto2. They were three seconds off at the start of their rookie season and a few tenths off by the end. They changed from a screamer engine to a big-bang engine, provided numerous revised frames (it's much easier to modify a tubular steel frame) and generally worked with their usual pragmatism to keep moving forward at a remarkable rate.

But KTM's success is also MotoGP's. The Austrian factory admitted that they may never have come into the class if it hadn't been for the introduction of control software, because otherwise they would have taken too long to get their heads around the most complicated aspect of MotoGP.

The control software has given more control back to the riders, which has made them happier and made the racing better. The simultaneous introduction of Michelins has also supercharged the thrill and unpredictability of the class, with the French company providing alternative compounds that are very close to each other, which results in different riders choosing different compounds and therefore a bigger mix of race performances.

MotoGP is in rude health at the moment. It's hard to imagine 2018 providing better racing than 2017, but with Lorenzo up to full speed and Yamaha no doubt reacting to their worst season in years, you never know…

ABOVE | *Iannone struggled for much of the year and somehow seemed distracted. Suzuki finally turned their season around with a test in September*

BELOW, LEFT-RIGHT | *Aprilia had an up and down season, with Espargaro fast but flawed and Lowes struggling in his rookie season; Espargaro and Smith found that KTM could make incredibly rapid progress in its rookie MotoGP season*

HONDA, KINGS OF THE PREMIER CLASS SINCE 1983

FREDDIE SPENCER 1983, 1985
WAYNE GARDNER 1987
EDDIE LAWSON 1989

MICK DOOHAN 1994, 1995, 1996, 1997, 1998
ALEX CRIVILLE 1999
VALENTINO ROSSI 2001, 2002, 2003

NICKY HAYDEN 2006
CASEY STONER 2011
MARC MARQUEZ 2013, 2014, 2016, 2017

WWW.HONDAPRORACING.COM

OBITUARIES

ANGEL | NIETO

The second most successful motorcycle racer in history and the man who single-handedly invented Spanish motorcycling.

He won 27 50cc GPs, one 80cc and 62 125cc races. Nieto's championships started with the 50cc crown in 1969 on a Derbi, retaining the title next season, winning his first 25 crown in '71 and doing the double in '72. In '75 he won the 50s for Kreidler, and for the next two years for Bultaco. Then it was the 125 title in '79, '81, '82, '83 and '84 for Minarelli and Garelli.

Nieto wasn't just a racer, he was an icon during Spain's years

JOHN | SURTEES

John Surtees' achievements are so singular, so unrepeatable that no-one is ever likely to be World Champion on two and four wheels again.

The very idea of anyone equalling that feet today is almost ridiculous. Yet this is what Surtees did. First he finished the work started by Les Graham at MV Agusta, then he used his understanding of all-things Italian to win at Ferrari, and then he used his sheer bloody mindedness to become an F1 constructor and team owner. He won MV their first 500cc world title in 1956, going on to the 500/350cc double in

NICKY | HAYDEN

America's last World Champion, universally admired as a great racer and an even greater human being.

The 2006 World Champion died after a road cycling accident in Italy aged 35. He was the only man to beat Valentino Rossi under the first 990cc MotoGP formula. It is a title that looks better and better with perspective; achieved in a last-round showdown after the most dramatic of seasons, on a prototype bike unlike any other Honda on the grid and with a rookie crew chief. Some achievement. As Nicky said, "I didn't just beat the kid round the corner." It was the most emotional of isolation under Franco - daring, dangerous, glamorous, a kid from the sticks who made it big. He was Spain's first champion and he rode Spanish bikes, as tough as they come and a genius of a tactician, ruthless on and off the track, the rock upon which that country's current domination of the sport was built. Laterly he mellowed into a genial elder statesman. Always in the public eye, he became a friend of King Juan Carlos and was instrumental in Dorna's purchase of the commercial rights to Grand Prix motorcycle racing. He died aged 70 on Ibiza, where he lived, after a road traffic accident.

Today's Spanish racers simply refer to him as Maestro - Master. His influence and legacy cannot be overestimated; just never say he won 13 titles, always say 12+1.

'58, '59 and 60. He then turned his attention to four wheels, becoming F1 champion in 1964 for Ferrari.

Marriage and family didn't alter John Surtees' single-minded attitude to motorsport but it mellowed him enormously as a person. It is not too big a stretch to say that while he was racing he was universally respected but in his later years he was universally loved.

All of which makes the courage and dignity with which he faced the death of his 18-year-old son Henry all the more humbling. That, and the energy he subsequently put into the Henry Surtees Foundation, was as remarkable as anything he did on a race track.

win in recent years and Hayden remains the last American to win the title.

He arrived in MotoGP as the youngest ever AMA Superbike Champion and a veteran of the oval dirt tracks, no-one drifted through a fast lefthander better than Nicky. From a large family of racers, he was brought up with impeccable manners, had natural charm by the boatload and was unfailingly polite no matter what the circumstances. It is fair to say that, uniquely, it was impossible to find anyone in the paddock with a bad word to say about Nicky Hayden, Champion of the USA, Champion of the World and as fine a sportsman as you could ever hope to meet.

RIDERS' RIDER OF THE YEAR

EVERY RIDER WHO RODE IN MORE THAN ONE MotoGP RACE VOTES IN OUR ANNUAL POLL. THIS IS WHAT THEY REALLY THINK OF EACH OTHER.

For only the second time the MotoGP riders have decided that their Rider of the Year is not the World Champion but the man who finished second, Andrea Dovizioso.

Only one voter did not select either of them as their top choice. The margin between first and second was small but significant and the gap was there from the first votes to the last. Dovi received double the number of first-place nominations compared to Marc, with that statistic being reversed when you count second places. One voter placed Dovi fourth, Marc had a fourth and two thirds. The only other year the champ has not won was 2006 when Nicky Hayden was beaten by the narrowest of margins by Loris Capirossi.

This year's voting produced an unusually clear pattern. Every rider who rode in more than one race was asked to name their

top six MotoGP ridivals in order, ten points were then allocated for each first place, down to one point for a sixth to echo the sliding scale in the real world championship. The front two received nearly twice the voting points of third-place man Johann Zarco who was also well clear of fourth-paced Maverick Vinales. It is highly unusual for a rider at the top of this poll to be so much higher than in the World Championship table. This is not the case lower down our top ten, especially this year as the men in the lower half of our top ten did not generally receive nominations for places higher than fourth.

Behind the top four came Valentino Rossi – the only man in our poll whose position is the same in both tables - and Danilo Petrucci with only a couple of points between them but with the majority of the voters naming both of them anywhere from

| 3 | **#5 JOHAN ZARCO** |
| 4 | **#25 MAVERICK VIÑALES** |

#93 MARC MARQUEZ

| 6 | **#9 DANILO PETRUCCI** |
| 7 | **#99 JORGE LORENZO** |

#46 VALENTINO ROSSI

| 9 | **#26 DANI PEDROSA** |
| 10 | **#94 JONAS FOLGER** |

#41 ALEIX ESPARGARO

second to sixth. The only man to get a first-place nomination apart from Marquez and Dovizioso was Johann Zarco, yet another manifestation of the impact the rookie has had on the MotoGP class this season.

The order in the lower reaches of our top ten should be treated with caution because of the small numbers of points involved but there is no doubt that Aleix Espargaro's eighth place, as opposed to his real-life 15th is an indication of his rivals' regard for his skills. It is also tempting to wonder where Jonas Folger would be if his illness hadn't ruined the second half of his season and where Dani Pedrosa might have been if his second win of the year had come earlier. Only five riders other than out top-ten got any votes.

There has never been a more clear-cut Riders' Rider of the Year result. Not just for the winner but all the way down our top ten. And the fact that it couldn't have happened to a better professional is probably relevant.

2017 TOP TEN

	RIDER	NAT	TEAM	NO.
1	Andrea Dovizioso	ITA	Ducati Team	#4
2	Marc Marquez	SPA	Repsol Honda Team	#93
3	Johann Zarco	FRA	Monster Yamaha Tech 3	#5
4	Maverick Viñales	SPA	Movistar Yamaha MotoGP	#25
5	Valentino Rossi	ITA	Movistar Yamaha MotoGP	#46
6	Danilo Petrucci	ITA	OCTO Pramac Racing	#9
7	Jorge Lorenzo	SPA	Ducati Team	#99
8	Aleix Espargaro	SPA	Aprilia Racing Team Gresini	#41
9	Dani Pedrosa	SPA	Repsol Honda Team	#26
10	Jonas Folger	GER	Monster Yamaha Tech 3	#94

PREVIOUS WINNERS

YEAR	RIDER	YEAR	RIDER
2004	Valentino Rossi	2010	Jorge Lorenzo
2005	Valentino Rossi	2012	Jorge Lorenzo
2006	Loris Capirossi	2013	Marc Marquez
2007	Casey Stoner	2014	Marc Marquez
2008	Valentino Rossi	2015	Valentino Rossi
2009	Valentino Rossi	2016	Marc Marquez

CHASING THE DRAGON

2017 FIM MotoGP

THREE OF THE FACTORIES COMPETING IN MotoGP ARE WELL-ESTABLISHED WINNERS, BUT THREE ARE NEWCOMERS. SO, HOW DO THEY CATCH UP?

Motorcycle racing is very lucky to have six factories now competing in the top class, MotoGP. Each approaches the same problem, how to get a rider and his machine around a race track for 45 minutes faster than anyone else, in a slightly different way. However, although there are six different approaches there are two broad headings under which this development takes place. There are factories that start with lots of power then try to make things handle. And there are factories that get the bike handling then gently add power.

In current engineering terms it's actually quite easy to beat the peak horsepower of current MotoGP power plants, what isn't so easy is to make that power usable in a racing motorcycle. If we look at the last of the normally aspirated F1 power plants, the 2.4 litre V8s, these made just under 800bhp at their peak, so on a simple proportional basis 320bhp should be achievable from a 1000cc four using similar technology.

This experiment has been carried out. The Aprilia Cube, using three cylinders of a Cosworth V8 F1 engine, was first tried back in 2002. Regis Laconi was the rider but history doesn't record his precise words after that first ride, but several people who were present still smile at the force of his reaction. The Cube wasn't ever fully sorted, but by the time Aprilia withdrew from MotoGP

racing three years later it was making 80bhp less peak power, didn't rely as much on electronic controls and had a heavier crankshaft, all in the cause of making the power 'rider friendly'. And the handling...

One of the major changes over the last decade has been the adoption of control tyres. These represent a major break with the past as the tyre design is now set and it is the job of the factories to get their bikes to work with them. In the past, motorcycle manufacturers and tyre companies worked together, so tyres were made specifically for each make of bike. Now the tyre company arrives with tyres and it is up to the factory and its race team to make their bike work with them.

Much of the science is focussed on to putting the right pressure on the tyres to increase their contact patch at the correct times. That means getting the static weight distribution right, then making sure the bike pitches at exactly the right rate to achieve those pressures on each tyre all the way round the circuit, and for the chassis to flex just enough at high lean angles to allow the tyres to work when the suspension can't help.

The lessons are clear. In a car application you can go for maximum power but for a motorcycle application a chassis that works the tyres to get the best out of them together with

an engine that provides an accurate and graduated throttle response are what matter.

The question, then, is how do you decide which tactic to adopt when you go racing for the first time? Do you make loads of power and try to contain it? Or do you make the best handling bike you can and try to increase power slowly, making sure you don't upset the handling each time the power goes up?

Of course it is not quite that simple, much depends on your starting point and a lot more depends on your budget. In recent years three factories have joined MotoGP (or rejoined actually as they've all been in MotoGP before), and they've all had to do it differently.

Deciding to compete for the first time in MotoGP is not easy; you have to balance the risks of putting your company's reputation on the line with the potential PR benefits that might result. But to do that you have to be confident that you can build a decent racing motorcycle, and that's not easy. You need good people and effective management, and they all need to understand the sport.

The latest rules also make a big difference, new factories are given time to get competitive. New entrants get substantial concessions on testing, engine design and engine numbers until they have had some good results. In addition, the software advantage previously enjoyed by Honda and Yamaha has been removed with the arrival for the 2016 season of the control ECU and its matching software.

Then you have to decide the strategy. Just how are you going to attack the challenge of the MotoGP championship? You are going to need a team, you will need a bike, and you will need riders; some personnel may be better suited to different phases of the operation than others. All cost a lot of money, and all have to work together seamlessly, so it is important you choose well and in the right order.

There are two main parts of the bike, the engine, and the chassis. You need power, but you also need handling, and each is typically built by a different engineering team. Typically the best organised factories have good relationships between the two engineering groups. But even in the best cases you then have to decide how to prioritise; what is your initial priority; the power or the handling?

You will also need electronics, and the control system now in use has at least reduced the complexity; but good people are needed to get the best out of that too. There are areas where you can make life easier; you can use parts that are already popular on your machine, at least you then know that they work, and that someone in the paddock knows how to set them up.

Three 'new' teams have started in recent years, Suzuki – returning from their years of self-imposed exile. Aprilia, returning after an extended period competing in the World Superbike Championship, and last, but certainly not least KTM, making a proper debut after a bit of a misfire with an engine-only deal back in 2005.

So how did each approach the series; and how is it working out?

SUZUKI | GENTLE STEPS

Suzuki left MotoGP at the end of 2010 and took three years to develop a new in-line four-cylinder reverse-rotating engine to replace their old V4. They also built a chassis with some unique features to provide better levels of lateral flex while keeping the required levels of braking and torsional rigidity. The plan was clearly to build a chassis that worked and then slowly increase power. Once the riders were on the bike they found one weak spot very quickly: the engine. Several were lost at the first test but after exhaustive dyno tests between Valencia and the first test in Sepang the cause, most likely oil pickup related, was isolated and dealt with. There was no doubt the bike went round corners but it took a while to deliver more power. Each time a new engine tune was introduced the bike was fitted with a torque sensor to check throttle behaviour before and after the change. Each step was small; just enough to be faster, not enough to upset the throttle response at full lean.

Suzuki went through the same chassis woes as everyone else as the Michelins arrived but soon settled on a design that is very similar to the one used in the Bridgestone years. It is an unusual combination of aluminium beam and carbon-fibre front engine mounts, designed to allow more lateral flex without losing rigidity on braking or the resistance to twist under power. In 2016 a Suzuki ridden by Maverick Viñales won at Silverstone, that's a circuit that values handling and agility more than power. It suited the Suzuki perfectly, or so we thought. Maverick scored well on the Suzuki, indeed he was on the podium three more times, but his team mate Aleix Espargaro was having a harder time with front-end crashes.

For 2017 it was all change, Maverick Viñales was poached by Yamaha to replace Jorge Lorenzo and Espargaro went off to Aprilia. To replace them Suzuki employed Andrea Iannone and Alex Rins and it hasn't turned out to be the most comfortable year for anyone involved.

To race successfully you need several major components; a good chassis, a good engine and a good rider are the basics. It now seems that in Suzuki's case the rider that was winning things in 2016 was even better than they thought. He was modifying his riding style to accommodate one of the foibles of the Suzuki design, it wasn't so good at braking all the way to the apex of each corner. Viñales was braking in a straight line and then coming off the brakes before he turned in. The design of Michelin's 2017 front tyre included a softer carcass; and that exacerbated the problem. Now the Suzuki didn't have the top rider who had learned to brake in straight lines and had replaced him with one who seemingly wasn't going to change his style. The other was a rookie who was going to take a while to simply get used to the machinery.

It seems Suzuki hadn't understood the messages they were receiving from their 2016 riders. Maverick, who was fast, was actually riding around problems and it looks like Aleix, who crashed a lot and was clearly held responsible for those crashes, was actually the more reliable information source. Compounding that, the decision to have two new riders meant there was no rider memory of how the bike felt the previous year. The repercussions have been severe for at least one person, as there is a new boss. Shinichi Sahara, the ex-GSV-R track engineer returned as project leader half-a-dozen races into the year. By Silverstone new parts were arriving; they included a stronger chassis, a revised aero package, and better set-up software. It has taken a while to get the project back on track, but as the season closed there have been flashes of the form we expected at the start of the year.

ABOVE | Suzuki's Catalunya 2014 test; note absence of the external front engine mount

BELOW, LEFT-RIGHT | Suzuki celebrated 30 years of the GSX-R at the Sachsenring in 2015; With its travel wheels in, the GSX-RR awaits a new year; and new riders at Qatar 2017

APRILIA | DROPPED IN THE DEEP END WITH A TINY BUDGET

Down at Aprilia the story is similar but different. They were World Superbike Champions in 2014 with Sylvian Guintoli but for 2015 the rules were changing, and changing in a way that would have meant a major re-engineering job. There was an option; re-engineer the bike for MotoGP instead. Sure it should cost more, but the exposure and the rewards would be far greater. All the race operation had to do was keep the costs down and race intelligently.

So it was that the works part of the Aprilia Superbike team came back to MotoGP, a place most had left at the end of 2009 with the 250s. In the meantime there had been the ART programme; open class MotoGP racers built by Aprilia, a derivative of their very successful World Superbike RSV-R. The works MotoGP effort was to be different though. They took very few cues from the ART project and pretty much started again. The first year was spent on understanding the tyres, the then control tyres were Bridgestones and they were very different to the World Superbike Championship Pirelli control tyres the Aprilia chassis people were used to. A new chassis was in order, one able to deal with the far stiffer carcasses of the Bridgestones.

The MotoGP engine wouldn't be ready for a year, so a version of the World Superbike engine was fitted with pneumatic valve springs and used in its stead. It was way too heavy and didn't make enough power, but for a year of serious learning it was ideal. Released from the need to use a road-based chassis, several ideas were tried out in swift succession culminating is some of the longest front engine mounts ever seen. Most of these experiments were quite cheap, however, with existing chassis being cut and re-welded.

For 2016 progress slowed, it was the first year of the Michelins and the control software, and Aprilia now had a completely new bike to develop. Using Bradl and Bautista, Aprilia worked solidly all year developing software and getting used to the tyres. As the new engine was developed, power was increased slowly in several stages during the year. Towards the end of the year there was a new chassis with a raised engine making it deliberately less stable and therefore easier to change direction on. Aprilia's development took a bit of a knock when their top chassis engineer was lost to KTM.

For 2017, like Suzuki, Aprilia changed both riders with Suzuki refugee Aleix Espargaro and rookie Sam Lowes arriving. That possibly wasn't the best thing to do. Having two new riders means there is no source of information that can compare the feel of previous experiments with any new stuff; that's a problem. As it turns out, Aleix turned into the rider we thought he was and Sam Lowes had a nightmare discovering that MotoGP currently requires a riding style that is the antithesis of everything he has spent years perfecting.

Late in testing Aprilia debuted a chassis with revised weight distribution, designed to make it even more quick turning; it suited Aleix to perfection but appeared to make Lowes' situation even worse. Over the year attempts were made to increase power, or at least the rev limit, but caused several failures. By mid-season all seemed far better albeit with a top speed 5-6kph lower than the fastest bikes. Lowes found the aero fairing a great help in adding some stability, Espargaro didn't like the first version but the one that debuted in Misano was much more to his liking and he used it most of the time thereafter in conjunction with a chassis with wider range of headstock adjustment. The Aprilia has shown flashes of brilliance, but it's not yet a complete package. It will be interesting to see what they bring to the party in 2018.

ABOVE | The first RSV-R was a re-chassised Superbike. Pneumatic-valve-spring engines were fitted early on but suffered some teething problems

BELOW, LEFT-RIGHT | By the end of the first year the engine mounts were as long as possible; there was a new bike with a full MotoGP spec engine in 2016

KTM | WE WILL DO IT OUR WAY, STARTING WITH A LOT OF POWER (AND SOMEONE ELSE'S CHEQUE BOOK)

KTM have competed in and conquered most other classes of motorcycle competition. Long-time kings of off-road, they have become serious competitors on the road too, winning the Moto3 World Championship three times. Each time they have done it their own way and with their own technologies.

MotoGP, however, is the pinnacle and until very recently the competition would simply have been overpowering. Factories with 15 years experience of the electronics had a massive advantage. It is extremely difficult to build up the library of motorcycle problems and software solutions that allows you to sort out strategies during a race weekend. The introduction of a control ECU, and later on control software, has gone a long way to negating that advantage, and the sport is better for it.

KTM decided some years ago that they would enter MotoGP. One of the first things they decided was the engine concept. It would be similar to their 2004 engine in being a V4 but different by having a 90-degree vee angle. The engine is very similar many ways to the Honda, except for one major thing. It still has a crankshaft that rotates forwards, just like the old, pre-2016 Honda. The rest of the bike is very much in the KTM house style. Suspension is from WP and the chassis is made of steel tubes painted orange. That makes KTM the only team in the class not using Ohlins suspension and with a non-aluminium chassis.

The engine spec includes a very lightweight crankshaft, as it has

to be if the bike is to turn well, but that light weight also makes for very abrupt throttle response. One method of alleviating this is to re-arrange the firing sequence so that all four cylinders fire in one revolution of the crank, 90 degrees after each other. That quick sequence evacuates the airbox and makes the engine less efficient so its response is slowed, exactly what you want if you use a crankshaft that is a little on the light side. It's not a cheap solution but only really requires a new crankshaft and camshafts for each engine.

KTM introduced the new motor at Jerez, the fourth race of the year, and it was a clear step forward. The bike had always been fast in a straight line, but for the first three races the riders simply couldn't get it off the corners so the speed didn't show up. From Jerez onwards the fastest KTM rider was usually around 5kph down on the fastest Ducatis but comfortably inside the top ten. At the same time a project was started to build a new motor with a reverse-rotating crankshaft, but that is a much bigger project, virtually a new engine.

Chassis wise, KTM started with two very similar designs. At Catalunya, however, a new version intended to allow far more lateral flex was introduced with tubes set higher. It helped but it wasn't enough. By Aragon there was another design, the high tubes remained but now the chassis had an open loop at the back. The lateral strut above the gear box was removed and the shock absorber was now mounted to a revised rear cylinder head. This made a big difference to the amount of lateral flex, suddenly the KTM riders were able to stay with other riders for longer, and to qualify better.

KTM have made giant strides this year, but it cannot have been cheap. There have been three major chassis concepts and, I am sure, many variations on each of those concepts. By the time testing starts after Valencia there will have been three major engine designs. It is only a matter of time before KTM will be visiting the rostrum.

ABOVE | The Valencia test 'black bike' didn't stay unchanged for long

BELOW, LEFT-RIGHT | By Catalunya it had a new chassis that raised the 'tube line' by 100mm, all the easier to make it flex; for Aragon the chassis adopted an 'open rear' design, look at the swingarm support area

NEW TYRE
MICHELIN POWER RS

© Michelin, GettyImages, iStock – Octobre 2017

UNLEASH YOUR
FULL POTENTIAL

MotorradTestCenter 1

OFFICIAL MotoGP™ CLASS TYRE

MICHELIN *POWER* RS

MICHELIN

DAINESE

We are proud to protect our champions from head to toe.

FRANCO MORBIDELLI
MOTO 2 | 2017 WORLD CHAMPION

JOAN MIR
MOTO 3 | 2017 WORLD CHAMPION

THE 2017 BIKES

HONDA | **RC213V**
22

YAMAHA | **YZR-M1**
24

DUCATI | **DESMOSEDICI GP**
26

SUZUKI | **GSX-RR**
28

KTM | **RC16**
30

APRILIA | **RS-GP**
32

HONDA | *RC213V*

In recent years the Honda has started the year clearly still a work in progress; it is as if the engine department in Japan is setting the chassis department (who make up the bulk of the travelling engineers) a deliberately difficult task for the year.

This year Honda had another new engine, the crankshaft was still reverse rotating but now lighter after the excessive weight and inertia of the 2016 version. The crank was also now a 'big-bang' arrangement with all four cylinders firing in one crankshaft revolution. This modification softens the power production by evacuating the airbox and blunting power delivery. And that power delivery needed to be blunted as Honda's engine builders had delivered an absolute missile of an engine. The new bike was notable for the very long exhaust system it needed for the best power.

Honda's engine designs are frozen during the year by regulation but they can still change the throttle bodies and exhausts. By the middle of the year there were shorter, smaller-diameter pipes, and probably throttle bodies that are longer and better calibrated to go with them. It is most likely that the original throttles were barrel type; the symptoms certainly suggest that and they have most likely been swapped for more conventional butterfly types which would give far more control at low revs but might not be quite as effective at full throttle openings.

For Pedrosa and the customer bikes there was a revised version of the new-generation chassis tested and raced by Crutchlow in the second half of 2016, Marquez, however, retained his favourite 2014-style chassis. As soon as the revised front Michelin came out at Mugello Marquez swapped over to the new-generation chassis, it clearly suits that tyre well. Honda have two aero packages, both very restrained, that seek to add a little downforce while maintaining as much manoeuvrability as possible. For all the development, however, this Honda needs to be kept on its limit to work well, it isn't an easy bike to ride.

1 | For Mugello and the new front Michelin, Marquez swapped over to the 'new-generation chassis - note the slim beams

2 | Aero arrived at Brno

3 | The long pipe was gone from Marquez's bike after just a few races, replaced by shorter, smaller-diameter pipes

4 | By Brno both Repsol bikes had aero additions, Marquez also had the latest carbon-outer-upper-tube Öhlins forks; Pedrosa stuck with the 2016 kit

YAMAHA | **YZR-M1**

From the outside the 2017 Yamaha looks very similar to the 2015 and 2016 versions sitting in the Tech 3 garage. The latest Yamaha looked superb in the first five races as new signing Maverick Viñales won three of them. The Yamaha, combined with the first version of the 2017 Michelin front tyre, suited Viñales perfectly.

At Mugello, however, all that changed. There was a new front tyre, brought in after a riders' vote, and the balance of power tipped. Ducati had a new chassis for Dovizioso and Honda promptly moved Marquez onto their new-generation chassis; both moves paid off. Yamaha was left struggling; a modified chassis appeared, then a new one, and finally the team went off to Misano and moved weight around the bike (the ECU went from on top of the airbox to under the fuel tank) in an attempt to get precisely the right weight in the right place to get the bike to pitch in the right way to make the front tyre work as they wanted. It is clear it still isn't right. Yamaha have always prized agility and handling above all else. Their ability to get the best out of the tyres has served them well in the past, but in late 2017 they had issues, especially with rear tyre grip late in the race. Half the time the bikes worked, half the time they didn't.

They do have some indications of how to fix the problem in that Zarco, riding for satellite team Tech 3 using the late 2016 chassis, has had many fewer problems than the works bikes. That bike holds its engine quite high, which works for Zarco because he is so smooth. Folger used an old 2015 chassis where the engine is held lower and suits his more abrupt riding style.

There were two sets of aerodynamic bodywork in the course of the year; both used ducts in the fairings to channel air over a set of wings.

1 | *By Silverstone there was a mark-two chassis, most of the difference was in the engine position*

2 | *The early season aero pioneered ducted wings*

3 | *The post-Brno version upped the wing count and added a wedge shaped cowling*

4 | *By Jerez the mark-one chassis had been modified for different behaviour on corner entry, note the welds in the middle of the beam*

5 | *Yamaha use the mass of the TV equipment in the seat unit as a tuned mass damper. This year the weight has moved, which will change the frequency of the damper*

DUCATI | **DESMOSEDICI GP**

The 2016 Ducati was long and low and bedecked with wings; it was a long way down the aerodynamics-first evolutionary path. The 2017 bike started off pretty much the same but without the wings. During testing, however, the changes started to come.

There were two new chassis. The early one that didn't use a 'lunchbox' tail was gone before testing was complete. The lunchbox tail version also had a swingarm-pivot area that was quite minimalistic and more flexible. Each time the bikes went out they seemed to be set higher, the front of the bikes were at least 25mm higher by the Jerez test (four races into the season) and the seats equally so. There were also new thinner-section swingarms.

The lunchbox tail is space for a mass damper of sorts. It most likely is a simple tuned mass damper like those used by all the other teams where the TV electronics are stored in the seat tail with the entire rear seat unit acting as a damper by vibrating out of phase with the rest of the bike. The precise frequency of the vibration is set by the rigidity of the seat unit and the distance the weight is from the seat-mounting lugs, so Ducati's large box allows some latitude for tuning.

Dovizioso received a special chassis at Mugello, and it immediately worked well with the new Michelin provided at the rider's request. This had a revised design with the upper frame member that connects the main beam to the headstock shrunk from a 40mm beam to a 7mm-thick piece of plate. This allowed a lot more flex and it seems the new front tyre liked that. There was a revised aero fairing too, in two sizes, both with a lot of downforce. Lorenzo used it a lot as he liked the steadying effects it brought. Dovizioso used it only sparingly to win at the Red Bull Ring and at Motegi.

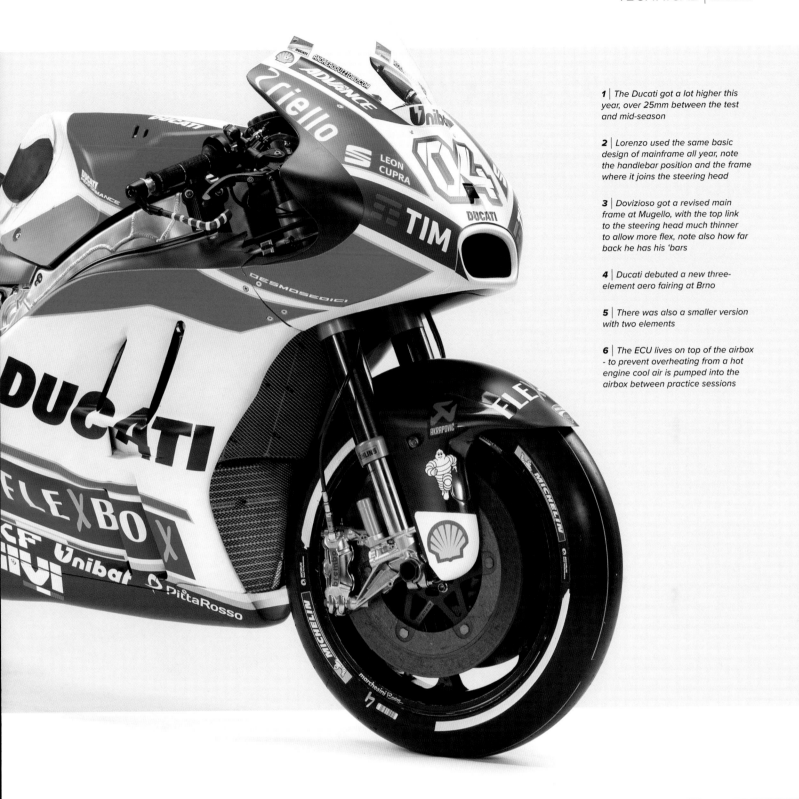

1 | The Ducati got a lot higher this year, over 25mm between the test and mid-season

2 | Lorenzo used the same basic design of mainframe all year, note the handlebar position and the frame where it joins the steering head

3 | Dovizioso got a revised main frame at Mugello, with the top link to the steering head much thinner to allow more flex, note also how far back he has his 'bars

4 | Ducati debuted a new three-element aero fairing at Brno

5 | There was also a smaller version with two elements

6 | The ECU lives on top of the airbox - to prevent overheating from a hot engine cool air is pumped into the airbox between practice sessions

SUZUKI | **GSX-RR**

Suzuki won a race in 2016, and we expected more of the same in 2017. But it was not to be. Both riders left at the end of 2016 leaving a void in reporting quality and certainly initially riding ability.

Suzuki's careful, handling-orientated development programme was knocked off track by riders with very different preferences. Andrea Iannone had only ridden Ducatis in MotoGP before taking the Suzuki ride and it is difficult to think of a more different machine. Alex Rins was a novice in the class, and one that has learned well, but his ability to develop the machine at this point of his career is seriously limited by his knowledge.

The Suzuki won in 2016 with a rider who modified his style, Maverick Viñales learned how to brake in a straight line coming up to corners and then let off the brakes before he peeled in. The 2017 front Michelin, especially the first iteration, needed the same kind of treatment. For Iannone, coming from Ducati, this was a nightmare; not only did the bike not want to brake to the apex, the tyres didn't either.

It took a while for the message to sink in, the bike would have to be redeveloped. Since then, however, Suzuki have been changing the specification of their bike quickly. A new chassis with a much reinforced swingarm pivot area has been in use since Silverstone. Before that the bike was equipped with the Akrapovič flapper-valve system so that the exhaust could be blocked, or at least partially blocked, by the ECU to provide additional engine braking on demand. The electronics have been addressed too, with additional help in the garage and a much improved traction-control system.

New aerodynamics have also been added with the second version providing much more downforce and clearly improving the feel of the bike.

1 | By Silverstone both riders had the use of a chassis that was stiffer near the swingarm pivot

2 | You can see the substantial additional metal here

3 | The first version of the aero fairing was a little too conservative

4 | Suzuki adopted a Ducati style flapper valve in the exhaust for more controllable engine braking after Jerez; you can see the operating cables under the 'U' of Suzuki.

5 | The later, more adventurous aero fairing arrived at Motegi

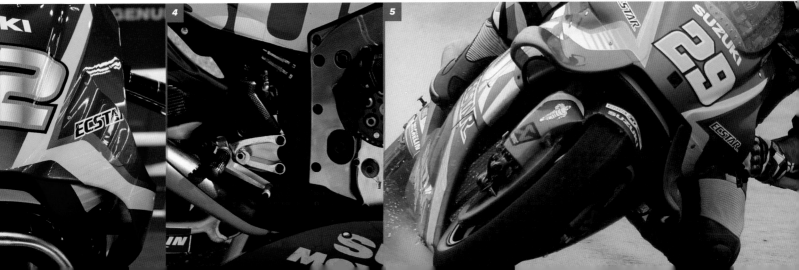

KTM | RC16

Compare the KTM that rolled out at the start of the year to the one on track now and its almost unrecognisable. The swingarm looks familiar but almost everything else is new. If nothing else KTM will have plenty of parts available for show bikes for the next few years. KTM have chosen to go against the mainstream with a steel tube chassis, in house WP suspension and an engine with a forward-rotating crankshaft.

The initial bike didn't seem to instil confidence in its riders; the first major modification was a new crankshaft giving a big-bang effect - all four cylinders firing in one revolution of the crank. That makes it difficult for the cylinders to all receive full charges of air from the airbox so the power take up is softer. At the same time a revised front cowl with wedge-type front was debuted and it stayed on pretty much all the time after that.

Once the throttle response was sorted the chassis was next. At Catalunya a completely revised chassis structure was introduced. The redesign was aimed at allowing far more lateral flex, what you need for grip on full lean. By Aragon there was another chassis, this time with an open rear section; the strut that linked the two sides of the chassis above the gearbox was gone. This weakens the structure and allows more flex. It is similar to most of the other bikes on the grid and made an immediate difference to the confidence of the riders. It is clear that the WP suspension and the choice of steel for the chassis haven't yet prevented KTM from improving; the team are now regular top-ten finishers.

But there is one major change still to come, an engine using a reverse-rotating crankshaft. That will allow a heavier crankshaft for more controllability and easier turning; we can expect that for 2018. These are substantial changes; most other factories would have spent two years to do what KTM have done in one.

1 | It didn't take long for the torque sensor to become standard equipment

2 | All water-cooled engines need a top up tank somewhere

3 | The second version of the chassis raised the main line of tubes to allow more room for flex

4 | WP suspension is a KTM owned company, and it's done just fine in Moto2 and Moto3

5 | The Aragon bike, note the reduced size of the area around the swingarm pivot and the bolt hole directly above, signifying the absence of the cross strut present in the previous versions.

APRILIA | RS-GP

Aprilia have been quietly working their way up the results sheets all year. Suzuki reject Aleix Espargaro has found the Aprilia RS-GP much more to his liking than the bike he rode in 2016. The Aprilia has been developed around his needs with the major changes being two new aero fairing designs, a new chassis at the start of the year followed by a stiffer swingarm and a bigger headstock for more adjustment mid-season.

The Aprilia engine is a 75-degree or thereabouts V4 (they won't confirm the vee angle), packaged to be very small with the cylinder heads looking particularly compact. Reliability has been a bit of an issue, however, with several engines being lost and some external components like fuel pumps being somewhat erratic.

The Aprilia's progress wasn't helped by the departure to KTM of their top chassis engineer Marco Bertolatti. His experience went all the way back to the three-cylinder Cube; it was a significant loss for Aprilia and an equally large gain for KTM. The 2016 RSV-R was criticised for being extremely stable, that's nice in a road bike but not what you want in a racer.

There was a chassis with a higher engine position in late 2016 and another at the end of pre-season testing this year. By the time the second steering-head modification was carried out mid-season the bike was where Espargaro wanted it. The Aprilia in this guise would have needed a fair amount of throttle and rear brake on use to hold it down in corners and make it manageable. This is perhaps one of the reasons why Lowes' bike always had the earlier aero fairing; just to add a little stability. At Misano a new aero fairing arrived as well, taking a few cues from the new Ducati fairing but, critically, by being far less extreme it worked very well for Espargaro.

1 | The RS-GP side on with its later aero bodywork

2 | Sam Lowes used the early aero for most of the season, he found it settled the bike down

3 | The later aero was inspired by Ducati's wings but having only two lower tiers is a better compromise for the less powerful Aprilia

4 | The engine mounts are bolt on, allowing the flex to be quickly adjusted

5 | The Aprilia is very slim, and the packaging is quite tight

ph: Milagro

JOHANN ZARCO MOTOGP - MONSTER YAMAHA TECH3

RT-RACE. THE CHOICE OF CHAMPIONS.

CE CERTIFICATION EN13634:2015

The RT-RACE is designed to offer the best riding performance both on track and on the road, it is equipped with the Double Flex Control System – a polyurethane frame that allows backward and forward controlled flexibility of the foot, while avoiding overextension of the ankle joint. The Fasten Fit Control, an internal fastening system, ensures that the upper wraps the foot, respecting the different foot anatomies and providing maximum fit precision and sensitivity while riding.

RT-RACE. THE ULTIMATE RACING EXPERIENCE.

TCX
FOCUS ON BOOTS

THE SEAON IN FOCUS

From the factory men to the wild cards, every MotoGP rider's season analysed.

2017 FIM MotoGP™ WORLD CHAMPIONSHIP

MotoGP™ WORLD CHAMPIONSHIP STANDINGS

	RIDER	NAT	TEAM	POINTS
1	Marc Marquez	SPA	Repsol Honda Team	298
2	Andrea Dovizioso	ITA	Ducati Team	261
3	Maverick Viñales	SPA	Movistar Yamaha MotoGP	230
4	Dani Pedrosa	SPA	Repsol Honda Team	210
5	Valentino Rossi	ITA	Movistar Yamaha MotoGP	208
6	Johann Zarco	FRA	Monster Yamaha Tech 3	174
7	Jorge Lorenzo	SPA	Ducati Team	137
8	Danilo Petrucci	ITA	OCTO Pramac Racing	124
9	Cal Crutchlow	GBR	LCR Honda	112
10	Jonas Folger	GER	Monster Yamaha Tech 3	84
11	Jack Miller	AUS	EG 0,0 Marc VDS	82
12	Alvaro Bautista	SPA	Pull&Bear Aspar Team	75
13	Andrea Iannone	ITA	Team SUZUKI ECSTAR	70
14	Scott Redding	GBR	OCTO Pramac Racing	64
15	Aleix Espargaro	SPA	Aprilia Racing Team Gresini	62
16	Alex Rins	SPA	Team SUZUKI ECSTAR	59
17	Pol Espargaro	SPA	Red Bull KTM Factory Racing	55
18	Loris Baz	FRA	Reale Avintia Racing	45
19	Tito Rabat	SPA	EG 0,0 Marc VDS	35
20	Karel Abraham	CZE	Pull&Bear Aspar Team	32
21	Bradley Smith	GBR	Red Bull KTM Factory Racing	29
22	Hector Barbera	SPA	Reale Avintia Racing	28
23	Michele Pirro	ITA	Ducati Team	25
24	Mika Kallio	FIN	Red Bull KTM Factory Racing	11
25	Sam Lowes	GBR	Aprilia Racing Team Gresini	5
26	Katsuyuki Nakasuga	JPN	Yamalube Yamaha Factory Racing	4
27	Sylvain Guintoli	FRA	Team SUZUKI ECSTAR	1
28	Michael van der Mark	NED	Monster Yamaha Tech 3	
29	Takuya Tsuda	JPN	Team SUZUKI ECSTAR	
30	Hiroshi Aoyama	JPN	EG 0,0 Marc VDS	
31	Broc Parkes	AUS	Monster Yamaha Tech 3	

1 #93 | MARC MARQUEZ

REPSOL HONDA TEAM | HONDA

NATIONALITY | SPANISH

DATE OF BIRTH | 17.02.1993

WEIGHT | 59 KG **HEIGHT** | 168 CM

2017 SEASON | 6 WINS, 12 ROSTRUMS,
8 POLE POSITIONS, 3 FASTEST LAPS

TOTAL POINTS | 298

A fourth MotoGP title at 24 years of age, all with a smile on his face as he makes yet another impossible save and laughing about it afterwards.

You would be forgiven for thinking he was immune to pressure. Seven races into a fraught start to the season and lying third in the championship table he went for a haircut only to be told his hair was dropping out. After Le Mans he told his team he simply wasn't enjoying riding the bike any more. Yes, things were that bad but with his team Marc turned the Honda back into a winner, although he had to explore the outer limits of the possible to effect the change. If a champion crashes half-a-dozen times in a season at this level, it is shocking. Marc crashed 27 times and by his own count came very close on another 50 or so occasions. His save in the final stages of the final race was the most breathtaking ever captured on film.

As usual Marc was willing to risk more than most, as the last corner attacks from almost hopeless positions showed so graphically. As usual he did things with a motorcycle that we have never seen before. He also maintained a cordial and sporting relationship with his rival. The scary thing is that it still feels as if we have yet to see the best of him and he shows no signs of getting bored with winning. His hairdresser will have to stay alert for a few more years and the records of Giacomo Agostini and Valentino Rossi will be in danger well before Marc reaches the age of 30. He now deserves to be considered in any discussion of the best rider we have ever seen. How many more titles could be his? Frankly, as many as he wants.

2 #4 | ANDREA DOVIZIOSO

DUCATI TEAM | DUCATI

NATIONALITY | ITALIAN

DATE OF BIRTH | 23.03.1986

WEIGHT | 67 KG **HEIGHT** | 167 CM

2017 SEASON | 6 WINS, 8 ROSTRUMS,
2 FASTEST LAPS

TOTAL POINTS | 261

You would have got very long odds against Andrea Dovizioso winning six races this year and taking the fight for the title to within six laps of the final flag.

Yet the man everyone thought would be second rider to Jorge Lorenzo at Ducati put in the season of his life. He has always been a good rider but this year he elevated himself to a greatness. The professionalism and precision had always been there, now he added that final element of mental toughness that saw him transformed into a championship contender. There were tracks on which Andrea had to ride within the limits imposed by the Ducati and there were tracks were he could unleash its power without worrying. He coped with these circumstances and all those in between with equanimity. The only sign of temper all season was a wonderfully dismissive flick of the wrist aimed at Marquez after a particularly leery last-corner attack in Austria. Even that was very understated, very Dovi. The applause and smiles that greeted him when he brought his crashed bike back to the pit in Valencia said it all. The combination of Dovi and the management skills of Gigi Dall'Igna took Ducati to the brink of something they've not done since the days of Casey Stoner.

Like the other standout surprise of the year, Johann Zarco, Andrea is a very normal person. No entourage, no bling, no attitude, team manager Davide Tardozzi had it right when he coined the phrase "Professor Dovizioso."

The hope of everyone who so admired him this season is that it was not a one-off and that he will take the form of 2017 into 2018.

3 #25 | **MAVERICK VIÑALES**

MOVISTAR YAMAHA MOTOGP | *YAMAHA*

Two races into the season you would have put the mortgage on Maverick being World Champion.

After dominating pre-season testing he won the first two races and after winning Le Mans led the championship, until he fell at Assen. He did not win another race and was a rare visitor to the podium in the second half of the year. By Austria he had dropped to third in the championship, what happened?

The answer is twofold. First, there was the change of frame at the factory Yamaha team. On Valentino Rossi's insistence both riders used a frame tested after Barcelona, on which Viñales crashed at Assen, and then there was the new, stiffer front tyre construction introduced at Mugello. Another chassis was used, on which Maverick was a close second at Silverstone, but that too only muddied the water. The ice-cool assassin of the first races turned into a fretful, nervous young man unsure of what to do. To be fair, he wasn't the only one. The other side of the garage wasn't in much better shape.

The second half of Maverick's season was characterised by serious grip problems in the wet and premature wear of the rear tyre in the dry, again a reflection of Rossi's problems. He set three fastest laps in the first half of the year at tracks as diverse as Le Mans and Mugello, but only one after the Summer break. It is now up to Yamaha to cure whatever ails the M1, restore Maverick's confidence and deliver a package with which Maverick can challenge the Ducatis and Hondas next season. He has the talent to be World Champion.

NATIONALITY | *SPANISH*

DATE OF BIRTH | *12.01.1995*

WEIGHT | *64 KG* **HEIGHT** | *171 CM*

2017 SEASON | *3 WINS, 7 ROSTRUMS, 5 POLE POSITIONS, 4 FASTEST LAPS*

TOTAL POINTS | *230*

---

4 #26 | **DANI PEDROSA**

REPSOL HONDA TEAM | *HONDA*

The perfect foil to his teammate's mercurial brilliance.

Yet again Dani Pedrosa set pole positions, made fastest laps and won a race, plus he helped Repsol Honda to the teams' championship and Honda to the constructors' title. There were also races where he simply didn't figure, like Australia, a dry race, and in the wet at Misano and Motegi. Both disappointments could be attributed to Dani's inability to get the tyres up to temperature, a consequence of his weight. His win came on a very slick Jerez track and he probably should have won at Aragon where a combination of factors delayed his move to the front.

That win in Jerez meant Dani has won a Grand Prix every season for the past 16 years, a unique achievement that dates back to the 125cc class of the Dutch TT in 2002 and takes in one 125cc and two 250cc titles.

For once, he stayed injury free but the fickle nature of the Honda, particularly at the start of the season when crashes in Argentina and Mugello bracketed three podium finishes, and the changes in tyre specification, blunted hopes of a championship challenge. Dani was briefly second in the championship after Le Mans, albeit 17 points behind Viñales, but was down to fifth a race later and never regained the ground. Nevertheless, it is impossible to imagine anyone doing a better job for his team than Dani. He is still one of the very few men who can guarantee you pole positions, regular podium finishes and, of course, at least one win a year.

NATIONALITY | *SPANISH*

DATE OF BIRTH | *29.09.1985*

WEIGHT | *51 KG* **HEIGHT** | *160 CM*

2017 SEASON | *2 WIN, 9 ROSTRUMS, 3 POLE POSITIONS, 2 FASTEST LAPS*

TOTAL POINTS | *210*

5 | #46 | VALENTINO ROSSI
MOVISTAR YAMAHA MOTOGP | *YAMAHA*

NATIONALITY | *ITALIAN*

DATE OF BIRTH | *16.02.1979*

WEIGHT | *65 KG* **HEIGHT** | *182 CM*

2017 SEASON | *1 WIN, 6 ROSTRUMS*

TOTAL POINTS | *208*

Valentino was a contender but injury and a recalcitrant Yamaha blunted his challenge.

Started the season well, although in the shadow of his new teammate Maverick Viñales, and led the championship after Texas and Spain. Then dropped to fifth in the championship before rallying with a classic win at Assen, the sort of grand old track on which he excels. After that there were thin pickings, although he put up great fights at Silverstone and Phillip Island where he used his experience in group fights. Indeed he looked, for most of the race, as if he was going to win in Great Britain, but slipped to third in the closing stages as Yamaha's problem with rear-tyre wear made itself apparent. There was also the not inconsiderable grip problem in wet weather, conditions that usually play to Valentino's vast experience. That got as close to making Valentino lose his cool in public as anything in his career has ever done.

Just one win in the season means that with 95 wins the chances of beating or equaling Giacomo Agostini's record of 122 victories in all classes, never mind that tenth world title, are diminishing. When the 2018 season starts, Valentino will be 39 years old and facing the toughest opposition imaginable. Will it be his last year? Who knows? Probably not even the man himself. There has been no sign of his motivation diminishing, as his miraculous return from a broken leg proved, but if he thinks winning is no longer possible he will retire from racing, not the sport, to concentrate on his academy and the VR46 orgainisation.

6 | #5 | JOHANN ZARCO
MONSTER YAMAHA TECH 3 | *YAMAHA*

NATIONALITY | *FRENCH*

DATE OF BIRTH | *16.07.1990*

WEIGHT | *66 KG* **HEIGHT** | *171 CM*

2017 SEASON | *3 ROSTRUMS, 2 POLE PSOITONS, 4 FASTEST LAPS*

TOTAL POINTS | *174*

The quiet man of MotoGP; independent team rider of the year and the best rookie since Marc Marquez.

No-one expected too much of Johann right up until he led the first six laps of the first race of the year and set the fastest lap. It was just a taster of what was to come, there were pole positions and podium finishes and there was absolutely no respect for the more experienced men. Valentino Rossi was on the wrong end of an ambitious move in Texas, Jorge Lorenzo was equally upset by a similar move in Japan and along the way most of the top men felt the rub of the Frenchman's fairing.

One of the images of the year was Johann listening to the anthem on the front row of his home race, his fans belted out the Marseillaise and he repaid them with his first MotoGP podium. He wasn't just aggressive, he was precise too. His aim was to be smooth and he was, his style enabled him to use the soft tyres where others couldn't and, as in Sepang, to get them to the podium. He did crash out of the lead in Qatar, but that was his only fall in a race. For a rookie in the same field as men like Marquez, Lorenzo and Rossi these are remarkable achievements.

All of this was achieved with an almost diffident approach so different from most of his peers: no bling, no tattoos, no ostentation whatsoever, not even a motorhome; he sleeps in a capsule hotel in the paddock. Johann is different, and he's got them worried.

7

#99 | **JORGE LORENZO**

DUCATI TEAM | *DUCATI*

A tricky first year with Ducati, but the signs are positive.

Did Jorge Lorenzo start to repay the millions Ducati, their sponsor and their owner have invested in him? The object, remember, is to win the world title, not just the odd race. The answer is a qualified yes. Jorge led many races, started from the front row more than once and made it to the podium as well. It's just that the progress didn't happen in a straight line. It started horribly when he was off the pace in Qatar then suddenly transformed with a podium in Jerez. Then there was a period where he'd be in contention but drop back as soon as he was passed, and there were a couple where he would be passed and drop back as usual then stage a comeback, but only after taking half-a-dozen laps to think about it.

That puzzled the team, but towards the end of the year the random pattern of results started to resolve into what looked like solid progress. There were still blips, like Australia where every Ducati suffered, but from Aragon where he finished top Ducati and on the podium it looked as if Jorge and the bike finally understood each other. Malaysia, where he did everything right as far as the team were concerned, could have been his first win but he was pressing on hard when he had a major moment. Misano, where he'd opened up a lead of over four seconds when he lost concentration and crashed, should have been that victory.

The task that faces Jorge now is to carry that form into next season, where he is expected to challenge not just for wins but for the championship.

NATIONALITY | *SPANISH*
DATE OF BIRTH | *04.05.1987*
WEIGHT | *64 KG* **HEIGHT** | *173 CM*
2017 SEASON | *3 ROSTRUMS*
TOTAL POINTS | *137*

8

#9 | **DANILO PETRUCCI**

OCTO PRAMAC RACING | *DUCATI*

As good as a third factory rider.

Danilo won the right to ride a 2017-spec Ducati in competition with his teammate last year, and he put it to very good use. He came within an ace both of pole position and of the win in Assen and had good reason to be disgruntled after getting baulked on the final lap. In Misano he again finished second and again he wasn't happy, but no-one could counter the sort of last-lap charge that Marc Marquez unleashed there. Better to concentrate on the happy third places at Mugello and Motegi. At home, he was as happy as you would expect any Italian to be having ridden an Italian motorcycle to a podium position; in Motegi he said he had the usual two problems, Marquez and Dovi and was content with third place.

As well as the stellar success there were also a few problems. His style is still very heavy on the rear tyre and Danilo often has to make a conscious effort to conserve his resources. When he adds a little subtlety to his all-or-nothing throttle style he will be even more dangerous.

Petrucci's ascent to MotoGP stardom has one major side effect. Like Cal Crutchlow and Moto2 champion Franky Morbidelli he did not arrive in GPs via the Moto3-Moto2 route. He was a motocrosser who came late to road racing and progressed through Superstock and some very uncompetitive MotoGP machinery to earn what is effectively a factory Ducati ride. That is a route to the top that has to give hope to any racer who didn't get to be a teenage factory rider in the Junior World Championship.

NATIONALITY | *ITALIAN*
DATE OF BIRTH | *24.10.1990*
WEIGHT | *77 KG* **HEIGHT** | *180 CM*
2017 SEASON | *4 ROSTRUMS*
TOTAL POINTS | *124*

9 | #35 | CAL CRUTCHLOW
LCR HONDA | HONDA

NATIONALITY | BRITISH

DATE OF BIRTH | 29.10.1985

WEIGHT | 70 KG

HEIGHT | 170 CM

2017 SEASON | 1 ROSTRUM

TOTAL POINTS | 112

This year Cal had an HRC contract for the first time, rather than with the LCR team, thanks to his form last year and his abilities as a test rider. But if you want an illustration of how recalcitrant the 2017-model Honda was, compare Cal's results this year with the previous season. In 2016 he won races in all conditions and stood on the podium four times. This season the best he could muster was a third place in Argentina, the second race of the year.

There were regular complaints about the front tyre not being hard enough - Marquez usually had the same opinion - and there were a few crashes as Cal, typically, had to over-ride the bike. When the situation demanded bravery, as in Assen, he was able to challenge for a podium finish. A tough season.

10 | #94 | JONAS FOLGER
MONSTER YAMAHA TECH 3 | YAMAHA

NATIONALITY | GERMAN

DATE OF BIRTH | 13.08.1993

WEIGHT | 68 KG

HEIGHT | 177 CM

2017 SEASON | 1 ROSTRUM, 2 FASTEST LAPS

TOTAL POINTS | 84

Not a lot was expected of the German, certainly not compared to the other rookies, but he exceeded expectations until a recurrent illness ended his season early. First he showed consistency, scoring points in every race up until Assen and then finishing a close second to Marc Marquez at home in Germany, having led the race for five laps. Jonas also set the fastest lap in Catalunya. Tech 3 team manager Herve Poncheral had wanted Jonas in his team for a while, his faith was completely justified.

After the Summer break Folger's form dropped and he reported getting tired so he trained harder. He was then diagnosed with a reoccurrence of the Epstein-Barr virus, which can cause all manner of problems, including the glandular fever that affected Jonas previously, and missed the last four races of the season.

11 | #43 | JACK MILLER
EG 0,0 MARC VDS | HONDA

NATIONALITY | AUSTRALIAN

DATE OF BIRTH | 18.01.1995

WEIGHT | 70 KG

HEIGHT | 175 CM

TOTAL POINTS | 82

Came to the end of his three-years with HRC, who sent him direct to MotoGP from Moto3 without touching down in Moto2. Was the experiment a success? Well Jack did win in the wet at Assen last year. This season he was again handicapped by injury, coming back from a broken leg a day quicker than Valentino Rossi to lead his home GP. He faded to seventh in Phillip Island but finished sixth in both Assen and Misano, underlining his wet-weather abilities.

Jack lost his HRC contract to his good friend Cal Crutchlow and therefore moves from Marc VDS to Ducati satellite team Pramac for 2018. It is worth noting that he was only 22 years old at the end of the season and has over 100 races under his belt, nearly half of them in the top class.

12 | #19 | ALVARO BAUTISTA
PULL&BEAR ASPAR TEAM | DUCATI

NATIONALITY | SPANISH

DATE OF BIRTH | 21.11.1984

WEIGHT | 60 KG

HEIGHT | 169 CM

TOTAL POINTS | 75

It is fair to say that not a lot was expected from Alvaro on his return to Aspar's team, it is also fair to say that he then reminded people why he'd been a World Champion with them. Although his old aversion to wet conditions did affect the end of his season there were races where he troubled the factory riders, notably a fourth place in Argentina where he was charging up to the leaders as the flag came out and a very impressive fifth at Mugello in front of Marc Marquez.

There were also a few crashes, Alvaro's youthful enthusiasm has never gone away, including one that swept up Jack Miller and led to a fracas in the sand trap. Alvaro wasn't concerned about the swipe aimed at him but did take exception to the kick aimed at his bike. He will be back next year, smiling as always.

13 | #29 | ANDREA IANNONE

TEAM SUZUKI ECSTAR | *SUZUKI*

NATIONALITY | *ITALIAN*

DATE OF BIRTH | *09.08.1989*

WEIGHT | *67 KG*

HEIGHT | *178 CM*

TOTAL POINTS | *70*

The loss of Maverick Viñales cast Suzuki adrift and they did not appear to be helped by their new lead rider, who took three rounds to score a point. The low point was Le Mans where Andrea was overtaken by Sylvain Guintoli, riding as a replacement for the injured Alex Rins. Iannone promptly dropped his lap times by well over a second-and-a-half. The team were distinctly unimpressed.

Things got worse as Andrea was equaled and at times outdone by the returning Rins – a rookie. Development parts did help and there were flashes of brilliance at Motegi and Phillip Island, two very different tracks, where Andrea ran with the leaders for most of both races.

Andrea will stay with Suzuki for the 2018 season and it will be a crucial year for his future, comparisons with Rins' form will be inevitable.

14 | #45 | SCOTT REDDING

OCTO PRAMAC RACING | *DUCATI*

NATIONALITY | *BRITISH*

DATE OF BIRTH | *04.01.1993*

WEIGHT | *78 KG*

HEIGHT | *185 CM*

2017 SEASON | *1 FASTEST LAP*

TOTAL POINTS | *64*

A very disappointing year in which Scott was overshadowed completely by his team mate Danilo Petrucci. A couple of seventh places really is not a lot to show for a man of his experience. There were some good weekends, but there was also the worst race of Scott's life in Germany, which almost reduced him to tears in post-race interviews. Too often he was lost in qualifying and even his usual wet-weather abilities seemed to desert him. He was top Ducati in Australia but that was only an 11th place finish and he took points off Andrea Dovizioso doing it.

Almost inevitably, Scott leaves the Pramac team to join Aprilia for 2018. It is to be hoped that he rediscovers his confidence. He is still young, just 24 years old at the end of the season, with victories in 125 and Moto2 plus podiums in MotoGP.

15 | #41 | ALEIX ESPARGARO

APRILIA RACING TEAM GRESINI | *APRILIA*

NATIONALITY | *SPANISH*

DATE OF BIRTH | *30.07.1989*

WEIGHT | *71 KG*

HEIGHT | *180 CM*

TOTAL POINTS | *62*

After being jilted by Suzuki, Aleix had a point to prove and he made it by giving that factory's riders a run for their money in the points table. Early in the season Aleix used the Aprilia's ability to make its tyres last to good effect, especially at the opening race in Qatar. Most of the rest of the first half of the season was an anticlimax, but in the second half bike and rider started to look like contenders. His ride to sixth at Aragon was particularly impressive.

Unfortunately, a crash in Australia gave Aleix a nasty fracture of his hand and compromised the end of his season. Without that he would have certainly given the three men above him in the table some serious pressure. It is not beyond the bounds of possibility that he would have overtaken the unfortunate Jonas Folger and made the top ten.

16 | #42 | ALEX RINS

TEAM SUZUKI ECSTAR | *SUZUKI*

NATIONALITY | *SPANISH*

D.O.B | *08.12.1995*

WEIGHT | *65 KG*

HEIGHT | *176 CM*

TOTAL POINTS | *59*

Suzuki's rookie missed pre-season testing with a nasty injury and then missed six races in the first half of the year through another equally unpleasant injury. He didn't score points in his first two races back, but after the Summer break he was very impressive and kept his out-of-sorts teammate honest. From Silverstone onwards he became a serious player, regularly going to the second qualifying session and finishing deep in the top ten. Like his team mate Andrea Iannone he was with the leaders all the way in Japan and Australia.

Given the unpredictable nature of his teammate, the man employed as the lead rider, Suzuki must be very happy with the investment they've made in Alex. It is not an exaggeration to say his form in the second half of the year held the team together.

17 | #44 | POL ESPARGARO

RED BULL KTM FACTORY RACING | *KTM*

NATIONALITY | *SPANISH* **D.O.B** | 10.06.1991
WEIGHT | *64 KG* **HEIGHT** | *171 CM*
TOTAL POINTS | 55

Led KTM's attack on the MotoGP class with the flair and enthusiasm you'd expect. Didn't finish a race lower than 11th in the second half of the year and regularly went to Q2.

18 | #76 | LORIS BAZ

REALE AVINTIA RACING | *DUCATI*

NATIONALITY | *FRENCH* **D.O.B** | 01.02.1993
WEIGHT | *79 KG* **HEIGHT** | *191CM*
TOTAL POINTS | 45

Unlucky to be leaving MotoGP after an impressive year when he was always a serious contender on wet tracks. Returns to World Superbike with a best MotoGP finish of fourth on his CV.

19 | #53 | TITO RABAT

EG 0,0 MARC VDS | *HONDA*

NATIONALITY | *SPANISH*

D.O.B | 25.05.1989 **WEIGHT** | 63 KG

HEIGHT | 178 CM **TOTAL POINTS** | 35

Ended his association with the Marc VDS team with a better season. Still a stranger to the top ten but put in plenty of points scoring rides although he only made QP2 once.

20 | #17 | KAREL ABRAHAM

PULL&BEAR ASPAR TEAM | *DUCATI*

NATIONALITY | *CZECH*

D.O.B | 02.01.1990 **WEIGHT** | 72 KG

HEIGHT | 181 CM **TOTAL POINTS** | 32

A much better return to MotoGP than anyone predicted, despite another nasty injury in Texas. Second on the grid in Argentina and a fighting seventh place at Assen were highlights.

21 | #38 | BRADLEY SMITH

RED BULL KTM FACTORY RACING | *KTM*

NATIONALITY | *BRITISH*

D.O.B | 28.11.1990 **WEIGHT** | 67 KG

HEIGHT | 179 CM **TOTAL POINTS** | 29

Still having trouble adjusting to Michelins but definite improvement by the end of season when he was regularly racing his teammate. Not helped by a horrible finger injury mid-season.

22 | #8 | HECTOR BARBERA

REALE AVINTIA RACING | *DUCATI*

NATIONALITY | *SPANISH*

D.O.B | 02.11.1986 **WEIGHT** | 61 KG

HEIGHT | 169 CM **TOTAL POINTS** | 28

Not a good final season in MotoGP. Struggled at the start with a bike designed for wings but now stripped of them. Will stay in the paddock with the Pons Moto2 team for 2018.

23 | #51 | MICHELE PIRRO

DUCATI TEAM | *DUCATI*

NATIONALITY | *ITALIAN*

D.O.B | 05.07.1986 **WEIGHT** | 69 KG

HEIGHT | 177 CM **TOTAL POINTS** | 25

Rode his usual schedule of three wild-card races and was quick every time. An integral part of Ducati's improvement and an advert for the benefits of a quick test rider.

24 | #36 | MIKA KALLIO

RED BULL KTM FACTORY RACING | *KTM*

NATIONALITY | *FINNISH*

D.O.B | 08.11.1982 **WEIGHT** | 58 KG

HEIGHT | 166 CM **TOTAL POINTS** | 11

KTM's test rider made four wild-card appearances, and on each occasion gave the factory's regular riders something to think about. Will no doubt do the same next year.

25 | #22 | SAM LOWES

APRILIA RACING TEAM GRESINI | *APRILIA*

NATIONALITY | *BRITISH*

D.O.B | *14.09.1990* **WEIGHT** | *66 KG*

HEIGHT | *168 CM* **TOTAL POINTS** | *5*

With hindsight, it is clear that employing a rookie while a bike is being developed was never a good idea. However, did lots of good work in testing and well liked by his team mate. Back in Moto2 for 2018.

26 | #21 | KATSUYUKI NAKASUGA

YAMALUBE YAMAHA FACTORY RACING | *YAMAHA*

NATIONALITY | *JAPANESE*

D.O.B | *09.08.1981* **WEIGHT** | *NA*

HEIGHT | *NA* **TOTAL POINTS** | *4*

Yamaha's tester and triple 8 Hour winner had his customary wild-card ride at Motegi and as usual was quick enough to finish well in the points. More valuable information for the M1 development program.

27 | #50 | SYLVAIN GUINTOLI

TEAM SUZUKI ECSTAR | *SUZUKI*

NATIONALITY | *FRENCH*

D.O.B | *24.06.1982* **WEIGHT** | *62 KG*

HEIGHT | *179 CM* **TOTAL POINTS** | *1*

Replaced Alex Rins for the French, Italian and Catalan GPs, scoring a point in his home race and beating regular riders in the others. Did the team a major favour at Le Mans by giving Andrea Iannone a big hurry-up.

28 | #60 | MICHAEL VAN DER MARK

MONSTER YAMAHA TECH 3 | *YAMAHA*

NATIONALITY | *DUTCH*

D.O.B | *26.10.1992* **WEIGHT** | *54 KG*

HEIGHT | *175 CM* **TOTAL POINTS** | *0*

Scheduled to replace Rossi at Aragon but never got a chance to ride thanks to Valentino's miraculous comeback. Got his chance when he replaced Jonas Folger for the final two rounds and acquitted himself well.

29 | #12 | TAKUYA TSUDA

TEAM SUZUKI ECSTAR | *SUZUKI*

NATIONALITY | *JAPANESE*

D.O.B | *27.04.1984* **WEIGHT** | *NA*

HEIGHT | *NA* **TOTAL POINTS** | *0*

Suzuki's young star replaced Alex Rins at Jerez. It was his first experience of MotoGP and it couldn't have been trickier. Stayed on for the post-race test, a useful bonus for development work.

30 | #7 | HIROSHI AOYAMA

EG 0,0 MARC VDS | *HONDA*

NATIONALITY | *JAPANESE*

D.O.B | *25.10.1981* **WEIGHT** | *57 KG*

HEIGHT | *165 CM* **TOTAL POINTS** | *0*

Honda's veteran test rider replaced Jack Miller at Motegi and expected to do well in the wet, but an early incident and bad tyre choice meant he did not score points.

31 | #23 | BROC PARKES

MONSTER YAMAHA TECH 3 | *YAMAHA*

NATIONALITY | *AUSTRALIAN*

D.O.B | *24.12.1981* **WEIGHT** | *64 KG*

HEIGHT | *170 CM* **TOTAL POINTS** | *0*

The Australian veteran, nowadays a part of Yamaha's endurance efforts, replaced Jonas Folger at the Australian GP. As you'd expect he did a solid professional job and got it to the flag.

32 | #31 | KOHTA NOZANE

MONSTER YAMAHA TECH 3 | *YAMAHA*

NATIONALITY | *JAPANESE*

D.O.B | *???* **WEIGHT** | *NA*

HEIGHT | *NA* **TOTAL POINTS** | *0*

Yamaha's young star got the call up for Motegi when Folger was declared unfit. Impressed in practice but hurt himself in qualifying and crashed in the race. A name to note.

THE 2017 CALENDAR

THE NEED FOR SPEED

Maverick Viñales lives up to the pre-season hype by winning from pole as Ducati finish second again, Honda suffer and rookies impress.

It could have been more dramatic, but I'm not sure how. Rain in the desert wiped out qualifying and nearly forced a postponement of the race. Yamaha's factory new boy rode to a cool, calculated victory while their grand old boy again rescued what looked like a hopeless position with a podium. Yamaha's satellite team new boy barged his way to the front at the first corner and led for half–a-dozen laps. Yamaha's old boy, meanwhile, had a very low-key race with his new Italian employers. All this and yet the rider of the day was arguably Aleix Espargaro who found he had plenty of tyre left at the end of the race and used it to catapult the Aprilia up to sixth.

The weather affected the Hondas most. After qualifying was rained off it looked as if the race would find a gap in the weather but as the bikes sat on the grid it came down again. There was much unseemly bickering about the course of action but after a delay of 45 minutes the race was started, albeit with the distance reduced by two laps. Worries about the dew point, after which the track gets very slippery very quickly, prompted most Honda riders to swap off the hard front tyre. This turned out to be a bad move, limiting the factory team's performance.

Anyone expecting an anticlimax when the race started were

quickly disabused as Johann Zarco, showing scant regard for reputations, elbowed his way to the front at the first corner. And then he pulled away steadily from the pack, setting the fastest lap of the race fourth time round. By lap six Johann had a lead of over one-and-a-half seconds and decided to stop pressing. However, next time round he fell at Turn 2, caught out by a small bump slightly off-line. It did nothing to reduce the impact of the double-Moto2 champion's first race in MotoGP. The reverse could be said of the five-times World Champion Jorge Lorenzo, having his first race for Ducati after that big-money transfer from Yamaha. His 12th-place start was the first time he'd been of the first two rows at Losail, and then he got a nudge in the first corner. Nevertheless, 11th only just in front of the customer Ducatis of Baz and Barbera was hardly impressive.

As this was all playing out, Ducati's nearly-man, Andrea Dovizioso, took over at the front and opened up a lead of a second over Marc Marquez. Then the factory Yamahas started to move forward. Viñales had spent the early part of the race in fifth and at half-distance found himself third thanks to Zarco and Iannone's crashes. Maverick then put the hammer down and jumped across the gap to Marquez, who was now in damage-limitation mode and found himself passed by both factory Yamahas almost simultaneously. Valentino Rossi had attached himself to Viñales' rear wheel very early on, but after they'd passed the Honda he couldn't hang on as Maverick took just two laps to get to Dovizioso. There followed a ferocious dice, which for once this race followed the script in that the Yamaha was better round corners and the Ducati had more grunt on the straight. The outcome wasn't clear until the penultimate lap, when the Spaniard opened up a gap of just over a quarter of a second and doubled it on the last lap. Andrea Dovizioso was second for the third year in a row, but managed to hide any disappointment very well. He may also have been deriving a little satisfaction from the sudden cessation of comments about Ducati keeping the wrong Andrea.

Not that Andrea Iannone had a bad first race for Suzuki. He started in second, the best ever qualifying by a Suzuki rider at Losail, and crashed out when he tailgated Marquez. He claimed to have been surprised by how slow the Honda was going into a corner, perhaps underestimating how well he was getting the

ABOVE, LEFT-RIGHT Johann Zarco shocked and amazed by leading for five laps; Andrea Dovizioso finished second despite qualifying on the second row; Aleix Espargaro's late-race pace made him a candidate for rider of the day

LEFT Jorge Lorenzo had a lack-lustre debut for Ducati

MAIN Maverick Viñales backed up his winter testing form with a win in his first race for Yamaha

'IT WAS EVEN MORE IMPORTANT THAN THE
FIRST MOTOGP VICTORY, BECAUSE THERE
WAS SO MUCH PRESSURE'

MAVERICK VIÑALES

CLIPPED WINGS

After the technical upheaval of recent seasons, the only significant rule change for the 2017 season was the banning of aerodynamic wings – for a mix of safety and cost reasons. Ducati, the factory that had spent more time and effort on aerodynamics than anyone, were not happy. The new rule allowed for the homologation of a new fairing after the start of the season as well as the design homologated at this race. The use of last year's design, sans winglets, was also allowed. The new rule specifically bans external devices, targeting the wings that proliferated last year, but allows internal aerodynamic devices such as aerofoils within ducts.

Everyone except KTM had been seen to try a new design in

Suzuki into corners. In their first MotoGP race, both factory KTM riders brought their bikes home out of the points, and frankly anything more would have been a major achievement on their competition debut. They closed the gap to the front men with every session, however the Austrians will have cast envious glances at Aprilia, whose Aleix Espargaro showed the year-old project had made serious advances.

It is always dangerous to read too much into the results of the first race of the year. No-one had any doubts about Viñales' potential, but Johann Zarco's form was a genuine shock. His fourth place on the grid was the best qualifying by a rookie since 2008 when two of them headed the grid; Jorge Lorenzo was on pole in Qatar with James Toseland second, but not everyone thought the Frenchman would carry his form into the rest of the season. It is also worth noting that but for Zarco the form of his fellow rookies Folger and Rins would have attracted considerable attention.

One thing was definitively underlined; Maverick Viñales is the real deal. His form in pre-season testing didn't evaporate as soon as race day dawned despite suffering his first Yamaha crash in FP2. He took his first pole in MotoGP, making him the first rider to start from pole position in all three current classes, and the win made him the second youngest rider ever to win top-class races on different makes of motorcycle. Only Mike Hailwood did it younger (on Norton and MV Agusta). In the race he had to keep calm after a tricky start and then overhaul two top men. There is also no reason why he should not be a championship contender. If Valentino Rossi felt any sense of relief when Jorge Lorenzo departed for Ducati, it certainly didn't last long.

MAIN | Johann Zarco shocked and amazed by leading for five laps

LEFT, TOP-BOTTOM | Hector Barbera's race was comprised by a recent collarbone injury: raincoats in pit lane; Never count him out, Valentino Rossi on his way to the podium

testing, with Ducati's being the most radical – no surprise there, but only Suzuki brought their 'aero' fairing to Losail. It was a relatively conservative design with intake vents on either side inside which aerodynamic 'blades' are mounted. Both Suzuki riders tried both designs with no apparent difference in top speed.

It is now generally accepted that wings were designed primarily as anti-wheelie aids but as with any aerodynamic device there is always a trade off between downforce and drag. No-one really expected any aero fairings to be raced at Losail, drag generated on the long, fast straight would negate any advantage gained in corner exit and most riders did not seem concerned about losing the wings, with the exception of Ducati's pilots. Anyone hoping for some radical bodywork was disappointed, and no factory showed any inclination to show their hand.

1 | QATAR

RACE RESULTS

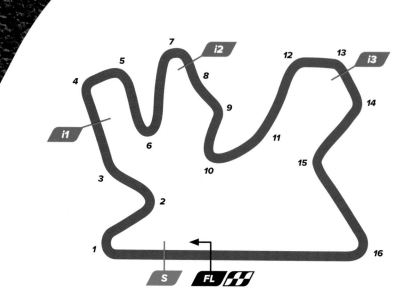

Sectors
Speed Trap
Finish Line

WINNER | MAVERICK VIÑALES

CIRCUIT LENGTH | 5.4 KM | 3.34 MILES

NO. OF LAPS | 22*

RACE DISTANCE | 118.4 KM* | 73.5 MILES*

CIRCUIT RECORD LAP | 1'54.927 | 168.5 KM/H
JORGE LORENZO (2016)

CIRCUIT BEST LAP | 1'53.927 | 170.0 KM/H
JORGE LORENZO (2008)

RACE CONDITION | DRY

AIR | 21°C

HUMIDITY | 96%

GROUND | 22°C

TISSOT SWISS WATCHES SINCE 1853 | MotoGP
OFFICIAL TIMEKEEPER

MICHELIN | MotoGP
OFFICIAL MotoGP™ CLASS TYRE

FRONT TYRES
SOFT
MEDIUM
HARD

REAR TYRES
SOFT
MEDIUM
HARD

< MILD   **TYRE SEVERITY**   SEVERE >

COMBINED FREE PRACTICE TIMES

	RIDER	NAT	TEAM	MACHINE	FP/TIME	GAP 1ST/PREV	
1	Maverick Viñales	SPA	Movistar Yamaha MotoGP	YAMAHA	FP1 1'54.316		
2	Andrea Iannone	ITA	Team SUZUKI ECSTAR	SUZUKI	FP3 1'54.848	0.532	0.532
3	Marc Marquez	SPA	Repsol Honda Team	HONDA	FP1 1'54.912	0.596	0.064
4	Johann Zarco	FRA	Monster Yamaha Tech 3	YAMAHA	FP3 1'55.008	0.692	0.096
5	Andrea Dovizioso	ITA	Ducati Team	DUCATI	FP3 1'55.042	0.726	0.034
6	Scott Redding	GBR	OCTO Pramac Racing	DUCATI	FP2 1'55.085	0.769	0.043
7	Dani Pedrosa	SPA	Repsol Honda Team	HONDA	FP3 1'55.113	0.797	0.028
8	Jonas Folger	GER	Monster Yamaha Tech 3	YAMAHA	FP2 1'55.208	0.892	0.095
9	Cal Crutchlow	GBR	LCR Honda	HONDA	FP3 1'55.211	0.895	0.003
10	Valentino Rossi	ITA	Movistar Yamaha MotoGP	YAMAHA	FP2 1'55.414	1.098	0.203
11	Danilo Petrucci	ITA	OCTO Pramac Racing	DUCATI	FP3 1'55.435	1.119	0.021
12	Jorge Lorenzo	SPA	Ducati Team	DUCATI	FP3 1'55.461	1.145	0.026
13	Alvaro Bautista	SPA	Pull&Bear Aspar Team	DUCATI	FP2 1'55.581	1.265	0.120
14	Loris Baz	FRA	Reale Avintia Racing	DUCATI	FP1 1'55.624	1.308	0.043
15	Aleix Espargaro	SPA	Aprilia Racing Team Gresini	APRILIA	FP3 1'55.634	1.318	0.010
16	Jack Miller	AUS	EG 0,0 Marc VDS	HONDA	FP2 1'55.959	1.643	0.325
17	Karel Abraham	CZE	Pull&Bear Aspar Team	DUCATI	FP2 1'56.003	1.687	0.044
18	Alex Rins	SPA	Team SUZUKI ECSTAR	SUZUKI	FP2 1'56.179	1.863	0.176
19	Tito Rabat	SPA	EG 0,0 Marc VDS	HONDA	FP2 1'56.368	2.052	0.189
20	Hector Barbera	SPA	Reale Avintia Racing	DUCATI	FP1 1'56.725	2.409	0.357
21	Sam Lowes	GBR	Aprilia Racing Team Gresini	APRILIA	FP3 1'56.854	2.538	0.129
22	Pol Espargaro	SPA	Red Bull KTM Factory Racing	KTM	FP2 1'57.116	2.800	0.262
23	Bradley Smith	GBR	Red Bull KTM Factory Racing	KTM	FP3 1'57.654	3.338	0.538

Qualifying practice cancelled due to rain, final grid positions based on combined free practice times

1 | MAVERICK VIÑALES
Lost ground at the start from his first MotoGP pole after contact with Zarco, so had to fight back from fifth. Kept calm as others crashed and closed down Marquez and Dovizioso. A lesson in how to deal with pressure.

2 | ANDREA DOVIZIOSO
Swapped to the soft rear tyre on the grid. Led the middle portion of the race after Zarco crashed and then put up spirited resistance to Viñales but had to settle for second for the third year in a row here.

3 | VALENTINO ROSSI
Looked lost in practice, as he had done pre-season, and started from tenth, but brought all his experience to bear. Said he was happy when he got to fifth but was delighted with the podium finish.

4 | MARC MARQUEZ
Swapped to the medium front tyre when the race was shortened to minimise crash risk, this turned out to be a major mistake and Marc actually seemed happy to finish fourth.

5 | DANI PEDROSA
Like his teammate, used the medium front and regretted it. Rode to conserve the tyre but then had to fend off Aleix Espargaro in the closing laps.

6 | ALEIX ESPARGARO
Probably the ride of the day. Started back on the fifth row and finished seven-and-a-half seconds behind the winner. The Aprilia seems to conserve tyres well and in the final laps Aleix charged, even passing Pedrosa with three laps to go.

7 | SCOTT REDDING
A promising start to the year after problems in warm up. Lost time when Zarco pushed past at the first corner then had a good dice with Miller.

8 | JACK MILLER
His best dry-weather MotoGP finish, bearing out the promise of pre-season testing. Given the weather on the second and third days, Jack reckoned his FP1 crash prevented an even better showing.

9 | ALEX RINS
First rookie home; a really solid MotoGP debut. Learnt a lot in the race and was able to pass Folger on the final corner.

10 | JONAS FOLGER
Started nervously and dropped back to eighteenth before working his way up to tenth. Under normal circumstances, a top-ten for a rookie on debut would create some excitement, but not this year!

11 | JORGE LORENZO
Not a stellar start to his Ducati career. Hung out to dry at Turn 1 then lapped well before losing some confidence in his tyres when he found the bike very physical.

12 | LORIS BAZ
Closer to the winner than he'd ever been in a dry race but hampered by severe arm pump from the start. That prevented him from holding off Lorenzo at the finish.

RACE LAP CHART

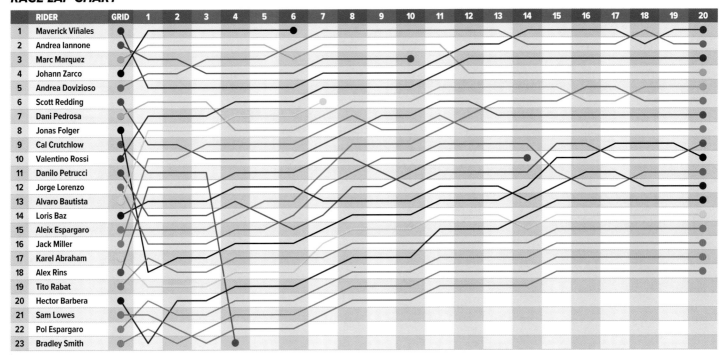

RIDER	GRID	1	2	3	4	5	6	7	8	9	10	11	12	13	14	15	16	17	18	19	20
1 Maverick Viñales																					
2 Andrea Iannone																					
3 Marc Marquez																					
4 Johann Zarco																					
5 Andrea Dovizioso																					
6 Scott Redding																					
7 Dani Pedrosa																					
8 Jonas Folger																					
9 Cal Crutchlow																					
10 Valentino Rossi																					
11 Danilo Petrucci																					
12 Jorge Lorenzo																					
13 Alvaro Bautista																					
14 Loris Baz																					
15 Aleix Espargaro																					
16 Jack Miller																					
17 Karel Abraham																					
18 Alex Rins																					
19 Tito Rabat																					
20 Hector Barbera																					
21 Sam Lowes																					
22 Pol Espargaro																					
23 Bradley Smith																					

RACE CLASSIFICATION AFTER 20 LAPS - 107.6 KM*

	RIDER	NAT	TEAM	MACHINE	TIME	+ GAP	TYRES
1	Maverick Viñales	SPA	Movistar Yamaha MotoGP	YAMAHA	38'59.999		M/M
2	Andrea Dovizioso	ITA	Ducati Team	DUCATI	39'00.460	0.461	M/S
3	Valentino Rossi	ITA	Movistar Yamaha MotoGP	YAMAHA	39'01.927	1.928	M/M
4	Marc Marquez	SPA	Repsol Honda Team	HONDA	39'06.744	6.745	M/M
5	Dani Pedrosa	SPA	Repsol Honda Team	HONDA	39'07.127	7.128	M/M
6	Aleix Espargaro	SPA	Aprilia Racing Team Gresini	APRILIA	39'07.660	7.661	M/S
7	Scott Redding	GBR	OCTO Pramac Racing	DUCATI	39'09.781	9.782	M/M
8	Jack Miller	AUS	EG 0,0 Marc VDS	HONDA	39'14.485	14.486	M/M
9	Alex Rins	SPA	Team SUZUKI ECSTAR	SUZUKI	39'14.787	14.788	M/M
10	Jonas Folger	GER	Monster Yamaha Tech 3	YAMAHA	39'15.068	15.069	M/M
11	Jorge Lorenzo	SPA	Ducati Team	DUCATI	39'20.515	20.516	M/S
12	Loris Baz	FRA	Reale Avintia Racing	DUCATI	39'21.254	21.255	M/M
13	Hector Barbera	SPA	Reale Avintia Racing	DUCATI	39'28.827	28.828	M/S
14	Karel Abraham	CZE	Pull&Bear Aspar Team	DUCATI	39'29.122	29.123	M/S
15	Tito Rabat	SPA	EG 0,0 Marc VDS	HONDA	39'29.469	29.470	M/M
16	Pol Espargaro	SPA	Red Bull KTM Factory Racing	KTM	39'33.600	33.601	M/S
17	Bradley Smith	GBR	Red Bull KTM Factory Racing	KTM	39'39.703	39.704	M/M
18	Sam Lowes	GBR	Aprilia Racing Team Gresini	APRILIA	39'47.130	47.131	M/S
NC	Danilo Petrucci	ITA	OCTO Pramac Racing	DUCATI	27'31.191	6 laps	M/M
NC	Andrea Iannone	ITA	Team SUZUKI ECSTAR	SUZUKI	19'34.409	10 laps	M/M
NC	Alvaro Bautista	SPA	Pull&Bear Aspar Team	DUCATI	13'46.030	13 laps	S/S
NC	Johann Zarco	FRA	Monster Yamaha Tech 3	YAMAHA	11'44.661	14 laps	M/S
NC	Cal Crutchlow	GBR	LCR Honda	HONDA	8'44.974	16 laps	M/M

CHAMPIONSHIP STANDINGS

	RIDER	NAT	TEAM	POINTS
1	Maverick Viñales	SPA	Movistar Yamaha MotoGP	25
2	Andrea Dovizioso	ITA	Ducati Team	20
3	Valentino Rossi	ITA	Movistar Yamaha MotoGP	16
4	Marc Marquez	SPA	Repsol Honda Team	13
5	Dani Pedrosa	SPA	Repsol Honda Team	11
6	Aleix Espargaro	SPA	Aprilia Racing Team Gresini	10
7	Scott Redding	GBR	OCTO Pramac Racing	9
8	Jack Miller	AUS	EG 0,0 Marc VDS	8
9	Alex Rins	SPA	Team SUZUKI ECSTAR	7
10	Jonas Folger	GER	Monster Yamaha Tech 3	6
11	Jorge Lorenzo	SPA	Ducati Team	5
12	Loris Baz	FRA	Reale Avintia Racing	4
13	Hector Barbera	SPA	Reale Avintia Racing	3
14	Karel Abraham	CZE	Pull&Bear Aspar Team	2
15	Tito Rabat	SPA	EG 0,0 Marc VDS	1
16	Pol Espargaro	SPA	Red Bull KTM Factory Racing	
17	Bradley Smith	GBR	Red Bull KTM Factory Racing	
18	Sam Lowes	GBR	Aprilia Racing Team Gresini	
19	Danilo Petrucci	ITA	OCTO Pramac Racing	
20	Andrea Iannone	ITA	Team SUZUKI ECSTAR	
21	Alvaro Bautista	SPA	Pull&Bear Aspar Team	
22	Johann Zarco	FRA	Monster Yamaha Tech 3	
23	Cal Crutchlow	GBR	LCR Honda	

*Race shortened to 20 laps due to weather conditions

13 HECTOR BARBERA
Raced just 20 days after a collarbone injury required a complicated operation. Short of bike time and far from fit, so happy to score points.

14 KAREL ABRAHAM
Scored points in MotoGP for the first time since 2014 with a smart ride that could have been even better had he not suffered problems with the visor of his helmet.

15 TITO RABAT
Happy to score a point after a winter interrupted by injury but couldn't respond when the Ducatis of Abraham and Barbera came past.

16 POL ESPARGARO
Finished 30 seconds behind the leader, which Pol had to be reminded is not a bad effort for a new machine, especially at a circuit they knew would be tough for the KTM.

17 BRADLEY SMITH
Improved on his practice time in the race and followed his teammate home. Happy to have done the best he could under the circumstances.

18 SAM LOWES
Somewhere between the pits, two warm-up laps and the grid, Sam's bike's electronics got confused and he did the race with incorrect throttle response. Did well to finish.

DID NOT FINISH

DANILO PETRUCCI
Felt something amiss on the warm-up laps. Victim of a mechanical malfunction just after he'd passed Lorenzo with five laps to go.

ANDREA IANNONE
Got the hole shot from second on the grid. Looked to be in the fight for the podium but crashed out when he appeared to touch Marquez's Honda. A sad end to a promising debut ride for Suzuki.

ALVARO BAUTISTA
Crashed out of an impressive sixth place at the last corner; not happy with the race being started so close to the Dew Point. Wanted it run on Monday.

JOHANN ZARCO
A brutal first corner put him in the lead and Johann pulled out a lead of over 1.5sec before deciding to back off a little and promptly crashing. An astonishing declaration of intent from a rookie.

CAL CRUTCHLOW
Like the factory Honda riders, he swapped to the medium front. Again, it was the wrong decision and he crashed and remounted, only to crash again when the throttle stuck open.

INTO THE DANGER ZONE

Maverick Viñales makes it two in a row as Yamaha pack the top six; Honda and Ducati suffer again.

So the four pre-season tests and the first race of year weren't a fluke. Maverick Viñales showed he will be a genuine championship contender as he calmly won again. That looked anything but a foregone conclusion right up until the fourth lap of the race, as on Saturday Marc Marquez maintained his one-hundred–percent pole-position record in Argentina and on Sunday opened up a lead of two-and-a-half seconds. Viñales had cut through from his sixth place – and top Yamaha – on the grid by then and the crowd looked forward to the first proper head-to-head battle between the two young masters. It didn't happen.

As soon as Viñales moved past Cal Crutchlow to take second, Marquez lost the front on the succession of small bumps at Turn 2, replicating the crash he'd had on the first day of practice. Marc was not happy and the lap times bear out his insistence that he was not pushing hard. His teammate, Dani Pedrosa, would have exactly the same crash before half-distance.

As in Qatar, practice and qualifying had been disrupted by the weather leaving a grid that looked very different from usual. The top Ducati was Karel Abraham in the middle of the front row while the factory bikes of Dovizioso and Lorenzo started from 13th and 16th, respectively, and there was no Yamaha in the top five for the first time in over two years. There was also a bit of tyre trouble to deal with. In order to avoid a repeat of 2016's disaster, which led to a two-part race, Race Direction instructed every rider to make a five-lap run on the hard rear tyre during practice on pain of a two-row grid penalty. Michelin had also planned to bring a new front tyre based on the stiffer construction trialed at Valencia as a fourth option but a general strike delayed their arrival, so the riders voted not to use it. Naturally, this all took place amid muttered theories about tyres being built to favour certain riders but as usual the whole affair had more of the cock-up than conspiracy about it.

Viñales then had most of the race left to make mistakes but showed no signs of weakness. He was inch perfect, wheels in line everywhere and appeared to be controlling the gap back to, first, Cal Crutchlow and then Valentino Rossi. The Englishman, now flying the flag for Honda, gradually lost ground hampered, he reported, by occasional warning lights on his dash. He didn't specify exactly what the problem might be, but the team hinted strongly that fuel consumption was the problem. The gap had grown to over two-and-a-half seconds by lap 18, after which Valentino Rossi came past. Viñales maintained his rhythm and, far from shrinking, the gap grew to over three seconds. It was an immaculate demonstration from a young man who gave every impression of being immune to pressure. However, it was very noticeable that Rossi was much happier with his bike than he had been in Qatar. He may not have been quite too happy to note how well the Tech 3 team's rookies did. Johann Zarco looked like the anti-Viñales as he spun the back wheel and went sideways at every corner on his way though the pack to an eventual fifth. He would be followed home by his teammate but both were passed in the closing stages by a charging Alvaro Bautista who was doing a very good impersonation of Aleix Espargaro in Qatar. The Aprilia rider had looked as if he might manage the same trick again but, as he caught up to the hectic fight for fourth place, he crashed braking for the first corner and scooped up Andrea Dovizioso, who must think Argentina has got it in for him. Dovi refused to blame Aleix, instead having a few harsh words for Danilo Petrucci's riding which, he said was ridiculous given he'd obviously ruined his rear tyre.

It is true, however, that the factory Ducatis' problems were caused by their low qualifying positions. Arguably, Dovi wouldn't have been in the scrap for fourth if he'd dealt with the mixed conditions

LEFT Karel Abraham's second place on the grid was a reward for a gutsy ride

MAIN The fight for second place; Crutchlow chases Rossi

BELOW, LEFT-RIGHT Zarco had another spectacular ride, this time to the finish; Bautista's late charge took him to fourth; Argentina continued to jinx Dovizioso who was involved in someone else's crash for the second year running

in qualifying better, but Jorge Lorenzo didn't even make it past the first corner after he tailgated Iannone. However, both the rider and team were surprisingly upbeat, claiming to have made solid progress during the weekend largely through reverting to the bike's original riding position. Confident noises about what would happen when they got back to Europe started to emerge.

It was not a good weekend for any factory other than Yamaha, with the exception of KTM. Against all expectations, both riders finished in the points in the bike's third GP (remember Mika Kallio made a wild-card entry at Valencia 2016). True they only beat one bike home, and that was Iannone's Suzuki after a jump-start penalty, but this time they weren't tailed off and chased Rabat and Barbera home.

It's always unwise to predict anything on the evidence provided by the first two or three races of the year, but already the '17 season is looking a little weird. Only one Honda rostrum in the first two races? And that was Cal Crutchlow's Team LCR satellite bike. Tech 3 Yamaha's rookies on satellite Yamahas threatening the factory bikes? Lorenzo and Iannone, the big transfer stories of the previous year, both struggling? Strange days indeed. Yet the Yamaha factory look entirely unconcerned. Maverick Viñales appears to be the real deal and Valentino Rossi ageless. The pair are handily clear of the opposition at the top of the points table after just two races followed by the Ducatis of Dovizioso and Scott Redding. Surely the Honda fight back will start at the next race.

MAIN | *Duelling cava - Rossi and Viñales exchange fire on the podium*

BELOW, LEFT-RIGHT | *Lorenzo's race lasted just one corner; Valentino continued to amaze*

LEFT, TOP TO BOTTOM | *Cal Crutchlow kept the Honda flag flying with third place; the dice for the final points; Andrea Iannone had the definition of a bad weekend*

BIG NUMBERS

It is easy to get blasé about the career of Valentino Rossi. He is such a fixture in the paddock that it's hard to recall the place without him, and indeed equally difficult to envisage the future without him. The Argentine Grand Prix was Valentino's 350th GP start. As there have been a total of 888 Grand Prix events (events note, not races) since the World Championship started in 1949, Rossi has ridden in 39.4% of all the GPs ever. This table shows all the riders who have made over 250 starts since the inception of the championship and graphically illustrates the scope of Valentino's career – so far!

RIDER	TOTAL	MotoGP 500cc	350cc	250cc Moto2	125cc Moto3	80cc 50cc
Valentino Rossi	349	289		30	30	
Loris Capirossi	328	217		84	27	
Jack Findlay	282	157	83	34	6	2
Alex Barros	276	245		14		17
Angel Nieto	265	1		16	160	88
Bruno Kneubuhler	264	71	46	52	86	9
Alex de Angelis	262	61		136	65	
Dani Pedrosa	260	182		32	46	
Andrea Dovizioso	259	161		49	49	
Randy de Puniet	253	140		80	33	
Jorge Lorenzo	251	157		48	46	

2 | ARGENTINA

RACE RESULTS

WINNER | MAVERICK VIÑALES

CIRCUIT LENGTH | 4.8 KM | 2.99 MILES

NO. OF LAPS | 25

RACE DISTANCE | 120.2 KM | 74.8 MILES

CIRCUIT RECORD LAP | 1'39.019 | 174.7 KM/H
VALENTINO ROSSI (2015)

CIRCUIT BEST LAP | 1'37.683 | 177.1 KM/H
MARC MARQUEZ (2014)

RACE CONDITION | DRY

AIR | 20°C

HUMIDITY | 60%

GROUND | 25°C

Sectors
Speed Trap
Finish Line

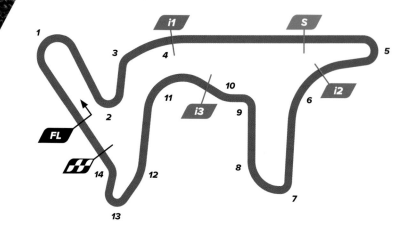

TISSOT SWISS WATCHES SINCE 1853 / motoGP

OFFICIAL TIMEKEEPER

MICHELIN / motoGP

OFFICIAL MotoGP™ CLASS TYRE

FRONT TYRES
SOFT
MEDIUM
HARD

REAR TYRES
SOFT
MEDIUM
HARD

< MILD   **TYRE SEVERITY**   SEVERE >

QUALIFYING RESULTS

	RIDER	NAT	TEAM	MACHINE	QP/TIME		GAP 1ST/PREV	
1	Marc Marquez	SPA	Repsol Honda Team	HONDA	Q2	1'47.512		
2	Karel Abraham	CZE	Pull&Bear Aspar Team	DUCATI	Q2	1'48.275	0.763	0.763
3	Cal Crutchlow	GBR	LCR Honda	HONDA	Q2	1'48.278	0.766	0.003
4	Danilo Petrucci	ITA	OCTO Pramac Racing	DUCATI	Q2	1'48.908	1.396	0.630
5	Dani Pedrosa**	SPA	Repsol Honda Team	HONDA	Q2	1'49.008	1.496	0.100
6	Maverick Viñales	SPA	Movistar Yamaha MotoGP	YAMAHA	Q2	1'49.218	1.706	0.210
7	Valentino Rossi**	ITA	Movistar Yamaha MotoGP	YAMAHA	Q2	1'49.272	1.760	0.054
8	Aleix Espargaro	SPA	Aprilia Racing Team Gresini	APRILIA	Q2	1'49.323	1.811	0.051
9	Loris Baz	FRA	Reale Avintia Racing	DUCATI	Q2	1'49.630	2.118	0.307
10	Alvaro Bautista	SPA	Pull&Bear Aspar Team	DUCATI	Q2	1'49.724	2.212	0.094
11	Jonas Folger	GER	Monster Yamaha Tech 3	YAMAHA	Q2	1'49.825	2.313	0.101
12	Andrea Iannone	ITA	Team SUZUKI ECSTAR	SUZUKI	Q2	1'50.725	3.213	0.900
13	Andrea Dovizioso	ITA	Ducati Team	DUCATI	Q1	1'49.488	*0.253	0.067
14	Johann Zarco	FRA	Monster Yamaha Tech 3	YAMAHA	Q1	1'49.916	*0.681	0.428
15	Scott Redding	GBR	OCTO Pramac Racing	DUCATI	Q1	1'50.048	*0.813	0.132
16	Jorge Lorenzo	SPA	Ducati Team	DUCATI	Q1	1'50.310	*1.075	0.262
17	Jack Miller	AUS	EG 0,0 Marc VDS	HONDA	Q1	1'50.319	*1.084	0.009
18	Pol Espargaro	SPA	Red Bull KTM Factory Racing	KTM	Q1	1'50.673	*1.438	0.354
19	Bradley Smith	GBR	Red Bull KTM Factory Racing	KTM	Q1	1'50.676	*1.441	0.003
20	Tito Rabat	SPA	EG 0,0 Marc VDS	HONDA	Q1	1'50.910	*1.675	0.234
21	Hector Barbera	SPA	Reale Avintia Racing	DUCATI	Q1	1'51.058	*1.823	0.148
22	Sam Lowes	GBR	Aprilia Racing Team Gresini	APRILIA	Q1	1'51.199	*1.964	0.141
23	Alex Rins	SPA	Team SUZUKI ECSTAR	SUZUKI	Q1	1'52.340	*3.105	1.141

*Gap to the fastest rider in the Q1 session
** Went forward from Q1 to Q2*

1 | MAVERICK VIÑALES
Started from the second row, needed two laps to get past Crutchlow then inherited the lead when Marquez fell. From then on, he put on a remarkably assured demonstration of smooth, controlled riding to make it two out of two. Unlike others, his wheels were never out of line.

2 | VALENTINO ROSSI
Like his teammate, came through after bad qualifying thanks to good work from his team. Where have we heard that before? Latched on to his teammate from the start but couldn't get past Crutchlow quickly. Happy with the podium in his 350th GP.

3 | CAL CRUTCHLOW
A great comeback after Qatar. Qualified on the front row, followed early leaders Marquez and Viñales but saw a warning lamp on his dash intermittently – fuel consumption? – and couldn't hold off Rossi, although he did give him a fight.

4 | ALVARO BAUTISTA
Tangled up with the big fight for fourth place in the first half of the race but in the final laps charged towards the top three on his soft tyres. A candidate for ride of the day.

5 | JOHANN ZARCO
His first MotoGP finish after an aggressive and impressive ride from the fifth row of the grid. Burnt his tyres up and couldn't hold off Bautista.

6 | JONAS FOLGER
A great start followed by a clever race. Saw that Petrucci was using up his tyres so tried to conserve his rubber and overtook the Italian with two laps to go.

7 | DANILO PETRUCCI
As aggressive as usual but that meant he used up his tyres very quickly. According to Dovizioso, that caused his crash with Espargaro and it certainly was the reason he was caught by Folger.

8 | SCOTT REDDING
Pleased with his result after disappointing qualifying and front-tyre troubles early on. When it all came right, Scott enjoyed a spirited dice with Miller and found himself fourth in the points table.

9 | JACK MILLER
Found more speed on race day than he had in practice or qualifying but still not happy with a full tank of petrol.

10 | KAREL ABRAHAM
Started a career-best second on the grid but on his second bike after a warm-up crash. Struggled early on but was then involved in an entertaining fight with Miller and Baz.

11 | LORIS BAZ
Lost his chance of capitalising on his grid position when he was caught up in Lorenzo's first-corner crash. Then wore out his front tyre so couldn't attack the group he caught. Thought he had the pace to be with Folger and Petrucci.

RACE LAP CHART

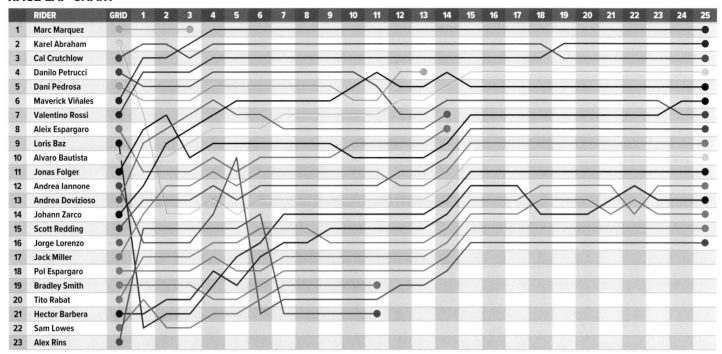

	RIDER	GRID	1	2	3	4	5	6	7	8	9	10	11	12	13	14	15	16	17	18	19	20	21	22	23	24	25
1	Marc Marquez																										
2	Karel Abraham																										
3	Cal Crutchlow																										
4	Danilo Petrucci																										
5	Dani Pedrosa																										
6	Maverick Viñales																										
7	Valentino Rossi																										
8	Aleix Espargaro																										
9	Loris Baz																										
10	Alvaro Bautista																										
11	Jonas Folger																										
12	Andrea Iannone																										
13	Andrea Dovizioso																										
14	Johann Zarco																										
15	Scott Redding																										
16	Jorge Lorenzo																										
17	Jack Miller																										
18	Pol Espargaro																										
19	Bradley Smith																										
20	Tito Rabat																										
21	Hector Barbera																										
22	Sam Lowes																										
23	Alex Rins																										

RACE CLASSIFICATION AFTER 25 LAPS - 120.15 KM

	RIDER	NAT	TEAM	MACHINE	TIME	+ GAP	TYRES
1	Maverick Viñales	SPA	Movistar Yamaha MotoGP	YAMAHA	41'45.060		M/M
2	Valentino Rossi	ITA	Movistar Yamaha MotoGP	YAMAHA	41'47.975	2.915	M/M
3	Cal Crutchlow	GBR	LCR Honda	HONDA	41'48.814	3.754	H/M
4	Alvaro Bautista	SPA	Pull&Bear Aspar Team	DUCATI	41'51.583	6.523	M/M
5	Johann Zarco	FRA	Monster Yamaha Tech 3	YAMAHA	42'00.564	15.504	M/H
6	Jonas Folger	GER	Monster Yamaha Tech 3	YAMAHA	42'03.301	18.241	M/M
7	Danilo Petrucci	ITA	OCTO Pramac Racing	DUCATI	42'05.106	20.046	H/H
8	Scott Redding	GBR	OCTO Pramac Racing	DUCATI	42'10.540	25.480	M/H
9	Jack Miller	AUS	EG 0,0 Marc VDS	HONDA	42'10.725	25.665	H/M
10	Karel Abraham	CZE	Pull&Bear Aspar Team	DUCATI	42'11.463	26.403	H/M
11	Loris Baz	FRA	Reale Avintia Racing	DUCATI	42'12.012	26.952	M/M
12	Tito Rabat	SPA	EG 0,0 Marc VDS	HONDA	42'26.935	41.875	H/M
13	Hector Barbera	SPA	Reale Avintia Racing	DUCATI	42'27.830	42.770	M/M
14	Pol Espargaro	SPA	Red Bull KTM Factory Racing	KTM	42'28.145	43.085	M/M
15	Bradley Smith	GBR	Red Bull KTM Factory Racing	KTM	42'28.512	43.452	M/M
16	Andrea Iannone	ITA	Team SUZUKI ECSTAR	SUZUKI	42'31.279	46.219	M/M
NC	Andrea Dovizioso	ITA	Ducati Team	DUCATI	23'31.497	11 laps	H/M
NC	Aleix Espargaro	SPA	Aprilia Racing Team Gresini	APRILIA	23'31.661	11 laps	H/H
NC	Dani Pedrosa	SPA	Repsol Honda Team	HONDA	21'48.977	12 laps	H/M
NC	Sam Lowes	GBR	Aprilia Racing Team Gresini	APRILIA	18'51.906	14 laps	H/H
NC	Alex Rins	SPA	Team SUZUKI ECSTAR	SUZUKI	19'14.623	14 laps	H/M
NC	Marc Marquez	SPA	Repsol Honda Team	HONDA	5'02.050	22 laps	H/M
NC	Jorge Lorenzo	SPA	Ducati Team	DUCATI		0 laps	M/M

CHAMPIONSHIP STANDINGS

	RIDER	NAT	TEAM	POINTS
1	Maverick Viñales	SPA	Movistar Yamaha MotoGP	50
2	Valentino Rossi	ITA	Movistar Yamaha MotoGP	36
3	Andrea Dovizioso	ITA	Ducati Team	20
4	Scott Redding	GBR	OCTO Pramac Racing	17
5	Cal Crutchlow	GBR	LCR Honda	16
6	Jonas Folger	GER	Monster Yamaha Tech 3	16
7	Jack Miller	AUS	EG 0,0 Marc VDS	15
8	Marc Marquez	SPA	Repsol Honda Team	13
9	Alvaro Bautista	SPA	Pull&Bear Aspar Team	13
10	Dani Pedrosa	SPA	Repsol Honda Team	11
11	Johann Zarco	FRA	Monster Yamaha Tech 3	11
12	Aleix Espargaro	SPA	Aprilia Racing Team Gresini	10
13	Danilo Petrucci	ITA	OCTO Pramac Racing	9
14	Loris Baz	FRA	Reale Avintia Racing	9
15	Karel Abraham	CZE	Pull&Bear Aspar Team	8
16	Alex Rins	SPA	Team SUZUKI ECSTAR	7
17	Hector Barbera	SPA	Reale Avintia Racing	6
18	Jorge Lorenzo	SPA	Ducati Team	5
19	Tito Rabat	SPA	EG 0,0 Marc VDS	5
20	Pol Espargaro	SPA	Red Bull KTM Factory Racing	2
21	Bradley Smith	GBR	Red Bull KTM Factory Racing	1
22	Andrea Iannone	ITA	Team SUZUKI ECSTAR	
23	Sam Lowes	GBR	Aprilia Racing Team Gresini	

12 | TITO RABAT
An encouraging race after difficult qualifying. Came out on top of a four-man dice.

13 | HECTOR BARBERA
Back to full fitness but having the same chronic problems with the bike. Said he never did one corner the way he wanted to all weekend and was now clear he had to change his style not the bike's settings.

14 | POL ESPARGARO
Delighted to score points in the KTM's second race but realistic about the work ahead. A little more speed would have helped in the dice with Rabat and Barbera.

15 | BRADLEY SMITH
Struggled to lap in the 1min 41sec bracket in practice but did mid- to low-41s all race long. Happy with the progress being made.

16 | ANDREA IANNONE
A series of disasters. Rammed by Lorenzo at the first corner, which put him to the back of the field, and then given a ride-through penalty for jumping the start.

DID NOT FINISH

ANDREA DOVIZIOSO
An innocent victim of the domino effect at Turn 5. Hit by Espargaro's sliding Aprilia but put the blame on Petrucci. Thought he was on for fifth at least despite lack of grip.

ALEIX ESPARGARO
Started steadily but was making rapid progress through the group fighting for fourth and looking on for a repeat of his Qatar performance when he lost the front at Turn 5 and scooped up Dovizioso.

DANI PEDROSA
Tangled with Petrucci and Zarco early on then started to push and was closing on the top three when he fell a lap after setting his best lap of the race. Like his teammate, he went down at Turn 2 and blamed the bumps.

SAM LOWES
Stopped by a gearbox problem just before half distance.

ALEX RINS
Racing with an ankle injury incurred in training after Qatar. Was making good progress towards the points when he fell and aggravated the injury.

MARC MARQUEZ
Fell at Turn 2 of lap three when he lost the front, probably on a succession of small bumps. Maintained his 100% pole record at Termas and was leading, pushing hard to open a gap, when he fell.

JORGE LORENZO
Fell at the first corner trying to make up for his qualifying. Ran into Iannone's Suzuki.

GIVE ME FIVE!

Marc Marquez makes it five out of five at CoTA as Repsol Honda get both bikes on the podium again.

There was still a strong feeling that entropy was increasing in MotoGP with weather again disrupting practice and tyre choice changes on the grid as temperatures again went above anything the riders had seen all weekend. But this time things played out very much to the script. Marc Marquez started from pole for the fifth year in a row and duly took his fifth win, making it nine wins in a row on American tarmac. He was followed home by Valentino Rossi and his teammate; no surprises there, although the formbook strongly suggests a factory Honda one-two is the norm for the Texan circuit. So, things weren't quite as simple as usual.

First, Dani Pedrosa got out in front and looked like he was going to be able to exploit his medium front tyre in the final laps. Marquez, who had changed to a hard front on the grid with less than five minutes to go, needed time to assess his situation. He had only used the tyre briefly on the Friday so followed Dani for the opening eight laps and when he saw his teammate start to run into trouble, he went past. Pedrosa had been running a pace that he thought would conserve his rear tyre for the end of the race so was more than a little surprised when he started having trouble with the front tyre so early on. He had no defence to Marquez, or Rossi who shadowed the Honda for most of the race before passing three laps from the flag and opening a decisive gap.

Now there is nothing unusual about Valentino Rossi finishing on the podium, but this was his best result at the Circuit of The Americas and came from his first front-row start of the season. In a major change of direction, he gave a lot of the credit to the 2017 M1. Valentino had always maintained that it is quite normal to be slower on a new bike for a race or two than on the previous year's machine but that is assuming the rider can see the potential for improvement. This was the first time he was publicly positive about the new model, saying it now allowed him to attack "at the end of races."

There's no doubt he was in a good mood. Second place put Valentino to the top of the championship points table for the first time since the final race of the 2015 season. He was also the oldest man to lead the top championship since the 42-year old Jack Findlay in 1977! Valentino's joy will have been amplified by the fate of his teammate, and the man he took the points lead from. Maverick Viñales looked like he was going to carry on where he left off in Argentina. He started from the middle of the front row but got hung out to dry at the first corner and pushed back to fifth. On the second lap he took fourth off Jorge Lorenzo but fell at the long right towards the end of the lap, Turn 16, fortunately without injury. Neither rider nor team could find anything in the data to suggest there had been a mistake. There were the first signs of stress and suspicion about the front tyre.

Valentino's only moment of stress came when he was punted off track by a highly optimistic move by Johann Zarco. Again, the Frenchman demonstrated that he was not going to be intimidated, in fact he again demonstrated that the established stars should be the ones doing the worrying. His ability to run softer tyre options, a result of concentrating on smoothing out his riding, also raised a few eyebrows.

The other man who looked as if he might have a say in the podium positions was Cal Crutchlow. One of the few who switched to the hard front tyre, he closed in on Zarco but ran off track and had to regroup. There was time to catch and pass the Frenchman, but no more. However, fifth place for the most exciting rookie of recent years was no mean achievement and put him a close seventh in the championship. Rossi, never one to

LEFT | One size fits all

MAIN | Negotiating CoTA's first corner is always a fraught affair

BELOW, LEFT-RIGHT | Viñales made his first mistake on a Yamaha; Crutchlow beat Zarco for fourth; Lorenzo's race was better than you'd think from his finishing position

'FIVE MINUTES BEFORE THE START, I SAID TO MY CHIEF MECHANIC 'OKAY, LET'S USE THE HARD TYRE'

MARC MÁRQUEZ

PENALTY LOOP

When Johann Zarco made an ill-advised lunge at Valentino Rossi at Turn 3 on Lap 7 the Italian had to pick up and run across the paved area on the inside of the corner, the alternative was a collision. He rejoined at the next corner a little further ahead of the Frenchman. Far enough ahead for Race Direction to decide that he had gained an advantage and therefore announce that Rossi would be subject to a 0.3sec "correction" to his race time to negate the advantage.

Race Direction were very careful not to call it a "penalty" as Rossi had done nothing wrong, but it still seemed an unusual thing to do

waste ammunition, had more than a few words to say about their coming together; a sure sign that he sees Zarco as a threat if not now then in the immediate future.

Another slightly unexpected indicator of the chaotic nature of MotoGP at the moment was Jorge Lorenzo qualifying as fastest Ducati, one place ahead of his teammate. Jorge had to go through the first qualifying session and then got on the back of the second row, a major improvement on the first two races. In the race, the two Ducatis swapped position early on and looked set to finish that way until Jorge struck tyre problems and lost places in the final laps. Nevertheless, there were indications that rider and bike were starting to understand each other.

So the paddock headed back to Europe after the opening three flyaway races not really quite sure how the season was going to unfold. All the top men except Rossi had already failed to score points in one race and none of the manufacturers' 2017 bikes appeared to be problem free. The only bikes that appeared to work everywhere and under all conditions were the 2016 Yamahas of the Tech 3 team, something their rookies were gleefully exploiting. Most years you'd say that situation wouldn't last once MotoGP got back to Europe and the tracks the factories have massive amounts of data for. This year, no-one was quite so sure.

MAIN | *Another podium finish took Valentino Rossi to the top of the points table*

LEFT, TOP-BOTTOM | *Bautista crashed and remounted to take the last point; Kenny Roberts Jnr, the 2000 World Champion, was a visitor to the Suzuki pit; both factory Hondas made it to the podium - which felt normal*

at best and a terrible precedent at worst.

Fortunately, the gaps at the flag were such that the "correction" made no difference to anyone. Valentino himself said he didn't like "the principle" of the decision, "But for me the problem isn't Race Direction, it's Zarco." Valentino then delivered a short lecture on the difference between MotoGP and Moto2.

Johann wasn't bothered. He had seen Valentino make a small mistake at Turn 1, which was why there was a chance to attack at Turn 3. Yes it was risky, said Johann, but there was a gap.

One thing the flyaway races had shown was that Johann Zarco will enliven what is already a very entertaining season.

3 | USA

RACE RESULTS

WINNER | MARC MARQUEZ

CIRCUIT LENGTH | 5.5 KM | 3.43 MILES

NO. OF LAPS | 21

RACE DISTANCE | 115.8 KM | 72.0 MILES

CIRCUIT RECORD LAP | 2'03.575 | 160.6 KM/H
MARC MARQUEZ (2014)

CIRCUIT BEST LAP | 2'02.135 | 162.4 KM/H
MARC MARQUEZ (2015)

RACE CONDITION | DRY

AIR | 23°C

HUMIDITY | 31%

GROUND | 40°C

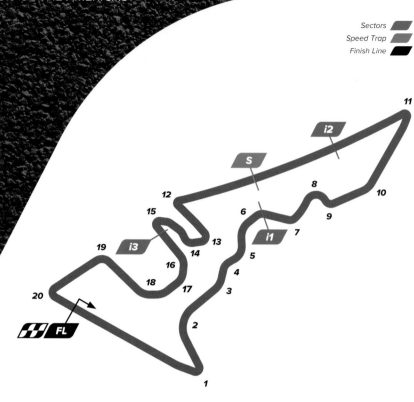

Sectors
Speed Trap
Finish Line

TISSOT | MotoGP
SWISS WATCHES SINCE 1853
OFFICIAL TIMEKEEPER

MICHELIN | MotoGP
OFFICIAL MotoGP™ CLASS TYRE

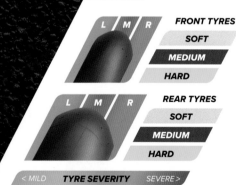

FRONT TYRES
SOFT
MEDIUM
HARD

REAR TYRES
SOFT
MEDIUM
HARD

< MILD   **TYRE SEVERITY**   SEVERE >

QUALIFYING RESULTS

	RIDER	NAT	TEAM	MACHINE	QP/TIME	GAP 1ST/PREV	
1	Marc Marquez	SPA	Repsol Honda Team	HONDA	Q2 2'02.741		
2	Maverick Viñales	SPA	Movistar Yamaha MotoGP	YAMAHA	Q2 2'02.871	0.130	0.130
3	Valentino Rossi	ITA	Movistar Yamaha MotoGP	YAMAHA	Q2 2'03.673	0.932	0.802
4	Dani Pedrosa	SPA	Repsol Honda Team	HONDA	Q2 2'03.866	1.125	0.193
5	Johann Zarco	FRA	Monster Yamaha Tech 3	YAMAHA	Q2 2'03.928	1.187	0.062
6	Jorge Lorenzo**	SPA	Ducati Team	DUCATI	Q2 2'04.151	1.410	0.223
7	Andrea Dovizioso	ITA	Ducati Team	DUCATI	Q2 2'04.431	1.690	0.280
8	Jonas Folger	GER	Monster Yamaha Tech 3	YAMAHA	Q2 2'04.623	1.882	0.192
9	Cal Crutchlow	GBR	LCR Honda	HONDA	Q2 2'04.661	1.920	0.038
10	Scott Redding	GBR	OCTO Pramac Racing	DUCATI	Q2 2'04.673	1.932	0.012
11	Andrea Iannone	ITA	Team SUZUKI ECSTAR	SUZUKI	Q2 2'05.741	3.000	1.068
12	Jack Miller**	AUS	EG 0,0 Marc VDS	HONDA	Q2 2'05.970	3.229	0.229
13	Danilo Petrucci	ITA	OCTO Pramac Racing	DUCATI	Q1 2'05.221	*0.783	0.010
14	Loris Baz	FRA	Reale Avintia Racing	DUCATI	Q1 2'05.231	*0.793	0.010
15	Hector Barbera	SPA	Reale Avintia Racing	DUCATI	Q1 2'05.541	*1.103	0.310
16	Tito Rabat	SPA	EG 0,0 Marc VDS	HONDA	Q1 2'05.920	*1.482	0.379
17	Karel Abraham	CZE	Pull&Bear Aspar Team	DUCATI	Q1 2'05.931	*1.493	0.011
18	Bradley Smith	GBR	Red Bull KTM Factory Racing	KTM	Q1 2'06.258	*1.820	0.327
19	Alvaro Bautista	SPA	Pull&Bear Aspar Team	DUCATI	Q1 2'06.295	*1.857	0.037
20	Sam Lowes	GBR	Aprilia Racing Team Gresini	APRILIA	Q1 2'07.232	*2.794	0.937
21	Pol Espargaro	SPA	Red Bull KTM Factory Racing	KTM	Q1 2'07.601	*3.163	0.369
22	Aleix Espargaro	SPA	Aprilia Racing Team Gresini	APRILIA	FP2 2'05.468	1.407	DNS

Gap to the fastest rider in the Q1 session
** Went forward from Q1 to Q2*

1 | MARC MARQUEZ
Five visits to the Circuit of The Americas, five wins from pole position. Risked changing to the hard front on the grid, took a few laps to get the feel then attacked his teammate and pulled away.

2 | VALENTINO ROSSI
Another stunning result from an unpromising weekend. Getting to grips with the new bike and very fast on used tyres to secure his best ever result at CoTA and go top of the Championship.

3 | DANI PEDROSA
Got the holeshot from the middle of the second row and led for eight laps before being taken by his teammate. Finished the right side of his medium front tyre by the time Rossi arrived and after that avoided a repeat of Argentina's crash.

4 | CAL CRUTCHLOW
A great result from ninth on the grid. Quickly became entangled in a fight with Zarco then ran off track after getting past. Despite which, Cal was very close to another podium finish.

5 | JOHANN ZARCO
Lost places at the first corner but was combative again as he made up places, so much so that he drew criticism from Valentino Rossi for one move. Johann was unapologetic and stayed with the multiple-champion for most of the race.

6 | ANDREA DOVIZIOSO
Definitely a race of damage limitation on a track where not one of the Ducati riders was ever happy. Expected better but never had the pace he hoped for.

7 | ANDREA IANNONE
A decent second half of the race after many troubles in practice and the first five laps of the race. Lapped at the same pace as the top five and scored his first points for Suzuki.

8 | DANILO PETRUCCI
A great result after troubled qualifying. Credited his team with the decision to use the hard rear tyre, which helped him make great progress through the midfield in the second half of the race.

9 | JORGE LORENZO
Again happier than you'd have thought. Had good race pace following his teammate until some graining of the front tyre lost him two places in the closing laps.

10 | JACK MILLER
Another solid result but still complaining about lack of drive off the corners which prevented Jack from challenging Lorenzo. Also lost some feeling from the front.

11 | JONAS FOLGER
A tough race. Happy with the gap to the top men but not with the mistakes he made when the fuel load lightened.

12 | SCOTT REDDING
Destabilised by a warm-up crash. Chose the hard rear, like his teammate, but never found any grip. Consequently over-stressed the front trying to make up time.

RACE LAP CHART

----- Dashed line: Lapped rider

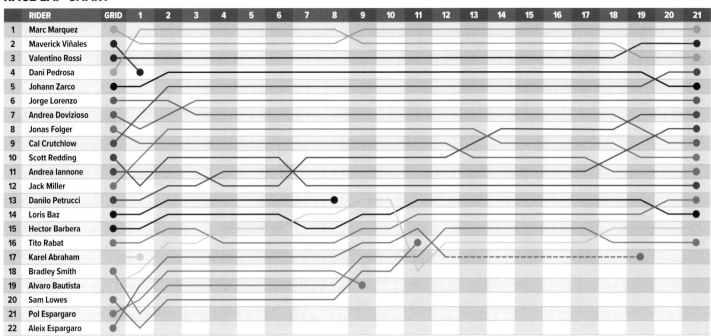

	RIDER	GRID	1	2	3	4	5	6	7	8	9	10	11	12	13	14	15	16	17	18	19	20	21
1	Marc Marquez																						
2	Maverick Viñales																						
3	Valentino Rossi																						
4	Dani Pedrosa																						
5	Johann Zarco																						
6	Jorge Lorenzo																						
7	Andrea Dovizioso																						
8	Jonas Folger																						
9	Cal Crutchlow																						
10	Scott Redding																						
11	Andrea Iannone																						
12	Jack Miller																						
13	Danilo Petrucci																						
14	Loris Baz																						
15	Hector Barbera																						
16	Tito Rabat																						
17	Karel Abraham																						
18	Bradley Smith																						
19	Alvaro Bautista																						
20	Sam Lowes																						
21	Pol Espargaro																						
22	Aleix Espargaro																						

RACE CLASSIFICATION AFTER 21 LAPS = 115.773 KM

	RIDER	NAT	TEAM	MACHINE	TIME	+ GAP	TYRES
1	Marc Marquez	SPA	Repsol Honda Team	HONDA	43'58.770		H/H
2	Valentino Rossi	ITA	Movistar Yamaha MotoGP	YAMAHA	44'01.839	3.069	M/M
3	Dani Pedrosa	SPA	Repsol Honda Team	HONDA	44'03.882	5.112	M/H
4	Cal Crutchlow	GBR	LCR Honda	HONDA	44'06.408	7.638	H/H
5	Johann Zarco	FRA	Monster Yamaha Tech 3	YAMAHA	44'06.727	7.957	M/M
6	Andrea Dovizioso	ITA	Ducati Team	DUCATI	44'12.828	14.058	M/S
7	Andrea Iannone	ITA	Team SUZUKI ECSTAR	SUZUKI	44'14.261	15.491	M/H
8	Danilo Petrucci	ITA	OCTO Pramac Racing	DUCATI	44'15.542	16.772	M/H
9	Jorge Lorenzo	SPA	Ducati Team	DUCATI	44'16.749	17.979	M/S
10	Jack Miller	AUS	EG 0,0 Marc VDS	HONDA	44'17.264	18.494	M/H
11	Jonas Folger	GER	Monster Yamaha Tech 3	YAMAHA	44'17.673	18.903	M/M
12	Scott Redding	GBR	OCTO Pramac Racing	DUCATI	44'27.505	28.735	M/H
13	Tito Rabat	SPA	EG 0,0 Marc VDS	HONDA	44'28.811	30.041	M/M
14	Hector Barbera	SPA	Reale Avintia Racing	DUCATI	44'30.134	31.364	M/S
15	Alvaro Bautista	SPA	Pull&Bear Aspar Team	DUCATI	45'05.317	66.547	M/S
16	Bradley Smith	GBR	Red Bull KTM Factory Racing	KTM	45'20.860	82.090	M/H
17	Aleix Espargaro	SPA	Aprilia Racing Team Gresini	APRILIA	45'43.993	2 laps	H/S
NC	Sam Lowes	GBR	Aprilia Racing Team Gresini	APRILIA	23'37.761	10 laps	H/H
NC	Pol Espargaro	SPA	Red Bull KTM Factory Racing	KTM	19'49.452	12 laps	M/M
NC	Loris Baz	FRA	Reale Avintia Racing	DUCATI	16'58.478	13 laps	M/S
NC	Maverick Viñales	SPA	Movistar Yamaha MotoGP	YAMAHA	2'07.393	20 laps	M/M
NC	Karel Abraham	CZE	Pull&Bear Aspar Team	DUCATI	2'11.727	20 laps	H/H
DNS	Alex Rins	SPA	Team SUZUKI ECSTAR	SUZUKI			

CHAMPIONSHIP STANDINGS

	RIDER	NAT	TEAM	POINTS
1	Valentino Rossi	ITA	Movistar Yamaha MotoGP	56
2	Maverick Viñales	SPA	Movistar Yamaha MotoGP	50
3	Marc Marquez	SPA	Repsol Honda Team	38
4	Andrea Dovizioso	ITA	Ducati Team	30
5	Cal Crutchlow	GBR	LCR Honda	29
6	Dani Pedrosa	SPA	Repsol Honda Team	27
7	Johann Zarco	FRA	Monster Yamaha Tech 3	22
8	Jonas Folger	GER	Monster Yamaha Tech 3	21
9	Scott Redding	GBR	OCTO Pramac Racing	21
10	Jack Miller	AUS	EG 0,0 Marc VDS	21
11	Danilo Petrucci	ITA	OCTO Pramac Racing	17
12	Alvaro Bautista	SPA	Pull&Bear Aspar Team	14
13	Jorge Lorenzo	SPA	Ducati Team	12
14	Aleix Espargaro	SPA	Aprilia Racing Team Gresini	10
15	Andrea Iannone	ITA	Team SUZUKI ECSTAR	9
16	Loris Baz	FRA	Reale Avintia Racing	9
17	Karel Abraham	CZE	Pull&Bear Aspar Team	8
18	Tito Rabat	SPA	EG 0,0 Marc VDS	8
19	Hector Barbera	SPA	Reale Avintia Racing	8
20	Alex Rins	SPA	Team SUZUKI ECSTAR	7
21	Pol Espargaro	SPA	Red Bull KTM Factory Racing	2
22	Bradley Smith	GBR	Red Bull KTM Factory Racing	1
23	Sam Lowes	GBR	Aprilia Racing Team Gresini	

13 | TITO RABAT
Three points-scoring rides in a row to start the year. Said he didn't push too hard at the start so had a little left later on for his fight with the Ducatis.

14 | HECTOR BARBERA
Still not happy with the wingless Ducati but starting to adjust his riding style. Happy to be in touch with some other Ducatis.

15 | ALVARO BAUTISTA
Crashed out of 13th and remounted to claim the last point. Like most Ducati riders, never happy with his set up.

16 | BRADLEY SMITH
Not surprisingly, suffered from a lack of data and raced on a tyre he hadn't done many laps on all weekend. Lost grip and couldn't hold off Bautista at the end.

17 | ALEIX ESPARGARO
Started last on the grid after missing qualifying and was making progress when he hit problems. Pitted to change the front tyre, after which he lapped at the pace he had been expecting.

DID NOT FINISH

SAM LOWES
Crashed out of 12th place while in the group fighting for points.

POL ESPARGARO
KTM's first mechanical problem in MotoGP turned out to be a broken clutch, which stopped Pol at half-distance.

LORIS BAZ
Ran off track when he found a false neutral then crashed trying to make time up on Scott Redding.

MAVERICK VIÑALES
Proved he is human after all with a second-lap crash at Turn 16. Lost the front.

KAREL ABRAHAM
A tale of two crashes. One in FP3 when he was hit by his teammate and injured an ankle then destroyed the bike on Lap 2 of the race

DID NOT START

ALEX RINS
Crashed in FP3 breaking both bones in his left forearm. Flew back to Barcelona for surgery.

DANI DOES IT AGAIN

Dani Pedrosa coped with the heat and worn-out tarmac better than the rest. Honda happy, Yamaha suffer, Lorenzo on the podium.

One of the perennial questions fans keep coming up with is why Dani Pedrosa keeps his ride at Repsol Honda. Jerez showed why, not that most sensible people asked the question in the first place. This was the 16th consecutive season in which Dani has won a GP and the 12th in MotoGP. Only Giacomo Agostini himself has equaled that run — from 1965-'76. And if you are HRC you need someone with such guaranteed form to back up the mercurial Marc Marquez and secure the Constructors and Teams championships. If you are Honda, that matters.

Yet again, the weather made life difficult for teams still trying to find a base setting and fully understand the Michelins on each new track. Rain interrupted Friday practice, again depriving teams of vital testing time. Then race day was considerably hotter than Friday and Saturday, sending the track temperature well over 40°C. The tarmac wasn't just into the temperature zone that sees tyres, any tyres, struggling to cope it was also worn out and very slick. The factory Yamaha men were already in serious trouble before the extreme conditions on race day, and this on a track that is always considered a Yamaha circuit.

In the spirit of this most confusing year, this Yamaha track produced an all-Honda front row and a runaway win for pole-man

ABOVE, LEFT-RIGHT | Johann Zarco ran with the top men again; Jorge Lorenzo started to repay Ducati's confidence in him; Valentino Rossi finished off the podium for the first time this season

MAIN | Perfect Pedrosa, Dani led every lap from pole and never gave the rest a chance

RIGHT | Lorenzo celebrates an unheralded podium finish

'I'M SUPER-HAPPY WITH THIS WIN IN JEREZ, A TRACK THAT I LOVE VERY MUCH, IN FRONT OF MY FAMILY, MY FRIENDS, AND ALL THESE AMAZING FANS'
DANI PEDROSA

Pedrosa who was only ever under pressure from his teammate Marc Marquez. This track is also supposed to expose the weak points of the Ducati, so how to explain Jorge Lorenzo's rostrum finish after a dispiriting start to his career with the Bologna factory? He too was a lot slower in the race than he was expecting, it's just that Jorge's slow lap was quicker than most people's. Significantly, he rode past both the factory Yamahas on consecutive laps before tracking Zarco's satellite bike for a few laps and then pulling away to a comfortable third place. His team reacted like they'd won the title, although it was easy to spot the signs of relief that ran through the celebrations. There were some very senior managers in the Ducati pit looking like some serious weight had been lifted from their shoulders.

In front of Jorge, Dani Pedrosa pulled out a lead of over one-and-a-half seconds in three laps then controlled the gap back to Marquez. The pair had fought tooth and nail for pole position and now Marquez again put the pressure on. As on Saturday, Dani responded and although the gap closed to just one second, Marc knew that he was pushing his luck. Crashing in qualifying is one thing, in the race quite another, so Marc decided not to push his luck. He knew he was in front of the other championship contenders and did not seem unhappy with twenty points, readily conceding that Dani is difficult to beat on a hot, slick track.

Both the factory Hondas used the hard front tyre but so did the factory Yamahas. Marquez said it wasn't hard enough, Dani said he'd probably have been quicker on the medium, and Maverick Viñales struggled not to say he'd got a faulty tyre. Valentino Rossi had an even worse time. As in every race so far this year, he was far from happy after qualifying but everyone expected another Sunday special where the team found an improvement in warm up and then Vale rode like, well, Valentino Rossi. This time they managed to make the bike worse, adding front-tyre problems to the lack of grip at the rear they'd had all weekend. Valentino was never a contender and in the third quarter of the race there was the shocking sight of Petrucci, Folger and Aleix Espargaro riding past him with ease.

MAIN Pedrosa is already gone as the pattern of the race emerges, the Yamahas would fade, Crutchlow and Iannone crash, leaving Marquez and Lorenzo to pick up the pieces

KTM GO BIG BANG

Having started the season with the last of the screamer engines, KTM had a rethink after a test. The riders were so keen on the new design that the team fitted them for Free Practice 1 and kept them.

The first motor had all the characteristics you'd expect of a screamer: vicious, difficult to control, prone to wheelspin and wheelies. It looked and sounded like a pre-big bang Honda. The new engine was so much more usable that Pol Espargaro practically had to be sedated so excited was he after cracking the top ten in FP3. It sounded different, the firing order had obviously

Not surprisingly, Valentino seemed less in love with the 2017-model M-1 than he had after the previous race. He was also anxious to try the stiff-construction front tyre that was supposed to be tried in Argentina. Valentino and everyone else got the chance to do that on the Monday after the race at the first test of the season.

Obviously this wasn't just a case of one tyre suiting the conditions and another not. What worked on the factory Hondas didn't on the factory Yamahas. And just to muddy the waters even further, the satellite Yamahas both went with the mediums and had no problems. Again Zarco was wonderfully aggressive in the opening laps as he pushed his way from sixth to third on Lap 2 and second two laps later. Just to show he hadn't adjusted his attitude one little bit after the coming together in Texas, Johann was particularly tough with Rossi.

The other technical talking point was aero fairings, as Yamaha and Suzuki tried their similar designs, tall vents on the fairing flanks with internal vanes. Yamaha didn't use them for the race, Suzuki did. One Aprilia rider, Sam Lowes, tested and raced what he called a "downforce fairing" with big pods either side of the central air intake. As with KTM's stubby winglets, this seemed to be a design the factory would persevere with on most tracks. There also seemed to be final agreement that their primary function was anti-wheelie out of slower corners.

One thing about the continuing chaos that everyone enjoyed is the way it has spread the wins – and crashes – around thus concertinaing the top men together at the top of the points table. Rossi just kept his championship lead from Viñales but Marquez closed to within four of the leader and Pedrosa to within ten. Anyone who thought we were going to start seeing patterns emerging when the championship got back to Europe turned out to be wrong. Again.

LEFT, TOP TO BOTTOM | *Scott Redding rode to good points thanks to finding some grip late on; Bautista and Miller came together at Turn 1, Alvaro's fault, Jack's retaliation*

been closed up, probably with a rephased crankshaft, and looked much, much steadier on track.

That might sound like a simple engine swap, but after just four races the KTM factory was able to get their electronics to do the job straight away. That was not the case at Honda when they made a similar change. It is impossible to overstate how difficult it is to take a racing project from a standing start to the level of Honda, Yamaha and Ducati. The Austrian factory says this is a five-year project, and it has to be said that their commitment cannot be doubted. They are a racing factory that is used to winning and they already have power and reliability. Now the really difficult bit starts.

4 | SPAIN

RACE RESULTS

WINNER | DANI PEDROSA

CIRCUIT LENGTH | 4.4 KM | 2.75 MILES

NO. OF LAPS | 27

RACE DISTANCE | 119.4 KM | 74.3 MILES

CIRCUIT RECORD LAP | 1'38.735 | 161.2 KM/H
JORGE LORENZO (2015)

CIRCUIT BEST LAP | 1'37.910 | 162.6 KM/H
JORGE LORENZO (2015)

RACE CONDITION | DRY

AIR | 28°C

HUMIDITY | 25%

GROUND | 41°C

Sectors
Speed Trap
Finish Line

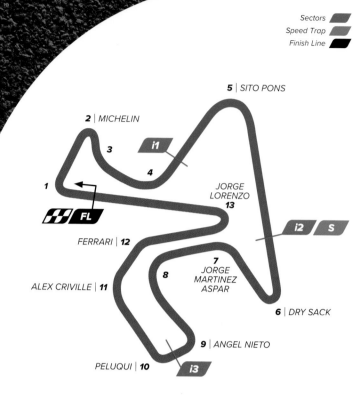

TISSOT
SWISS WATCHES SINCE 1853 | MotoGP™

OFFICIAL TIMEKEEPER

MICHELIN | MotoGP™

OFFICIAL MotoGP™ CLASS TYRE

FRONT TYRES
L M R
SOFT
MEDIUM
HARD

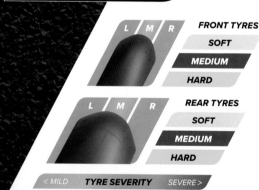

REAR TYRES
L M R
SOFT
MEDIUM
HARD

< MILD **TYRE SEVERITY** SEVERE >

QUALIFYING RESULTS

	RIDER	NAT	TEAM	MACHINE	QP/TIME		GAP 1ST/PREV	
1	Dani Pedrosa	SPA	Repsol Honda Team	HONDA	Q2	1'38.249		
2	Marc Marquez	SPA	Repsol Honda Team	HONDA	Q2	1'38.298	0.049	0.049
3	Cal Crutchlow	GBR	LCR Honda	HONDA	Q2	1'38.453	0.204	0.155
4	Maverick Viñales	SPA	Movistar Yamaha MotoGP	YAMAHA	Q2	1'38.677	0.428	0.224
5	Andrea Iannone**	ITA	Team SUZUKI ECSTAR	SUZUKI	Q2	1'38.744	0.495	0.067
6	Johann Zarco	FRA	Monster Yamaha Tech 3	YAMAHA	Q2	1'38.861	0.612	0.117
7	Valentino Rossi	ITA	Movistar Yamaha MotoGP	YAMAHA	Q2	1'38.908	0.659	0.047
8	Jorge Lorenzo	SPA	Ducati Team	DUCATI	Q2	1'38.910	0.661	0.002
9	Jonas Folger	GER	Monster Yamaha Tech 3	YAMAHA	Q2	1'39.108	0.859	0.198
10	Jack Miller	AUS	EG 0,0 Marc VDS	HONDA	Q2	1'39.125	0.876	0.017
11	Scott Redding	GBR	OCTO Pramac Racing	DUCATI	Q2	1'39.152	0.903	0.027
12	Aleix Espargaro**	SPA	Aprilia Racing Team Gresini	APRILIA	Q2	1'39.400	1.151	0.248
13	Danilo Petrucci	ITA	OCTO Pramac Racing	DUCATI	Q1	1'39.090	*0.171	0.148
14	Andrea Dovizioso	ITA	Ducati Team	DUCATI	Q1	1'39.255	*0.336	0.165
15	Pol Espargaro	SPA	Red Bull KTM Factory Racing	KTM	Q1	1'39.282	*0.363	0.027
16	Bradley Smith	GBR	Red Bull KTM Factory Racing	KTM	Q1	1'39.321	*0.402	0.039
17	Alvaro Bautista	SPA	Pull&Bear Aspar Team	DUCATI	Q1	1'39.462	*0.543	0.141
18	Tito Rabat	SPA	EG 0,0 Marc VDS	HONDA	Q1	1'39.564	*0.645	0.102
19	Karel Abraham	CZE	Pull&Bear Aspar Team	DUCATI	Q1	1'39.678	*0.759	0.114
20	Loris Baz	FRA	Reale Avintia Racing	DUCATI	Q1	1'39.824	*0.905	0.146
21	Hector Barbera	SPA	Reale Avintia Racing	DUCATI	Q1	1'39.906	*0.987	0.082
22	Sam Lowes	GBR	Aprilia Racing Team Gresini	APRILIA	Q1	1'40.213	*1.294	0.307
23	Takuya Tsuda	JPN	Team SUZUKI ECSTAR	SUZUKI	Q1	1'40.386	*1.467	0.173

*Gap to the fastest rider in the Q1 session
** Went forward from Q1 to Q2*

1 | DANI PEDROSA
A perfect weekend: pole, fastest lap and the win. Went with the hard front even though he preferred the medium and managed the situation perfectly to win the 3000th Grand Prix race. Frankly, the result was never in doubt as long as Dani didn't make a mistake.

2 | MARC MARQUEZ
Felt even the hard front was too soft for him. Knew from FP1 that Pedrosa was strong, tried to push him in every session but had to concede in the race after a few scares. Checked where the Yamahas were and knew he'd be back in Championship contention.

3 | JORGE LORENZO
Typically aggressive early laps put him behind Zarco; Jorge then spent a few laps behind the Yamaha before out-braking him and pulling steadily away for his first rostrum as a Ducati rider. It was Ducati's 100th MotoGP podium.

4 | JOHANN ZARCO
Another remarkable race. Smashed his way up to second by Lap 4 then, contrary to expectations, made his soft tyres last the distance. Realised Lorenzo had better pace in the final stages and rode accordingly.

5 | ANDREA DOVIZIOSO
Like his teammate, made up a lot of places in the early laps after average qualifying. Settled in to a fight with the factory Yamahas and took advantage of their problems. Delighted with the result at a track that has never favoured the Ducati.

6 | MAVERICK VIÑALES
Confused by the effects of the temperature rise. Felt like he was going to crash in every corner. The hard front tyre, perfect in warm up, was far from it in the race. Only just held off Petrucci.

7 | DANILO PETRUCCI
Didn't start well but fought his way forward with great race pace. Took two laps to get past Rossi, which cost Danilo a chance of attacking Viñales on the run to the flag.

8 | JONAS FOLGER
Four points-scoring rides, three in the top ten, in his first four MotoGP races. Again disappointed with his early pace, especially as his lap times matched his teammate on worn tyres.

9 | ALEIX ESPARGARO
Claimed he hadn't used his knee-sliders such was the lack of grip. Didn't qualify well and started cautiously. Once he realised he wasn't going to catch Folger, Aleix shut up shop.

10 | VALENTINO ROSSI
A nightmare of a weekend-never higher than fifth. For once, the set-up changes for Sunday didn't work and he had no rear grip as well as the existing front-tyre problems. Simply had no defence in the closing stages and only just managed to hold off Redding.

11 | SCOTT REDDING
Started badly, dropping to 20th thanks to no rear grip and a shove from Baz. From ten laps in, he found good grip and pace.

RACE LAP CHART

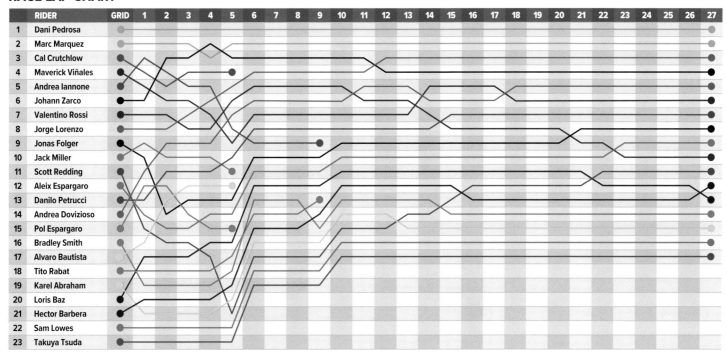

RIDER	GRID	1	2	3	4	5	6	7	8	9	10	11	12	13	14	15	16	17	18	19	20	21	22	23	24	25	26	27
1 Dani Pedrosa																												
2 Marc Marquez																												
3 Cal Crutchlow																												
4 Maverick Viñales																												
5 Andrea Iannone																												
6 Johann Zarco																												
7 Valentino Rossi																												
8 Jorge Lorenzo																												
9 Jonas Folger																												
10 Jack Miller																												
11 Scott Redding																												
12 Aleix Espargaro																												
13 Danilo Petrucci																												
14 Andrea Dovizioso																												
15 Pol Espargaro																												
16 Bradley Smith																												
17 Alvaro Bautista																												
18 Tito Rabat																												
19 Karel Abraham																												
20 Loris Baz																												
21 Hector Barbera																												
22 Sam Lowes																												
23 Takuya Tsuda																												

RACE CLASSIFICATION AFTER 27 LAPS = 119.421 KM

	RIDER	NAT	TEAM	MACHINE	TIME	+ GAP	TYRES
1	Dani Pedrosa	SPA	Repsol Honda Team	HONDA	45'26.827		H/M
2	Marc Marquez	SPA	Repsol Honda Team	HONDA	45'32.963	6.136	H/H
3	Jorge Lorenzo	SPA	Ducati Team	DUCATI	45'41.594	14.767	M/M
4	Johann Zarco	FRA	Monster Yamaha Tech 3	YAMAHA	45'44.428	17.601	M/M
5	Andrea Dovizioso	ITA	Ducati Team	DUCATI	45'49.740	22.913	H/M
6	Maverick Viñales	SPA	Movistar Yamaha MotoGP	YAMAHA	45'51.383	24.556	H/M
7	Danilo Petrucci	ITA	OCTO Pramac Racing	DUCATI	45'51.786	24.959	H/M
8	Jonas Folger	GER	Monster Yamaha Tech 3	YAMAHA	45'54.548	27.721	M/M
9	Aleix Espargaro	SPA	Aprilia Racing Team Gresini	APRILIA	45'58.060	31.233	H/M
10	Valentino Rossi	ITA	Movistar Yamaha MotoGP	YAMAHA	46'05.509	38.682	H/M
11	Scott Redding	GBR	OCTO Pramac Racing	DUCATI	46'07.806	40.979	H/M
12	Hector Barbera	SPA	Reale Avintia Racing	DUCATI	46'10.026	43.199	M/M
13	Loris Baz	FRA	Reale Avintia Racing	DUCATI	46'10.038	43.211	H/M
14	Bradley Smith	GBR	Red Bull KTM Factory Racing	KTM	46'14.791	47.964	H/M
15	Karel Abraham	CZE	Pull&Bear Aspar Team	DUCATI	46'18.106	51.279	H/M
16	Sam Lowes	GBR	Aprilia Racing Team Gresini	APRILIA	46'35.712	68.885	H/H
17	Takuya Tsuda	JPN	Team SUZUKI ECSTAR	SUZUKI	46'54.277	87.450	H/M
NC	Andrea Iannone	ITA	Team SUZUKI ECSTAR	SUZUKI	15'19.450	18 laps	H/M
NC	Tito Rabat	SPA	EG 0,0 Marc VDS	HONDA	15'24.810	18 laps	H/M
NC	Cal Crutchlow	GBR	LCR Honda	HONDA	8'29.685	22 laps	H/H
NC	Jack Miller	AUS	EG 0,0 Marc VDS	HONDA	8'33.241	22 laps	H/M
NC	Alvaro Bautista	SPA	Pull&Bear Aspar Team	DUCATI	8'33.277	22 laps	H/M
NC	Pol Espargaro	SPA	Red Bull KTM Factory Racing	KTM	8'35.892	22 laps	H/M

CHAMPIONSHIP STANDINGS

	RIDER	NAT	TEAM	POINTS
1	Valentino Rossi	ITA	Movistar Yamaha MotoGP	62
2	Maverick Viñales	SPA	Movistar Yamaha MotoGP	60
3	Marc Marquez	SPA	Repsol Honda Team	58
4	Dani Pedrosa	SPA	Repsol Honda Team	52
5	Andrea Dovizioso	ITA	Ducati Team	41
6	Johann Zarco	FRA	Monster Yamaha Tech 3	35
7	Cal Crutchlow	GBR	LCR Honda	29
8	Jonas Folger	GER	Monster Yamaha Tech 3	29
9	Jorge Lorenzo	SPA	Ducati Team	28
10	Danilo Petrucci	ITA	OCTO Pramac Racing	26
11	Scott Redding	GBR	OCTO Pramac Racing	26
12	Jack Miller	AUS	EG 0,0 Marc VDS	21
13	Aleix Espargaro	SPA	Aprilia Racing Team Gresini	17
14	Alvaro Bautista	SPA	Pull&Bear Aspar Team	14
15	Loris Baz	FRA	Reale Avintia Racing	12
16	Hector Barbera	SPA	Reale Avintia Racing	12
17	Andrea Iannone	ITA	Team SUZUKI ECSTAR	9
18	Karel Abraham	CZE	Pull&Bear Aspar Team	9
19	Tito Rabat	SPA	EG 0,0 Marc VDS	8
20	Alex Rins	SPA	Team SUZUKI ECSTAR	7
21	Bradley Smith	GBR	Red Bull KTM Factory Racing	3
22	Pol Espargaro	SPA	Red Bull KTM Factory Racing	2
23	Sam Lowes	GBR	Aprilia Racing Team Gresini	

---

12 | HECTOR BARBERA
Starting to understand the bike and get some feel for the first time. A step forward?

13 | LORIS BAZ
Followed an aggressive start with a good race enlivened by a spirited dice with his teammate over the final five laps.

14 | BRADLEY SMITH
Another learning experience with a hard front tyre in extreme conditions. The highlight of the weekend was

nearly going direct to the final qualifying session.

15 | KAREL ABRAHAM
No feeling at the front and handicapped by his foot injury from the USA. Admitted that he was lucky to inherit the final point thanks to others' crashes.

16 | SAM LOWES
Probably chose the wrong front tyre but had no grip at the rear either. Like his teammate, just had to try and get it to the flag.

17 | TAKUYA TSUDA
Suzuki's test rider replaced the injured Rins and finished the race, his first experience of MotoGP

DID NOT FINISH

ANDREA IANNONE
Good qualifying and a fighting first few laps – he was as high as third. Andrea's pace dropped off after four laps and he crashed at Criville on Lap 7.

TITO RABAT
Another victim of the low grip levels. Lost the front just after taking 13th place off Bradley Smith.

CAL CRUTCHLOW
Qualified on the front row and was looking good in fourth place behind Zarco when he lost the front at Criville. Annoyed to have lost what he saw as an opportunity for another podium finish.

ALVARO BAUTISTA
Lost the front going into Turn 1 and took out Miller. Not too worried about the push but did not like Miller kicking his bike.

JACK MILLER
Involved in the hectic midfield dice and looking good, only to be scooped up by Bautista. Gave the Spaniard a shove in the gravel trap and incurred a fine.

POL ESPARGARO
Got a little over-excited with the potential of the new motor and crashed while optimistically aiming for a top-ten finish.

DID NOT RACE

ALEX RINS
Recovering from the broken arm sustained in Texas. Replaced by factory tester Tsuda.

RETURN OF THE MACK

Maverick Viñales won to retake the points lead as Rossi fell and Zarco thrilled the home crowd.

The abiding image of Le Mans 2017 (well, the happy one) will be Johann Zarco's face as he sat on the front row of the grid and listened to the French national anthem. A Le Mans crowd is rowdy at the best of times, belting out La Marseillaise they looked and sounded like they were about to storm the barricades in defence of their revolution. Johann soaked it all in and thought "Why not hear it again after the race?"

On a commercial note, Tech 3 had obviously sold a lot of merchandise. The stands at any GP are usually tinted yellow, at Le Mans they were black with flashes of Monster's green. The record crowd got what it came for. Despite practice and qualifying again being disrupted by rain, Johann qualified third and led the first six laps. Once Maverick Viñales came past Johann hung on to him despite having started on the soft tyres while the factory bikes were on mediums. But Valentino Rossi had saved something for the finale. Six laps from home he slid past Zarco and closed in on his young teammate. It looked very much as if the old master had got the job done when he put in an inch-perfect pass at the Dunlop Chicane, even more so when Viñales ran straight-on at Chemin aux Boeufs. He rejoined the track but did not attract a penalty as, according to Race Direction, he gained no advantage. Later microanalysis using helicopter pictures showed it was a correct decision.

That set up an astounding last lap. Viñales closed in but surely the master of the last-lap duel wouldn't make a mistake with victory so close? He didn't; he made two. First, he ran wide going in to Garage Vert leaving a big gap that Viñales promptly took advantage of. Maverick went on to set a new lap record on that final circuit of the resurfaced Bugatti Circuit. Rossi was closing all the way to the esses where he lost the rear of his Yamaha and slid out. He was unable to restart. As Valentino said afterwards, it was an odd crash; it's the front you worry about at Le Mans not the rear.

Zarco surfed home on a wave of French pride over four seconds in front of Dani Pedrosa who scored his third podium in three races. He'd been stranded way back on the fifth row of the grid and lain awake most of Saturday night thinking about how to get through the Dunlop Chicane on the first lap. He managed to do it unscathed and at least stopped Yamaha sweeping both the front row and the podium as they celebrated their 500th win across all GP classes. Marc Marquez had one of those weekends when nothing really looked right. His Honda was snapping sideways on the brakes and he lost the front twice in practice. It happened again in the race, but he had already been passed by his teammate and was clearly not happy with the medium front tyre, which is never hard enough for Marc. Like others, especially Honda riders, he was anxious to see if the stiffer front casing would help him.

Behind Pedrosa's now rather solitary third place Cal Crutchlow and Andrea Dovizioso had an entertaining duel, with Jorge Lorenzo and Jonas Folger a safe distance behind. This was the race where Jorge thought he would first be able to show his potential with the Ducati, a track where the Desmosedici has good form. That idea was ruined by the weather on Friday and Saturday but on race day he made his way stealthily through the field, shadowed much of the way by Danilo Petrucci until he became another victim of a rash of mechanical failures that afflicted the private Ducatis. It was actually an impressive ride from Lorenzo, making up ten places on his starting position. Pedrosa also made up ten, mainly thanks to a brilliant first lap

'TODAY I FELT REALLY GOOD, WHICH WAS IMPORTANT AFTER TWO RACES WHERE I FELT NOT SO GOOD. TODAY THE BIKE FELT GREAT AND WE DID A GOOD JOB'

MAVERICK VIÑALES

MAIN | *Maverick Viñales reasserted his authority and went back to the top of the points standings*

THE FRENCH CONNECTION

The surprise of the early part of the season was undoubtedly the form of Tech 3 Yamaha's rookie Johann Zarco. His thrilling ride to the podium at his home race was hardly a shock given his form and especially his willingness to go toe-to-toe with the established stars. Less than 2 months ago team principal Herve Poncheral called a press conference to bemoan the difficulty in attracting talented young riders to a satellite teams even when they'd be riding probably the best balanced bike on the grid. The form of the Frenchman and his teammate and fellow rookie Jonas Folger, 27 and 24 years old respectively, altered most people's thinking on the subject, and not surprisingly Poncheral rapidly signed both of them to extended contracts. It is worth noting that but for Zarco's form everyone would have been raving about the speed and consistency of the German.

– or, more precisely, a brilliant first chicane. Even taking into account the crashes in front of them, this was impressive from both men. The crashes and mechanical problems left Tech 3's other rookie, Jonas Folger, as the only man in MotoGP who's scored points in every race. If it weren't for Zarco everyone would be raving about his achievements.

So the crowd got what they wanted and celebrated Zarco's first MotoGP podium raucously. In fact most of the paddock joined in, and it felt like a relief. The Grand Prix was overshadowed by news of Nicky Hayden's accident, and the paddock grapevine knew just how serious the situation was. The 2016 World Champion had a cycling accident near the Misano circuit and was now in Bufalini Hospital in Cesena with grievous injuries. On Friday, with the circuit enveloped in grey drizzle, it felt like everyone involved would much rather be somewhere else – anywhere else. That feeling didn't go away until race day when the old Le Mans buzz took over, and once the motards had belted out The Marseillaise it was business as normal. Or as normal as this season gets. Viñales was now back at the top of the points table with Dani Pedrosa second. Maybe as importantly, it felt like Maverick was also back in charge of the Yamaha team. While Valentino Rossi was starting to doubt the 2017 chassis, despite his earlier statements, Maverick was, unsurprisingly, happy with it. His troubles at Jerez had generated the first signs of tension but now he was back in the iceman persona he exhibited after the first two wins at the start of the year. But the one thing we've learnt so far is just when you think you understand this season something will happen that proves you haven't got a clue.

LEFT, TOP-BOTTOM | *Ducati's challenge for the podium never materialised, Dovizioso did make fourth after a fight with Crutchlow; Loris Baz made it a great day for French fans with a great ride to ninth; Sylvain Guintoli replaced the injured Rins and made it three French points scorers at the French GP*

Zarco isn't just remarkable on track, he is very different from most other motorcycle races with a lifestyle more akin to a Shaolin monk. He has no motorhome and lives in a capsule hotel in the paddock, no tattoos, no residence in a tax haven, and a tendency to stand up for the interests of Moto3 and Moto2 riders in Safety Commission meetings. None of this is normal in the paddock. He is very much an independent thinker, for instance in his search for a smooth riding style he has stopped riding motocross as it makes him too abrupt in his input to the motorcycle. No doubt this is a good part of the reason Johann is often able to use the softest tyres in the allocation.

Johann's form may not change the paddock's obsession with youth but his achievements are already giving hope to riders in the smaller classes, and other paddocks, who are no longer teenagers.

5 | FRANCE

RACE RESULTS

WINNER | MAVERICK VIÑALES

CIRCUIT LENGTH | 4.2 KM | 2.6 MILES

NO. OF LAPS | 28

RACE DISTANCE | 117.2 KM | 72.8 MILES

CIRCUIT RECORD LAP | 1'32.309 | 163.2 KM/H
MAVERICK VIÑALES (2017)

CIRCUIT BEST LAP | 1'31.975 | 163.8 KM/H
JORGE LORENZO (2016)

RACE CONDITION | DRY

AIR | 21°C

HUMIDITY | 50%

GROUND | 37°C

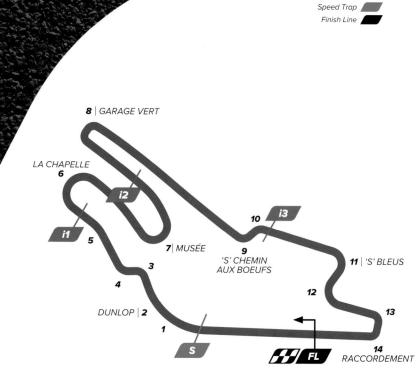

Sectors
Speed Trap
Finish Line

8 | GARAGE VERT
LA CHAPELLE
6
i2
10 i3
i1
5
7 | MUSÉE
11 | 'S' BLEUS
9
'S' CHEMIN AUX BOEUFS
3
12
4
13
DUNLOP | 2
1
14
S
FL
RACCORDEMENT

TISSOT
SWISS WATCHES SINCE 1853

OFFICIAL TIMEKEEPER

MICHELIN

OFFICIAL MotoGP™ CLASS TYRE

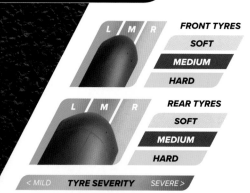

FRONT TYRES
SOFT
MEDIUM
HARD

REAR TYRES
SOFT
MEDIUM
HARD

< MILD **TYRE SEVERITY** SEVERE >

QUALIFYING RESULTS

	RIDER	NAT	TEAM	MACHINE	QP/TIME		GAP 1ST/PREV	
1	Maverick Viñales	SPA	Movistar Yamaha MotoGP	YAMAHA	Q2	1'31.994		
2	Valentino Rossi	ITA	Movistar Yamaha MotoGP	YAMAHA	Q2	1'32.100	0.106	0.106
3	Johann Zarco**	FRA	Monster Yamaha Tech 3	YAMAHA	Q2	1'32.229	0.235	0.129
4	Cal Crutchlow	GBR	LCR Honda	HONDA	Q2	1'32.300	0.306	0.071
5	Marc Marquez	SPA	Repsol Honda Team	HONDA	Q2	1'32.493	0.499	0.193
6	Andrea Dovizioso**	ITA	Ducati Team	DUCATI	Q2	1'32.726	0.732	0.233
7	Scott Redding	GBR	OCTO Pramac Racing	DUCATI	Q2	1'33.119	1.125	0.393
8	Pol Espargaro	SPA	Red Bull KTM Factory Racing	KTM	Q2	1'33.399	1.405	0.280
9	Karel Abraham	CZE	Pull&Bear Aspar Team	DUCATI	Q2	1'33.517	1.523	0.118
10	Bradley Smith	GBR	Red Bull KTM Factory Racing	KTM	Q2	1'33.629	1.635	0.112
11	Jack Miller	AUS	EG 0,0 Marc VDS	HONDA	Q2	1'33.756	1.762	0.127
12	Loris Baz	FRA	Reale Avintia Racing	DUCATI	Q2	1'33.955	1.961	0.199
13	Dani Pedrosa	SPA	Repsol Honda Team	HONDA	Q1	1'32.415	*0.117	0.048
14	Alvaro Bautista	SPA	Pull&Bear Aspar Team	DUCATI	Q1	1'32.484	*0.186	0.069
15	Jonas Folger	GER	Monster Yamaha Tech 3	YAMAHA	Q1	1'32.695	*0.397	0.211
16	Jorge Lorenzo	SPA	Ducati Team	DUCATI	Q1	1'32.830	*0.532	0.135
17	Andrea Iannone	ITA	Team SUZUKI ECSTAR	SUZUKI	Q1	1'32.844	*0.546	0.014
18	Aleix Espargaro	SPA	Aprilia Racing Team Gresini	APRILIA	Q1	1'33.187	*0.889	0.343
19	Danilo Petrucci	ITA	OCTO Pramac Racing	DUCATI	Q1	1'33.231	*0.933	0.044
20	Hector Barbera	SPA	Reale Avintia Racing	DUCATI	Q1	1'33.233	*0.935	0.002
21	Sam Lowes	GBR	Aprilia Racing Team Gresini	APRILIA	Q1	1'33.817	*1.519	0.584
22	Tito Rabat	SPA	EG 0,0 Marc VDS	HONDA	Q1	1'33.875	*1.577	0.058
23	Sylvain Guintoli	FRA	Team SUZUKI ECSTAR	SUZUKI	Q1	1'34.082	*1.784	0.207

* Gap to the fastest rider in the Q1 session
** Went forward from Q1 to Q2

1 | MAVERICK VIÑALES
His third win of the year. Fought Zarco in the early laps and then forced Valentino Rossi into a mistake on the last lap to secure Yamaha's 500th Grand Prix victory and go back to the top of the championship.

2 | JOHANN ZARCO
Lit up the whole weekend. Qualified on the front row, led the race for six laps and was never dropped by the factory bikes. Used the soft tyres and didn't fade. The first rostrum in MotoGP for the fastest rookie in years.

3 | DANI PEDROSA
A brilliant start after disastrous qualifying followed by an aggressive middle of the race and then a cautious finish as he started to feel some chatter. Went to second in the championship.

4 | ANDREA DOVIZIOSO
Not really happy with his race; thought he should at least have been fighting Pedrosa for the final podium place. Slowed by arm pump mid-race.

5 | CAL CRUTCHLOW
Used the hard front, like Marquez, for better braking stability but it hampered him mid-corner. Survived a barge from Pedrosa and couldn't catch Dovi in the closing laps but more than happy with the result.

6 | JORGE LORENZO
This was the race Jorge thought would see his first success on Ducati but that was scuppered by the wet practice and qualifying. Pleased with his race pace and ability to make passes in early laps.

7 | JONAS FOLGER
Now the only rider in the class to have scored points in every race. Nevertheless, his stunning pace in the second half highlighted the fact that he has trouble getting up to speed in the opening laps.

8 | JACK MILLER
Survived a horrific crash in FP4 to equal his best finish of the season so far. Happily admitted he had profited from the misfortune of others but pointed out he was having a good weekend before his crash.

9 | LORIS BAZ
Never solved his front-end problems on a circuit that doesn't suit him or the bike, but dug in to get a good result. Took a while to pass Pol Espargaro early on then had a real fight with Iannone at the end.

10 | ANDREA IANNONE
Another race where Andrea didn't have confidence in the bike. Not helped by the mixed conditions on Friday and Saturday. Rode for the finish.

11 | TITO RABAT
His best result of the season from the back row of the grid achieved, said Tito, because he kept calm and analysed things clearly. Close to Iannone at the flag.

12 | POL ESPARGARO
Did not feel too well on race day, so felt he didn't achieve his full potential. Amazingly, the whole team felt the same way after both bikes went straight through to final qualifying.

RACE LAP CHART

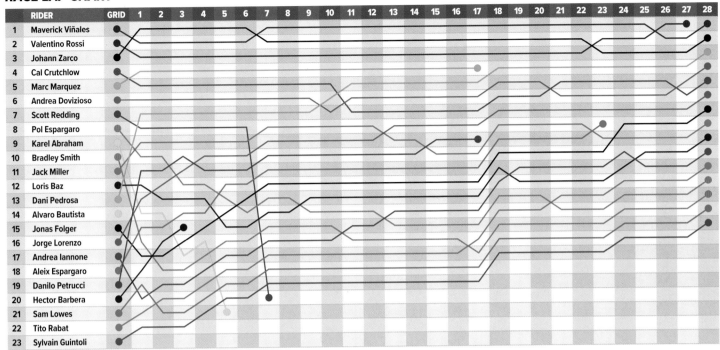

	RIDER	GRID	1	2	3	4	5	6	7	8	9	10	11	12	13	14	15	16	17	18	19	20	21	22	23	24	25	26	27	28
1	Maverick Viñales																													
2	Valentino Rossi																													
3	Johann Zarco																													
4	Cal Crutchlow																													
5	Marc Marquez																													
6	Andrea Dovizioso																													
7	Scott Redding																													
8	Pol Espargaro																													
9	Karel Abraham																													
10	Bradley Smith																													
11	Jack Miller																													
12	Loris Baz																													
13	Dani Pedrosa																													
14	Alvaro Bautista																													
15	Jonas Folger																													
16	Jorge Lorenzo																													
17	Andrea Iannone																													
18	Aleix Espargaro																													
19	Danilo Petrucci																													
20	Hector Barbera																													
21	Sam Lowes																													
22	Tito Rabat																													
23	Sylvain Guintoli																													

RACE CLASSIFICATION AFTER 28 LAPS = 117.18 KM

	RIDER	NAT	TEAM	MACHINE	TIME	+ GAP	TYRES
1	Maverick Viñales	SPA	Movistar Yamaha MotoGP	YAMAHA	43'29.793		M/M
2	Johann Zarco	FRA	Monster Yamaha Tech 3	YAMAHA	43'32.927	3.134	S/S
3	Dani Pedrosa	SPA	Repsol Honda Team	HONDA	43'37.510	7.717	M/S
4	Andrea Dovizioso	ITA	Ducati Team	DUCATI	43'41.016	11.223	M/M
5	Cal Crutchlow	GBR	LCR Honda	HONDA	43'43.312	13.519	H/M
6	Jorge Lorenzo	SPA	Ducati Team	DUCATI	43'53.795	24.002	M/M
7	Jonas Folger	GER	Monster Yamaha Tech 3	YAMAHA	43'55.526	25.733	S/S
8	Jack Miller	AUS	EG 0,0 Marc VDS	HONDA	44'02.396	32.603	S/S
9	Loris Baz	FRA	Reale Avintia Racing	DUCATI	44'15.577	45.784	M/S
10	Andrea Iannone	ITA	Team SUZUKI ECSTAR	SUZUKI	44'18.125	48.332	M/M
11	Tito Rabat	SPA	EG 0,0 Marc VDS	HONDA	44'19.829	50.036	S/S
12	Pol Espargaro	SPA	Red Bull KTM Factory Racing	KTM	44'22.454	52.661	M/S
13	Bradley Smith	GBR	Red Bull KTM Factory Racing	KTM	44'22.972	53.179	M/S
14	Sam Lowes	GBR	Aprilia Racing Team Gresini	APRILIA	44'25.225	55.432	M/S
15	Sylvain Guintoli	FRA	Team SUZUKI ECSTAR	SUZUKI	44'36.671	66.878	M/S
NC	Valentino Rossi	ITA	Movistar Yamaha MotoGP	YAMAHA	41'57.076	1 lap	M/M
NC	Aleix Espargaro	SPA	Aprilia Racing Team Gresini	APRILIA	36'08.128	5 laps	M/S
NC	Marc Marquez	SPA	Repsol Honda Team	HONDA	26'31.585	11 laps	M/M
NC	Danilo Petrucci	ITA	OCTO Pramac Racing	DUCATI	26'43.477	11 laps	M/M
NC	Scott Redding	GBR	OCTO Pramac Racing	DUCATI	11'47.236	21 laps	M/M
NC	Karel Abraham	CZE	Pull&Bear Aspar Team	DUCATI	8'17.534	23 laps	M/S
NC	Hector Barbera	SPA	Reale Avintia Racing	DUCATI	4'54.098	25 laps	S/S
NC	Alvaro Bautista	SPA	Pull&Bear Aspar Team	DUCATI			M/S

CHAMPIONSHIP STANDINGS

	RIDER	NAT	TEAM	POINTS
1	Maverick Viñales	SPA	Movistar Yamaha MotoGP	85
2	Dani Pedrosa	SPA	Repsol Honda Team	68
3	Valentino Rossi	ITA	Movistar Yamaha MotoGP	62
4	Marc Marquez	SPA	Repsol Honda Team	58
5	Johann Zarco	FRA	Monster Yamaha Tech 3	55
6	Andrea Dovizioso	ITA	Ducati Team	54
7	Cal Crutchlow	GBR	LCR Honda	40
8	Jorge Lorenzo	SPA	Ducati Team	38
9	Jonas Folger	GER	Monster Yamaha Tech 3	38
10	Jack Miller	AUS	EG 0,0 Marc VDS	29
11	Danilo Petrucci	ITA	OCTO Pramac Racing	26
12	Scott Redding	GBR	OCTO Pramac Racing	26
13	Loris Baz	FRA	Reale Avintia Racing	19
14	Aleix Espargaro	SPA	Aprilia Racing Team Gresini	17
15	Andrea Iannone	ITA	Team SUZUKI ECSTAR	15
16	Alvaro Bautista	SPA	Pull&Bear Aspar Team	14
17	Tito Rabat	SPA	EG 0,0 Marc VDS	13
18	Hector Barbera	SPA	Reale Avintia Racing	12
19	Karel Abraham	CZE	Pull&Bear Aspar Team	9
20	Alex Rins	SPA	Team SUZUKI ECSTAR	7
21	Pol Espargaro	SPA	Red Bull KTM Factory Racing	6
22	Bradley Smith	GBR	Red Bull KTM Factory Racing	6
23	Sam Lowes	GBR	Aprilia Racing Team Gresini	2
24	Sylvain Guintoli	FRA	Team SUZUKI ECSTAR	1

13 | BRADLEY SMITH
Gave the rest a head start by running off-track three times. Like his teammate, felt that the highlight of the weekend was going straight through to Qualifying 2. Still an impressive weekend for the whole KTM team.

14 | SAM LOWES
His first points in MotoGP after a strong weekend. Much happier with the gaps to the top ten and the leaders.

15 | SYLVAIN GUINTOLI
Replaced Rins. Enjoyed his home GP, surprised to finish less than 20 seconds behind his teammate.

DID NOT FINISH

VALENTINO ROSSI
Stalked his teammate and took the lead three laps from the flag. Ran wide at Garage Vert on the last lap then crashed at the esses when he lost the rear.

ALEIX ESPARGARO
Making an impressive charge through the pack after bad qualifying when his engine failed five laps from the flag. Looked like a top-end problem.

MARC MARQUEZ
Had already been passed by Pedrosa when he lost the front at the frightening first corner to add to two similar crashes in practice. Hoped the new Michelin front would change things a little from the next race.

DANILO PETRUCCI
Started well back on the grid, gained eight places on a brutal first lap and was closing in on Lorenzo when he was forced to stop thanks to an oil leak.

SCOTT REDDING
Much happier with the bike after a good test at Jerez and being fast all through the weekend. Stopped by a gearbox problem but looked more like his old self.

KAREL ABRAHAM
Qualified ninth and looked good until the bike got stuck in second gear a few laps into the race.

HECTOR BARBERA
Happy with the front end at last following a good test. Looked like he was going to have a good race but engine failure stopped Hector on Lap 4.

ALVARO BAUTISTA
Fell on the first lap when he ran a little wide at Chapelle.

DID NOT RACE

ALEX RINS
Recovering from operation to fix his broken arm. Replaced by Guintoli.

DESMODROMIC DOMINATION

Andrea Dovizioso wins for Ducati, Viñales second, Petrucci on the podium.

For the first time in the season, MotoGP enjoyed a weekend of unbroken sunshine, a joy enhanced by the venue being the most beautiful track in the calendar. There was also a feeling of profound loss following the death of Nicky Hayden, the 2006 World Champion. He was remembered in many ways; a minute's silence, his racing number on leathers and bikes, and a paddock display of his bikes. But the sun shone, and it illuminated a Grand Prix that brought joy to all of Italy, with the possible exception of some corners of Tavullia, as Italians won all three races.

Andrea Dovizioso rode a superbly controlled race to bring home Ducati's first win in Italy since the days of Casey Stoner and the first by an Italian rider on an Italian bike at the Italian GP (then called the GP des Nations) since 1974 when Gianfranco Bonera won on an MV Agusta at Imola. The Bologna factory's joy was unconfined, with senior managers including CEO Claudio Domenicali going crazy in the pit and parc fermé. There must have been a large dose of profound relief in amongst the celebrations, not least because of the performance of the remarkable Danilo Petrucci on the satellite bike and the sight of expensive new recruit Jorge Lorenzo starting off the front row and leading the race. The following week's phone calls with both owners and sponsors must have been considerably more relaxed than usual.

This was not an easy victory. Dovi had to control both factory Yamahas as well as the charging Petrucci over the course of the race, a task made even more difficult by the circuit being very physical and guaranteed to bring on arm pump if he pushed too hard. He also had a nasty dose of food poisoning that deprived him of sleep on Saturday night. The Desmosedici takes advantage of the long straight but is still far from perfect, as rider and team were keen to remind us once the initial fever had abated. Andrea was not the only Italian hero with health worries. Valentino Rossi had crashed a motocrosser ten days earlier with enough force to put him in hospital overnight, and there were serious doubts about his fitness to race. Fortunately there were no fractures, just serious abdominal bruising, and he was able to compete, albeit with some discomfort. However, it was no surprise that although he led the first three laps Valentino was pushed back to fourth and couldn't respond.

In among the Italian carnival it was easy to overlook Maverick Viñales, despite the fact he started on pole, set the fastest lap, finished second, and extended his championship lead. He did admit to checking where the Hondas were and deciding to settle for second and 20 points rather than take too many risks. It was another efficient, clinical job of work interrupted only by a big crash on Friday, which left him shaken.

Not as shaken as the Honda camp at the end of proceedings. After a test at Jerez the riders had voted by 20 to three to adopt Michelin's new, stiffer front-tyre construction. As usual, there were three choices of front at Mugello with the medium being asymmetric. The three men on the podium all used different combinations and Marc Marquez, like Dovi, went for the medium front. He said the harder rubber on the right side of the tyre was actually harder than the symmetric hard tyre. It didn't help, he never got higher than third, and then only for one lap, and soon dropped off the leaders. Marc reported that he did not like the feeling when the tyre transitioned from compound to compound. Tellingly, he could not respond to Alvaro Bautista when he came past on the satellite Aspar Ducati. That sixth place finish was the worst by Marquez in a race where he hasn't crashed or been penalised since the 125cc Czech GP of 2010. Just how bad was Honda's weekend? When Crutchlow and Pedrosa went down in a

LEFT *Maverick Viñales started from pole and finished second to increase his championship lead to 26 points, more than a race win's worth*

MAIN *He started from the front row, he led the race, but Valentino Rossi couldn't make the top three*

BELOW, LEFT-RIGHT *Alvaro Bautista had another combative ride through the field; An unhappy Cal Crutchlow walks away from the last-lap encounter with Pedrosa; Marc Marquez contemplates an unhappy day for anyone on a Honda*

'I WASN'T THE QUICKEST MAN OUT THERE, BUT I DID A PERFECT STRATEGY, AND I MOVED INTO THE RIGHT POSITION AT THE RIGHT MOMENT. I RODE REALLY SMOOTHLY'
ANDREA DOVIZIOSO

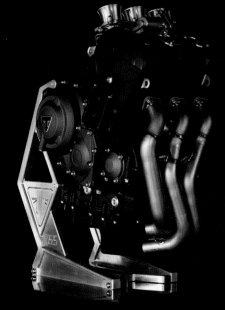

TRIUMPH ARE COMING

For the first time since the inception of the class in 2010, Moto2 will run with an engine other than a four-cylinder Honda CBR600RR from the 2019 season on. The new engine will be a 765cc three-cylinder Triumph, a modified version of the motor powering the new Speed Triple RS, which is rated at 121bhp. For Moto2, it will have similar modifications to the Honda; titanium valves, revised porting, stiffer valves, taller first gear, race alternator, and revised cases and sump.

The contract for a new, upgraded spec ECU has already been awarded to Magneti Marelli and it will be a much more sophisticated system than the very basic one Moto2 has had all its life. These changes mark a seismic change in the class that was

heap at Corentaio on the last lap they were squabbling over 11th place nearly ten seconds behind Marquez who was in turn nearly six seconds behind Dovizioso.

Danilo Petrucci's third place generated as much noise as Dovi's win. Danilo rode across a gap to the leaders and when he got there he thought that fourth would do. Then he remembered it was his home race and attacked, passing Rossi and Viñales on consecutive laps. His arrival corresponded with Dovi making his move to the front and Danilo quickly realised that trying another pass was not a good plan. By now he had, as he usually does, worn his rear tyre out and was more than happy to go to the podium at his home race. Hours later, still in his leathers, he could be found celebrating with his fan club. Dovi, for whom this was a third MotoGP win but his first in the dry, admitted to a great weight being lifted off his shoulders. His only fellow countrymen to have won in the top class at Mugello are Valentino Rossi and Loris Capirossi. One did not have to enter into the realms of Nostradamus to feel that the dam had been broken and more wins would follow.

Ducati's celebrations didn't stop at the track. Back in Bologna, on Monday one of the factory's external walls was draped with a giant picture of Andrea on the Desmosedici. The team and riders later celebrated with the workforce and handed out T-shirts bearing the slogan "Success Made in Italy." They will be popular on the production line for quite a while. It felt like most of Italy was celebrating, not least because in this most unpredictable of seasons Andrea Dovizioso had moved into second place in the points table. Could he be a genuine championship contender? Why not?

MAIN | *Andrea Dovizioso celebrates his first MotoGP win on a dry track*

LEFT, TOP-BOTTOM | *Maverick Viñales was the non-smiling interloper on a very smiley Italian podium; Most of Italy celebrated, even the ones dressed in yellow; Danilo Petrucci put the satellite-team Ducati on the podium alongside the works bike*

conceived in the throes of the global financial crisis and designed to be, above all else, cheap. There was a move to use Kawasakis, then the only street 600 with a cassette gearbox and as a bonus keep the factory in the paddock, but Honda stepped in when no other factory could be persuaded to show interest. The new bike will be more sophisticated, torquey and much, much more like a proper Grand Prix bike. It will also sound great. Ex-125cc World Champion Julian Simon is already testing a prototype and is suitably impressed.

Triumph have practically no history in GPs (just one podium in their entire history) but their beautiful air-cooled 750cc triples of the early 1970s competed in the four-stroke classes before Superbike's arrival. The British factory's arrival in 2019 is good news for all of motorcycle sport.

6 | ITALY

RACE RESULTS

WINNER | ANDREA DOVIZIOSO

CIRCUIT LENGTH | 5.2 KM | 3.26 MILES

NO. OF LAPS | 23

RACE DISTANCE | 120.6 KM | 75.0 MILES

CIRCUIT RECORD LAP | 1'47.639 | 175.4 KM/H
MARC MARQUEZ (2013)

CIRCUIT BEST LAP | 1'46.489 | 177.3 KM/H
ANDREA IANNONE (2015)

RACE CONDITION | DRY

AIR | 25°C

HUMIDITY | 58%

GROUND | 42°C

Sectors
Speed Trap
Finish Line

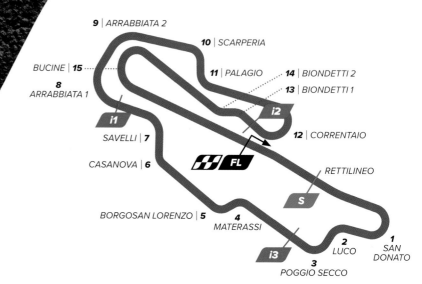

9 | ARRABBIATA 2
10 | SCARPERIA
BUCINE | 15
11 | PALAGIO
14 | BIONDETTI 2
8
ARRABBIATA 1
13 | BIONDETTI 1
i2
i1
12 | CORRENTAIO
SAVELLI | 7
FL
CASANOVA | 6
RETTILINEO
S
BORGOSAN LORENZO | 5
4
MATERASSI
2
1
i3
LUCO
SAN DONATO
3
POGGIO SECCO

OFFICIAL TIMEKEEPER

OFFICIAL MotoGP™ CLASS TYRE

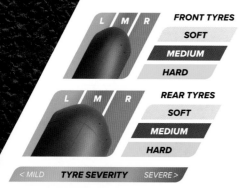

FRONT TYRES
SOFT
MEDIUM
HARD

REAR TYRES
SOFT
MEDIUM
HARD

< MILD   **TYRE SEVERITY**   SEVERE >

QUALIFYING RESULTS

	RIDER	NAT	TEAM	MACHINE	QP/TIME		GAP 1ST/PREV	
1	Maverick Viñales**	SPA	Movistar Yamaha MotoGP	YAMAHA	Q2	1'46.575		
2	Valentino Rossi	ITA	Movistar Yamaha MotoGP	YAMAHA	Q2	1'46.814	0.239	0.239
3	Andrea Dovizioso**	ITA	Ducati Team	DUCATI	Q2	1'46.835	0.260	0.021
4	Michele Pirro	ITA	Ducati Team	DUCATI	Q2	1'46.878	0.303	0.043
5	Dani Pedrosa	SPA	Repsol Honda Team	HONDA	Q2	1'46.999	0.424	0.121
6	Marc Marquez	SPA	Repsol Honda Team	HONDA	Q2	1'47.050	0.475	0.051
7	Jorge Lorenzo	SPA	Ducati Team	DUCATI	Q2	1'47.152	0.577	0.102
8	Alvaro Bautista	SPA	Pull&Bear Aspar Team	DUCATI	Q2	1'47.167	0.592	0.015
9	Danilo Petrucci	ITA	OCTO Pramac Racing	DUCATI	Q2	1'47.266	0.691	0.099
10	Tito Rabat	SPA	EG 0,0 Marc VDS	HONDA	Q2	1'47.282	0.707	0.016
11	Johann Zarco	FRA	Monster Yamaha Tech 3	YAMAHA	Q2	1'47.319	0.744	0.037
12	Aleix Espargaro	SPA	Aprilia Racing Team Gresini	APRILIA	Q2	1'47.475	0.900	0.156
13	Cal Crutchlow	GBR	LCR Honda	HONDA	Q1	1'47.220	*0.162	0.079
14	Hector Barbera	SPA	Reale Avintia Racing	DUCATI	Q1	1'47.272	*0.214	0.052
15	Jonas Folger	GER	Monster Yamaha Tech 3	YAMAHA	Q1	1'47.305	*0.247	0.033
16	Andrea Iannone	ITA	Team SUZUKI ECSTAR	SUZUKI	Q1	1'47.625	*0.567	0.320
17	Loris Baz	FRA	Reale Avintia Racing	DUCATI	Q1	1'47.809	*0.751	0.184
18	Pol Espargaro	SPA	Red Bull KTM Factory Racing	KTM	Q1	1'47.940	*0.882	0.131
19	Jack Miller	AUS	EG 0,0 Marc VDS	HONDA	Q1	1'47.961	*0.903	0.021
20	Scott Redding	GBR	OCTO Pramac Racing	DUCATI	Q1	1'47.975	*0.917	0.014
21	Karel Abraham	CZE	Pull&Bear Aspar Team	DUCATI	Q1	1'48.361	*1.303	0.386
22	Sam Lowes	GBR	Aprilia Racing Team Gresini	APRILIA	Q1	1'48.416	*1.358	0.055
23	Bradley Smith	GBR	Red Bull KTM Factory Racing	KTM	Q1	1'48.594	*1.536	0.178
24	Sylvain Guintoli	FRA	Team SUZUKI ECSTARR	SUZUKI	Q1	1'48.892	*1.834	0.298

Gap to the fastest rider in the Q1 session
** Went forward from Q1 to Q2*

1 | ANDREA DOVIZIOSO
A superb victory despite suffering from food poisoning. Measured his effort carefully to avoid over-stressing the tyres and used the Ducati's strengths brilliantly. Survived a massive tank-slapper at top speed, took the lead after half-distance and managed the race perfectly.

2 | MAVERICK VIÑALES
Started from pole, and in the leading group for the whole race. Admitted to thinking of the points situation rather than the win when he saw where the Hondas where. Lucky to escape uninjured from a big Friday crash.

3 | DANILO PETRUCCI
Came across the gap from the pack to join the leading group when he thought about settling for fourth, but not for long. Got to second and attacked Dovi but realised he was over-reaching and the rear tyre was gone.

4 | VALENTINO ROSSI
Couldn't ride as he wanted to due to the motocross crash that put him in hospital ten days before the race. Qualified on the front row for the first time this season and led the race but couldn't stay the distance. Called the result "a gift."

5 | ALVARO BAUTISTA
Qualified as best independent rider, didn't start well then ripped through the midfield. Made it past Marquez just before half-distance and held him off on last lap for what he called a "real" result, unlike Argentina.

6 | MARC MARQUEZ
A race conditioned by his asymmetric front tyre. Used the medium because he knew the hard wouldn't last. Pushed hard at the start but knew he had to ride for points. Couldn't get close enough to attack Bautista in closing stages.

7 | JOHANN ZARCO
It doesn't look as impressive as Le Mans, but he was by far the fastest rookie. Again fearless in the opening laps as he made up for mildly disappointing qualifying.

8 | JORGE LORENZO
Qualified on the front row and led a race for the first time on Ducati. When he started having trouble getting into corners he dropped back quickly.

9 | MICHELE PIRRO
Ruined his superb qualifying with a terrible start, but Ducati's test rider impressed again.

10 | ANDREA IANNONE
Looks much like Le Mans but in reality a much better showing.

Very competitive, especially on the brakes, in the first part of the race but his times suffered as tyre drop-off seriously affected the bike's behavior.

11 | TITO RABAT
Best ever MotoGP qualifying followed by a strong race in which he first shadowed Crutchlow and then Pedrosa. Lost rear-tyre grip five laps from home. Second Honda.

12 | SCOTT REDDING
With the group dice for most of the race but dropped off in the last three laps.

RACE LAP CHART

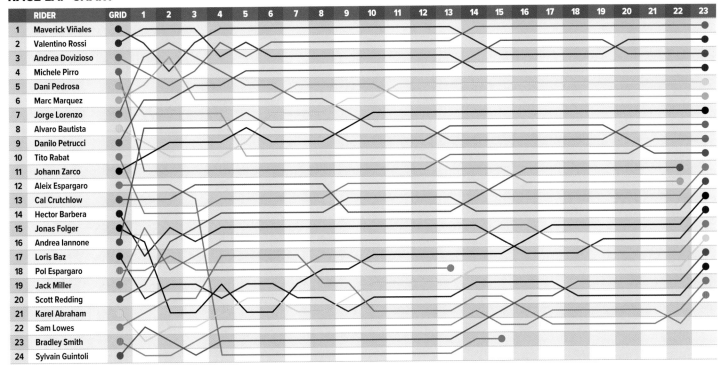

	RIDER	GRID	1	2	3	4	5	6	7	8	9	10	11	12	13	14	15	16	17	18	19	20	21	22	23
1	Maverick Viñales																								
2	Valentino Rossi																								
3	Andrea Dovizioso																								
4	Michele Pirro																								
5	Dani Pedrosa																								
6	Marc Marquez																								
7	Jorge Lorenzo																								
8	Alvaro Bautista																								
9	Danilo Petrucci																								
10	Tito Rabat																								
11	Johann Zarco																								
12	Aleix Espargaro																								
13	Cal Crutchlow																								
14	Hector Barbera																								
15	Jonas Folger																								
16	Andrea Iannone																								
17	Loris Baz																								
18	Pol Espargaro																								
19	Jack Miller																								
20	Scott Redding																								
21	Karel Abraham																								
22	Sam Lowes																								
23	Bradley Smith																								
24	Sylvain Guintoli																								

RACE CLASSIFICATION AFTER 23 LAPS = 120.635 KM

	RIDER	NAT	TEAM	MACHINE	TIME	+ GAP	TYRES
1	Andrea Dovizioso	ITA	Ducati Team	DUCATI	41'32.126		M/M
2	Maverick Viñales	SPA	Movistar Yamaha MotoGP	YAMAHA	41'33.407	1.281	H/H
3	Danilo Petrucci	ITA	OCTO Pramac Racing	DUCATI	41'34.460	2.334	H/M
4	Valentino Rossi	ITA	Movistar Yamaha MotoGP	YAMAHA	41'35.811	3.685	H/H
5	Alvaro Bautista	SPA	Pull&Bear Aspar Team	DUCATI	41'37.928	5.802	H/M
6	Marc Marquez	SPA	Repsol Honda Team	HONDA	41'38.011	5.885	M/M
7	Johann Zarco	FRA	Monster Yamaha Tech 3	YAMAHA	41'45.331	13.205	S/H
8	Jorge Lorenzo	SPA	Ducati Team	DUCATI	41'46.519	14.393	M/M
9	Michele Pirro	ITA	Ducati Team	DUCATI	41'47.006	14.880	M/M
10	Andrea Iannone	ITA	Team SUZUKI ECSTAR	SUZUKI	41'47.628	15.502	H/M
11	Tito Rabat	SPA	EG 0,0 Marc VDS	HONDA	41'54.130	22.004	H/M
12	Scott Redding	GBR	OCTO Pramac Racing	DUCATI	41'57.078	24.952	H/H
13	Jonas Folger	GER	Monster Yamaha Tech 3	YAMAHA	42'00.286	28.160	H/M
14	Hector Barbera	SPA	Reale Avintia Racing	DUCATI	42'02.802	30.676	H/H
15	Jack Miller	AUS	EG 0,0 Marc VDS	HONDA	42'02.905	30.779	H/M
16	Karel Abraham	CZE	Pull&Bear Aspar Team	DUCATI	42'14.432	42.306	H/M
17	Sylvain Guintoli	FRA	Team SUZUKI ECSTARR	SUZUKI	42'18.420	46.294	H/M
18	Loris Baz	FRA	Reale Avintia Racing	DUCATI	42'22.857	50.731	H/H
19	Sam Lowes	GBR	Aprilia Racing Team Gresini	APRILIA	42'22.866	50.740	H/S
20	Bradley Smith	GBR	Red Bull KTM Factory Racing	KTM	42'23.023	50.897	M/M
NC	Cal Crutchlow	GBR	LCR Honda	HONDA	39'58.963	1 lap	M/M
NC	Dani Pedrosa	SPA	Repsol Honda Team	HONDA	39'59.353	1 lap	H/M
NC	Aleix Espargaro	SPA	Aprilia Racing Team Gresini	APRILIA	27'58.615	8 laps	H/M
NC	Pol Espargaro	SPA	Red Bull KTM Factory Racing	KTM	23'52.621	10 laps	M/M

CHAMPIONSHIP STANDINGS

	RIDER	NAT	TEAM	POINTS
1	Maverick Viñales	SPA	Movistar Yamaha MotoGP	105
2	Andrea Dovizioso	ITA	Ducati Team	79
3	Valentino Rossi	ITA	Movistar Yamaha MotoGP	75
4	Marc Marquez	SPA	Repsol Honda Team	68
5	Dani Pedrosa	SPA	Repsol Honda Team	68
6	Johann Zarco	FRA	Monster Yamaha Tech 3	64
7	Jorge Lorenzo	SPA	Ducati Team	46
8	Danilo Petrucci	ITA	OCTO Pramac Racing	42
9	Jonas Folger	GER	Monster Yamaha Tech 3	41
10	Cal Crutchlow	GBR	LCR Honda	40
11	Scott Redding	GBR	OCTO Pramac Racing	30
12	Jack Miller	AUS	EG 0,0 Marc VDS	30
13	Alvaro Bautista	SPA	Pull&Bear Aspar Team	25
14	Andrea Iannone	ITA	Team SUZUKI ECSTAR	21
15	Loris Baz	FRA	Reale Avintia Racing	19
16	Tito Rabat	SPA	EG 0,0 Marc VDS	18
17	Aleix Espargaro	SPA	Aprilia Racing Team Gresini	17
18	Hector Barbera	SPA	Reale Avintia Racing	14
19	Karel Abraham	CZE	Pull&Bear Aspar Team	9
20	Michele Pirro	ITA	Ducati Team	7
21	Alex Rins	SPA	Team SUZUKI ECSTAR	7
22	Pol Espargaro	SPA	Red Bull KTM Factory Racing	6
23	Bradley Smith	GBR	Red Bull KTM Factory Racing	6
24	Sam Lowes	GBR	Aprilia Racing Team Gresini	2
25	Sylvain Guintoli	FRA	Team SUZUKI ECSTAR	1

13 | JONAS FOLGER
The pattern is now clear. Jonas lost all the time to his teammate on the opening five laps which saw him as far back as 21st, after which he was as fast as anyone. Kept his 100-per cent finishing record.

14 | HECTOR BARBERA
Chose the hard tyres, as opposed to the Ducatis on the podium, and had no grip so couldn't capitalise on good practice.

15 | JACK MILLER
A difficult weekend thanks mainly, like other Honda riders, to front-tyre difficulties. Not helped by missing the Barcelona test because of injury.

16 | KAREL ABRAHAM
Big problems at the test and then last on Friday. Things didn't get much better in qualifying but had good pace on race day.

17 | SYLVAIN GUINTOLI
Replaced Rins. Didn't score a point, unlike Le Mans, but starting to feel at home.

18 | LORIS BAZ
Wrecked the bike in warm up then had a severe headache and pain in both arms in the race.

19 | SAM LOWES
Impressive times for the first half-a-dozen laps then hit front-tyre issues for the first time in the weekend.

20 | BRADLEY SMITH
Took a few laps to get the feel of the new chassis but then had rear-brake problems, something the KTM needs. Still felt it was a better weekend than Texas with progress made.

DID NOT FINISH

CAL CRUTCHLOW
Fastest on Friday but that's as good as it got for anyone on a Honda. Spent the race managing the front tyre and was in 11th when he was brought down on the last lap by Pedrosa, with whom Cal was not happy.

DANI PEDROSA
Suffered with lack of grip at both ends all weekend and finished by crashing on the last lap and taking Crutchlow out.

ALEIX ESPARGARO
Jumped the start for the first time in his career then ran off-track trying to catch up. His lap times after the ride-through were very good, but the excursion led to gearchange problems and retirement.

POL ESPARGARO
Going well and in the dice with Miller and Folger when stopped by electrical problems. Disappointed not to take advantage of new parts including the chassis.

DID NOT RACE

ALEX RINS
Nearly recovered from his arm injury but the team want him fully fit before his return.

DOVI DOES THE DOUBLE

Andrea Dovizioso wins again amid chaos caused by the track surface.

There were eight years between Andrea Dovizioso's first and second wins in MotoGP and just seven days between the third and the fourth. Even in this season of complete unpredictability the Catalan Grand Prix was a stand-out thanks to a worn-out track, and temperatures so high that riders had to choose between a tyre that would last the race but have no grip or one that would work but only for half-a-dozen laps.

And, astonishingly, that might not even have been the most remarkable aspect of the weekend. That distinction may belong to the chicane. The previous year, MotoGP adopted the chicane before the final corner after the fatal accident that befell Luis Salom. It was already in place for the F1 race so, despite being far from perfect, was adopted so racing could go ahead. A new design was approved by riders, and the work was done over winter. The riders then decided they preferred the original F1 layout. They disliked the new one so much the switch back happened for Saturday morning's FP3.

As if that wasn't enough, everyone knew after a test two weeks earlier that the surface was doing that clever trick worn-out tarmac specialises in, being both low grip and highly abrasive. Now factor in track temperatures well over 50 degrees and bumps that appear to have multiplied over the previous 12 months and you had a recipe for a very strange race indeed.

ABOVE, LEFT-RIGHT | Conditions didn't prevent Jonas Folger from sealing a new lap record; Bradley Smith badly hurt a finger in qualifying and was unable to race; But for a few slow laps mid race Jorge Lorenzo would have been on the podium again

RIGHT | Dani Pedrosa qualified on pole and wasn't too happy with third place

MAIN | The Hondas and the factory Ducatis dominated proceedings

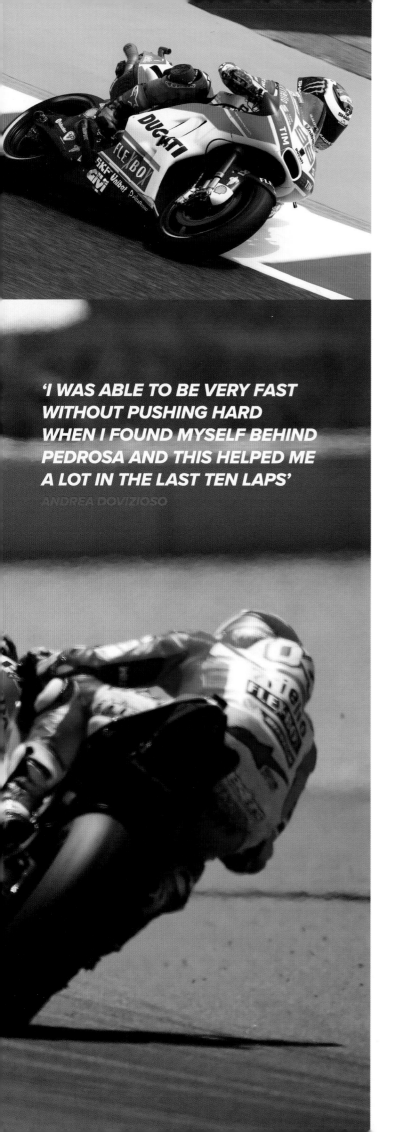

'I WAS ABLE TO BE VERY FAST WITHOUT PUSHING HARD WHEN I FOUND MYSELF BEHIND PEDROSA AND THIS HELPED ME A LOT IN THE LAST TEN LAPS'

ANDREA DOVIZIOSO

It wasn't simple though. Compare the fastest lap of the race, set by Jonas Folger third time round, with the sort of times he was doing 20 laps later trying to hold off his teammate. The difference was three-and-a-quarter seconds. For comparison, in the previous GP the difference between Maverick Viñales' fastest lap and his times a couple of laps from the flag was 0.2sec.

At the start there was enough grip for Folger to break the lap record set in 2016 by Maverick Viñales, at the end it was a matter of survival of the cleverest. First, we were treated to another chapter in the saga of Jorge Lorenzo. The previous week he'd led for a couple of corners, this time he led for the first five laps. Again he slid back quickly once he was overtaken and that, we assumed, would be the last we saw of Jorge. Marc Marquez took over at the front for two laps then Dani Pedrosa went through, followed by Andrea Dovizioso. There followed a phony war in which Pedrosa spent nine laps trying to ensure he had some rear tyre left at the end of the race while being shadowed by Dovi. Dani was all too aware that Andrea was shutting off very early to avoid driving past him and there would be nothing he could do when the Italian decided to make his move.

When Dovizioso went past Pedrosa at the end of the front straight, Marc Marquez took just two more laps to follow and give chase but realised very quickly that he wasn't going to catch Dovizioso without adding to his astonishing crash tally for the weekend. Marc had already crashed five times, including in warm up plus a comedy trip over a starter motor in pitlane, not surprisingly he decided to cut his losses. He could have been out of the race before the first corner, surviving a serious sideswipe from an out-of-control Danilo Petrucci who was starting from the front row for the first time. The Italian later received a warning from Race Direction and apologised to Marc.

Honda's usual deficit on acceleration to the Ducatis was emphasised by the track, but Yamaha were having an even worse time. Thanks to similar temperatures and conditions at Jerez, Yamaha already knew their 2017 M1 could not find grip on a hot, slick track. Only there it was front grip and at Catalunya

MAIN Andrea Dovizioso teased the Hondas for a while, but he always had the grip he needed to pull away

RIGHT, TOP-BOTTOM Cal Crutchlow had a tough weekend; Sylvain Guintoli stalks his temporary teammate Andrea Iannone; Catalunya is Marquez country

MAHINDRA QUIT Moto3

The Indian company Mahindra, winner of three Moto3 races, has decided to leave the MotoGP paddock at the end of the season. The company will switch resources to its Formula E effort having recently won its first race in that series.

Mahindra joined the then 125cc championship in 2011, the last year of the two-stroke formula and took the last ever pole position for a two-stroke in MotoGP racing at Valencia thanks to British rider Danny Webb. After a tough first year in the new four-stroke Moto3 class, Mahindra partnered with Suter Racing Technology for 2013 with Miguel Oliveira and Efren Vazquez riding. The Portuguese rider scored the factory's first ever podium at Sepang. In 2014 Mahindra riders stood on the podium three times and then in '15 they became a proper independent constructor supplying four customer teams.

it was mainly rear grip. And again the Tech 3 satellite team, using what is basically the 2016 bike, out-performed the factory team in both qualifying and the race. Valentino Rossi, up to now seemingly undecided about the new bike, at last went public with his dissatisfaction. It was, he said, not as "natural" to ride and did not feel like a Yamaha. The choice between grip for a few laps or, frankly, never having any represented by the medium/hard rear choice was hardest in the Movistar Yamaha garage. In Jerez they had gone for hard tyres whereas both Tech 3 riders had gone softer and fared better. In Barcelona all four Yamahas used mediums front and rear but again the satellite bikes used them best. As for the men on the rostrum, they all used the hard front and the medium rear but the Ducati clearly got some power down better even when lap times rose so dramatically.

Dovizioso said it was a very strange feeling to lead a race without actually pushing.

It was indeed a strange race but Andrea Dovizioso dealt with the very strange, changing conditions best. Just to add another twist to an already labyrinthine plot, the second factory Ducati, Jorge Lorenzo, hadn't disappeared from the leaders. He suddenly dropped his lap times by over one second and ripped from a distant eighth to a close fourth in four laps. If it weren't for four or five laps where Jorge clearly lost his focus, Ducati could have had an even better day.

As it was, they still left Catalunya having won two races in a row for the first time since the days of Casey Stoner, and were third in the Constructors' Championship a mere 17 points adrift of Yamaha. And Andrea Dovizioso, the quiet man who many thought Ducati should have let go rather than the other Andrea, was only seven points behind championship leader Viñales.

However, 2016 was the factory's greatest year with three wins against the toughest opposition from KTM and Honda. The first came at Assen from Pecco Bagnaia after one of the best races of that or any other season. The Italian added a wet weather win in Malaysia at the end of the year, sandwiching another distinctly damp win by John McPhee in the Czech Republic. The Scot's motorcycle was badged as a Peugeot but was a Mahindra.

Unfortunately the factory's fortunes nose-dived in 2017 and the decision was made to pull out.

As well as the three victories, Mahindra scored a total of 13 podium finishes. Not a bad record for a company that came to MotoGP with no experience of World-Championship motorsport and leave with the honour of being the first manufacturer from their country to win a Grand Prix.

7 | CATALUNYA

RACE RESULTS

WINNER | ANDREA DOVIZIOSO

CIRCUIT LENGTH | 4.7 KM | 2.94 MILES

NO. OF LAPS | 25

RACE DISTANCE | 118.2 KM | 73.5 MILES

CIRCUIT RECORD LAP | 1'45.969 | 158.1 KM/H
JONAS FOLGER (2017)

CIRCUIT BEST LAP | 1'43.589 | 161.7 KM/H
MARC MARQUEZ (2016)

RACE CONDITION | DRY

AIR | 33°C

HUMIDITY | 20%

GROUND | 54°C

OFFICIAL TIMEKEEPER

OFFICIAL MotoGP™ CLASS TYRE

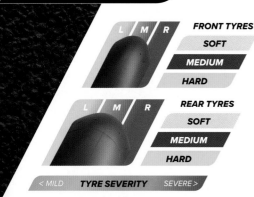

QUALIFYING RESULTS

	RIDER	NAT	TEAM	MACHINE	QP/TIME		GAP 1ST/PREV	
1	Dani Pedrosa	SPA	Repsol Honda Team	HONDA	Q2	1'43.870		
2	Jorge Lorenzo	SPA	Ducati Team	DUCATI	Q2	1'44.201	0.331	0.331
3	Danilo Petrucci	ITA	OCTO Pramac Racing	DUCATI	Q2	1'44.220	0.350	0.019
4	Marc Marquez	SPA	Repsol Honda Team	HONDA	Q2	1'44.320	0.450	0.100
5	Aleix Espargaro	SPA	Aprilia Racing Team Gresini	APRILIA	Q2	1'44.348	0.478	0.028
6	Hector Barbera	SPA	Reale Avintia Racing	DUCATI	Q2	1'44.381	0.511	0.033
7	Andrea Dovizioso	ITA	Ducati Team	DUCATI	Q2	1'44.451	0.581	0.070
8	Jonas Folger**	GER	Monster Yamaha Tech 3	YAMAHA	Q2	1'44.600	0.730	0.149
9	Maverick Viñales**	SPA	Movistar Yamaha MotoGP	YAMAHA	Q2	1'44.620	0.750	0.020
10	Alvaro Bautista	SPA	Pull&Bear Aspar Team	DUCATI	Q2	1'44.740	0.870	0.120
11	Scott Redding	GBR	OCTO Pramac Racing	DUCATI	Q2	1'44.852	0.982	0.112
12	Andrea Iannone	ITA	Team SUZUKI ECSTAR	SUZUKI	Q2	1'44.928	1.058	0.076
13	Valentino Rossi	ITA	Movistar Yamaha MotoGP	YAMAHA	Q1	1'44.661	*0.422	0.040
14	Johann Zarco	FRA	Monster Yamaha Tech 3	YAMAHA	Q1	1'44.681	*0.442	0.020
15	Jack Miller	AUS	EG 0,0 Marc VDS	HONDA	Q1	1'44.829	*0.590	0.148
16	Loris Baz	FRA	Reale Avintia Racing	DUCATI	Q1	1'44.919	*0.680	0.090
17	Cal Crutchlow	GBR	LCR Honda	HONDA	Q1	1'45.162	*0.923	0.243
18	Karel Abraham	CZE	Pull&Bear Aspar Team	DUCATI	Q1	1'45.641	*1.402	0.479
19	Tito Rabat	SPA	EG 0,0 Marc VDS	HONDA	Q1	1'45.741	*1.502	0.100
20	Pol Espargaro	SPA	Red Bull KTM Factory Racing	KTM	Q1	1'45.887	*1.648	0.146
21	Sam Lowes	GBR	Aprilia Racing Team Gresini	APRILIA	Q1	1'48.803	*4.564	2.916
22	Sylvain Guintoli	FRA	Team SUZUKI ECSTAR	SUZUKI	FP3	1'45.912	1.734	
23	Bradley Smith	GBR	Red Bull KTM Factory Racing	KTM	FP3	1'46.853	2.675	0.586

* Gap to the fastest rider in the Q1 session
** Went forward from Q1 to Q2

---

1 | ANDREA DOVIZIOSO
Consecutive wins for the first time in any class. Simply managed the conditions better than the others and made best use of the Ducati's speed advantage on the straight to pass long-time leader Pedrosa. Ducati's first back-to-back wins since the days of Casey Stoner.

2 | MARC MARQUEZ
Crashed five times in the weekend plus tripping over his starter motor in pit lane. Thought he could win and followed Dovizioso past Pedrosa only to realise, as he said, that it was Dovi's day.

3 | DANI PEDROSA
Pole and a podium at home, but still a little disappointed. Led for nine laps but knew Dovizioso was conserving his tyres and would pass when he wanted. After Dovi went past, Marquez followed next time round.

First front-row start, led the race for opening laps then dropped back, but this time after half-a-dozen laps he picked up four places in the final third. The first time he has finished within ten seconds of the winner.

5 | JOHANN ZARCO
A difficult weekend but Johann stuck at it from 14th on the grid and was able to make ground when others couldn't at the end of the race. Couldn't stay with Lorenzo but caught his teammate on last lap.

6 | JONAS FOLGER
The fastest Yamaha rider all weekend. With the leaders for the first half of the race, when he set the fastest lap, but caught and passed by his teammate on last lap, which took the gloss off proceedings for Jonas.

7 | ALVARO BAUTISTA
Rode conservatively to save his tyres but never out of the top ten. Lost the front at the first corner when he started to push then felt the rear lose grip as well. Happy to make up for previous two races.

8 | VALENTINO ROSSI
An awful weekend emphasising what we learned at Jerez – that the Yamaha can't find grip on hot, slippy tracks. Couldn't keep Zarco behind him. Valentino blamed the 2017 chassis.

9 | HECTOR BARBERA
Qualified on the second row, got barged off-track by Zarco at the chicane then had his best race of the season, passing Viñales on the last lap. Detected signs of understanding the bike; more cheerful than most at the finish.

10 | MAVERICK VIÑALES
The best that could be said is that Maverick left Barcelona still leading the Championship. Even at the start of the race he had problems and sank back to 16th.

11 | CAL CRUTCHLOW
Three crashes saw him qualify 17th, so 11th was a decent result. Chose a hard tyre thinking it wouldn't drop as much as the opposition's but "it wasn't even good on the warm-up lap." Happy for his old teammate Dovizioso.

4 | JORGE LORENZO

RACE LAP CHART

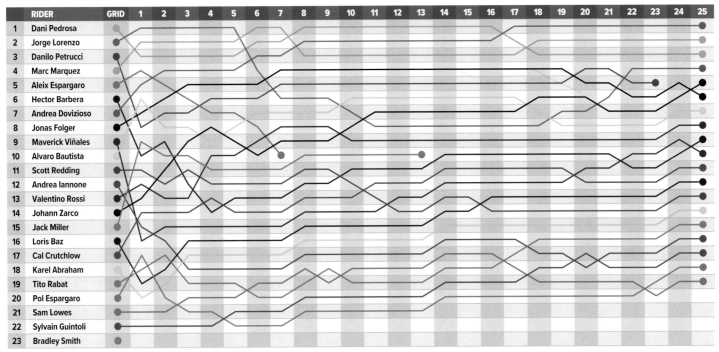

	RIDER	GRID	1	2	3	4	5	6	7	8	9	10	11	12	13	14	15	16	17	18	19	20	21	22	23	24	25
1	Dani Pedrosa																											
2	Jorge Lorenzo																											
3	Danilo Petrucci																											
4	Marc Marquez																											
5	Aleix Espargaro																											
6	Hector Barbera																											
7	Andrea Dovizioso																											
8	Jonas Folger																											
9	Maverick Viñales																											
10	Alvaro Bautista																											
11	Scott Redding																											
12	Andrea Iannone																											
13	Valentino Rossi																											
14	Johann Zarco																											
15	Jack Miller																											
16	Loris Baz																											
17	Cal Crutchlow																											
18	Karel Abraham																											
19	Tito Rabat																											
20	Pol Espargaro																											
21	Sam Lowes																											
22	Sylvain Guintoli																											
23	Bradley Smith																											

RACE CLASSIFICATION AFTER 25 LAPS = 116.375 KM

	RIDER	NAT	TEAM	MACHINE	TIME	+ GAP	TYRES
1	Andrea Dovizioso	ITA	Ducati Team	DUCATI	44'41.518		H/M
2	Marc Marquez	SPA	Repsol Honda Team	HONDA	44'45.062	3.544	H/M
3	Dani Pedrosa	SPA	Repsol Honda Team	HONDA	44'48.292	6.774	H/M
4	Jorge Lorenzo	SPA	Ducati Team	DUCATI	44'51.126	9.608	H/H
5	Johann Zarco	FRA	Monster Yamaha Tech 3	YAMAHA	44'55.356	13.838	M/M
6	Jonas Folger	GER	Monster Yamaha Tech 3	YAMAHA	44'55.439	13.921	M/M
7	Alvaro Bautista	SPA	Pull&Bear Aspar Team	DUCATI	44'58.281	16.763	M/M
8	Valentino Rossi	ITA	Movistar Yamaha MotoGP	YAMAHA	45'02.339	20.821	M/M
9	Hector Barbera	SPA	Reale Avintia Racing	DUCATI	45'05.470	23.952	M/M
10	Maverick Viñales	SPA	Movistar Yamaha MotoGP	YAMAHA	45'05.707	24.189	M/M
11	Cal Crutchlow	GBR	LCR Honda	HONDA	45'09.847	28.329	H/H
12	Loris Baz	FRA	Reale Avintia Racing	DUCATI	45'14.799	33.281	M/M
13	Scott Redding	GBR	OCTO Pramac Racing	DUCATI	45'16.718	35.200	H/H
14	Karel Abraham	CZE	Pull&Bear Aspar Team	DUCATI	45'20.954	39.436	M/M
15	Tito Rabat	SPA	EG 0,0 Marc VDS	HONDA	45'22.390	40.872	H/M
16	Andrea Iannone	ITA	Team SUZUKI ECSTAR	SUZUKI	45'24.739	43.221	H/M
17	Sylvain Guintoli	FRA	Team SUZUKI ECSTAR	SUZUKI	45'26.173	44.655	H/M
18	Pol Espargaro	SPA	Red Bull KTM Factory Racing	KTM	45'30.511	48.993	M/H
19	Sam Lowes	GBR	Aprilia Racing Team Gresini	APRILIA	45'37.010	55.492	M/M
NC	Danilo Petrucci	ITA	OCTO Pramac Racing	DUCATI	41'16.068	2 laps	H/H
NC	Jack Miller	AUS	EG 0,0 Marc VDS	HONDA	23'18.364	12 laps	H/M
NC	Aleix Espargaro	SPA	Aprilia Racing Team Gresini	APRILIA	12'33.993	18 laps	M/M

CHAMPIONSHIP STANDINGS

	RIDER	NAT	TEAM	POINTS
1	Maverick Viñales	SPA	Movistar Yamaha MotoGP	111
2	Andrea Dovizioso	ITA	Ducati Team	104
3	Marc Marquez	SPA	Repsol Honda Team	88
4	Dani Pedrosa	SPA	Repsol Honda Team	84
5	Valentino Rossi	ITA	Movistar Yamaha MotoGP	83
6	Johann Zarco	FRA	Monster Yamaha Tech 3	75
7	Jorge Lorenzo	SPA	Ducati Team	59
8	Jonas Folger	GER	Monster Yamaha Tech 3	51
9	Cal Crutchlow	GBR	LCR Honda	45
10	Danilo Petrucci	ITA	OCTO Pramac Racing	42
11	Alvaro Bautista	SPA	Pull&Bear Aspar Team	34
12	Scott Redding	GBR	OCTO Pramac Racing	33
13	Jack Miller	AUS	EG 0,0 Marc VDS	30
14	Loris Baz	FRA	Reale Avintia Racing	23
15	Andrea Iannone	ITA	Team SUZUKI ECSTAR	21
16	Hector Barbera	SPA	Reale Avintia Racing	21
17	Tito Rabat	SPA	EG 0,0 Marc VDS	19
18	Aleix Espargaro	SPA	Aprilia Racing Team Gresini	17
19	Karel Abraham	CZE	Pull&Bear Aspar Team	11
20	Michele Pirro	ITA	Ducati Team	7
21	Alex Rins	SPA	Team SUZUKI ECSTAR	7
22	Pol Espargaro	SPA	Red Bull KTM Factory Racing	6
23	Bradley Smith	GBR	Red Bull KTM Factory Racing	6
24	Sam Lowes	GBR	Aprilia Racing Team Gresini	2
25	Sylvain Guintoli	FRA	Team SUZUKI ECSTAR	1

12 | LORIS BAZ
Clutch problems at the start, arm pump at the finish. In between he tried to save his tyres but like most ended with no grip.

13 | SCOTT REDDING
His hard tyres lasted about six laps before he couldn't defend himself. Said the mediums would have lasted about ten laps. Horrible weekend.

14 | KAREL ABRAHAM
Very happy after an awful test here a couple of weeks previously. Knew that tyres would drop and had the maps ready, even so ended up using the emergency one.

15 | TITO RABAT
Another points-scoring race, every time he's finished this year he's scored. Fast at the end but still not quick at the start.

16 | ANDREA IANNONE
Had a dreadful weekend culminating in being passed by his temporary teammate, after which he rediscovered some of his missing pace. The team were not amused.

17 | SYLVAIN GUINTOLI
His final ride as replacement for Rins, and another professional job. Followed and passed his teammate, who promptly found some speed. Stayed on to help at the test.

18 | POL ESPARGARO
KTM had never tested at Catalunya, so this was a voyage into the unknown with the added complication of the conditions. Turning in long corners is a problem anyway, so here the problem was amplified.

19 | SAM LOWES
Didn't have a good weekend but only lost out to Espargaro's KTM on last four laps when his tyre performance dropped severely.

DID NOT FINISH

DANILO PETRUCCI
Started from the front row for the first time but went sideways off the start and hit Marquez. Fought back to fourth from 11th but again used up his rear tyre and crashed two laps from the flag thinking of a podium.

JACK MILLER
Fourth fastest in warm up and carried that pace into the race. Trying to save his tyres but crashed while closing on the Rossi group.

ALEIX ESPARGARO
Fast all weekend and with the Rossi/Zarco group when stopped by mechanical failure on the eighth lap.

DID NOT RACE

ALEX RINS
The team kept him out of the race but rode in the test in preparation for his return.

BRADLEY SMITH
Crashed in qualifying and badly injured his left little finger.

THE DOCTOR DELIVERS

Valentino Rossi reignites his championship chances with a win under pressure on a tricky surface. Marquez and Dovizioso play the odds, Petrucci feels aggrieved.

It was surreal. It started with the White Giant dancing on the grid and ended with the GOAT laughing on the podium. From Friday to Sunday, Assen's biggest crowd in years watched Valentino Rossi roll the years back, starting with his best Friday of the season, and on race day celebrated his first victory in over a year. But for starters they watched Wil Hartog, the first Dutchman to win the top class at Assen, parade his bike 40 years to the day after his historic victory. Then, still in his iconic white leathers - the very ones he wore on the great day, he jigged in delight with a bunch of flowers in his hand. After that the GOAT, aka the Greatest Of All Time, took over the entertainment and the magic kept coming.

It was just over a year since Valentino had won a race, so far this season his teammate was showing him the way, and that tenth world title seemed out of reach. In the course of one of the best races of recent times, Valentino dealt with each of his rivals, handing them a lesson in how to deal with the trickiest of conditions on what is still MotoGP's grandest old stage.

Rossi's biggest challenge came from a very feisty Danilo Petrucci, who was angry with himself for missing pole on Saturday and even more angry on Sunday with back markers (remember them?) getting in his way and preventing an attack on the final lap. Would he have won? Well, he'd have had a chance. All the other top contenders faded away, some more than others.

The man who led the championship coming into Assen, Maverick Viñales, was a victim of uncertain qualifying, he crashed in the chicane pressing to make places up. He knew he had the pace to run with the leaders and everyone expected him to be there. The only bit of luck involved was that Andrea Dovizioso was good enough to miss the sliding Spaniard. Maverick's early exit suddenly meant the championship lead was up for grabs, which is perhaps why his exit was signalled on a surprising number of pit-boards. It certainly concentrated the minds of Andrea Dovizioso and Marc Marquez. Before the dramatic denouement, that most startling of rookies, Johann Zarco, led a four-man breakaway. He was the only one on soft tyres and by half distance he had been passed by Rossi, Petrucci and Marc Marquez. The Doctor had gone from third to first on consecutive laps, never allowing Marquez to lead. And then the rain came.

Not a lot of rain, and not on all of the circuit. But enough to convince some that it was worth changing to their wet bikes. After all, when it starts to rain in Assen it always gets heavier, doesn't it? Sound reasoning, but in this case wrong. So Zarco was first into pit lane to swap bikes, followed by a handful of other hopefuls, all of whom were to be disappointed. The men who decided to ignore the rain, like Karel Abraham and Loris Baz, were well rewarded for their bravery. As were Cal Crutchlow and Andrea Dovizioso who also knew that they had to press even harder on the dry sections of track to keep enough heat in their tyres to cope with the wet section. Rain is always an encouragement to Danilo Petrucci, who continued to harass Rossi for the lead as Crutchlow and Dovizioso leapt across what had been a big gap to join the leaders.

Now it was a question of who was willing to risk most in the conditions, and the answer to that question quickly turned out to be Rossi and Petrucci. As soon as Dovi and Cal arrived at the front, the pair re-opened a gap. Marquez and Dovi both later said that they decided not to risk everything, although as usual Marc's last-lap pass on Cal for third didn't look like the work of a man who was particularly risk-averse. No-one is better than Andrea Dovizioso at playing the odds and while he finished on the back of the leading group, he also took the lead in the World Championship for the

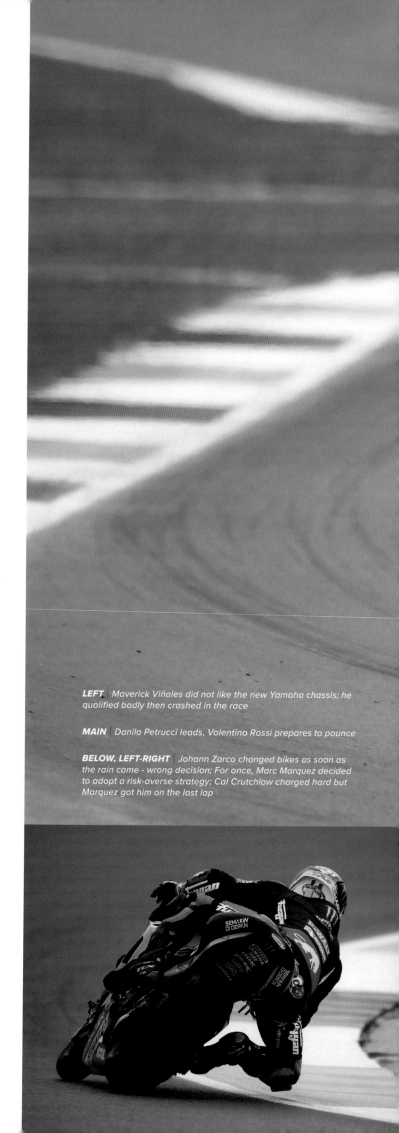

LEFT | Maverick Viñales did not like the new Yamaha chassis; he qualified badly then crashed in the race

MAIN | Danilo Petrucci leads, Valentino Rossi prepares to pounce

BELOW, LEFT-RIGHT | Johann Zarco changed bikes as soon as the rain came - wrong decision; For once, Marc Marquez decided to adopt a risk-averse strategy; Cal Crutchlow charged hard but Marquez got him on the last lap

'I RACE WITH MOTORCYCLES FOR THIS FEELING: FOR WHAT I FEEL IN THE FIVE OR SIX FINAL LAPS OF THE RACE. THAT'S ALWAYS GREAT AND ESPECIALLY AFTER A YEAR WITHOUT A VICTORY'
VALENTINO ROSSI

MAIN | Zarco leads before the rain cam

RIGHT, TOP-BOTTOM | Pol Espargaro gave KTM their best finish yet with 11th; Hector Barbera, a rain master, made the mistake of following Zarco to change bikes; The moment that cost Petrucci his victory?

FAR RIGHT | Petrucci tries to look happy with second place

BELOW, LEFT-RIGHT | Rossi celebrates his tenth win at Assen; Two Italians in parc ferme, one a little happier than the other

TESTING TIMES

Valentino Rossi's new-found optimism came from a chassis he tried at the test after the Catalan GP. Before that race he had said that the 2016 chassis was "more natural" to ride and then for the first time declared that there was a significant difference between the new and the old equipment - an unusually strong statement. For the Dutch TT the Yamaha riders had one old and one new chassis and in FP1 they compared them back-to-back. By now Valentino was in no doubt. The new chassis was the answer to his problems. His teammate Maverick Viñales was not so sure, earning a dismissive remark to the effect that "he doesn't know

first time in his MotoGP career. Not a bad bet.

It came down to a showdown between Rossi and Petrucci, who was able to use his Ducati's power to get past more than once on the ultra-fast run down to the final chicane. Rossi, using the chassis from the post-Barcelona test, looked every inch his old self, riding with total precision and making every pass look easy on the most demanding of tracks. However, circumstances robbed the crowd of the last lap they were expecting. First Hector Barbara and then, crucially, Alex Rins, who'd both swapped bikes, found themselves in Petrucci's way. Danilo encountered Rins in the fast run back to the pits on the penultimate lap, punting the Spaniard off track and losing over a third of a second. One lap later he lost the race by 0.063sec. Would he have won? Who knows, but Danilo surely would have had a chance to attack Rossi even if depriving the master of his tenth win in The Netherlands would have been a major undertaking.

The importance of Rossi's win cannot be over-stated. It put him right in contention for the championship lead and, more importantly, gave him renewed faith in his Yamaha and its potential.

what a Yamaha should feel like."

There were, of course, rumours that the "new" chassis was indeed an "old" chassis sourced from the Tech 3 garage. That is a little too simplistic, and it is in any case highly unlikely that this year's motor would bolt directly into last year's chassis. What is likely, however, is that the chassis brought to the Barcelona test incorporated stiffness ratios from the 2016 bike. It would also suggest, in view of Rossi's comments, that Yamaha were again listening to him rather than Viñales.

His M1, Rossi now said, felt like a Yamaha again. And he looked like his old self as well.

RACE RESULTS

WINNER | VALENTINO ROSSI

CIRCUIT LENGTH | 4.5 KM | 2.82 MILES

NO. OF LAPS | 26

RACE DISTANCE | 118.1 KM | 73.3 MILES

CIRCUIT RECORD LAP | 1'33.617 | 174.6 KM/H
MARC MARQUEZ (2015)

CIRCUIT BEST LAP | 1'32.627 | 176.5 KM/H
VALENTINO ROSSI (2015)

RACE CONDITION | WET

AIR | 18°C

HUMIDITY | 76%

GROUND | 25°C

Sectors
Speed Trap
Finish Line

5 | STRUBBEN
HAARBOCHT | 1
2 | MADIJK
4
3 | OSSEBROEKEN
i1
FL
18
GEERT TIMMER BOCHT | 16
17
VEENSLANG
S
RAMSHOEK | 15
6 | RUSKENHOEK
HOGE HEIDE | 13
7
MEEUWENMEER | 12
i2
i3
8 | STEKKENWAL
9 | DE BULT
DUIKERSLOOT | 11
10 | MANDEVEEN

TISSOT | motoGP
SWISS WATCHES SINCE 1853
OFFICIAL TIMEKEEPER

MICHELIN | motoGP
OFFICIAL MotoGP™ CLASS TYRE

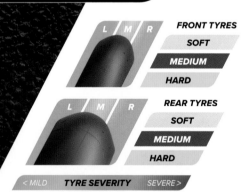

FRONT TYRES
SOFT
MEDIUM
HARD

REAR TYRES
SOFT
MEDIUM
HARD

< MILD **TYRE SEVERITY** SEVERE >

QUALIFYING RESULTS

	RIDER	NAT	TEAM	MACHINE	QP/TIME		GAP 1ST/PREV	
1	Johann Zarco	FRA	Monster Yamaha Tech 3	YAMAHA	Q2	1'46.141		
2	Marc Marquez	SPA	Repsol Honda Team	HONDA	Q2	1'46.206	0.065	0.065
3	Danilo Petrucci	ITA	OCTO Pramac Racing	DUCATI	Q2	1'46.526	0.385	0.320
4	Valentino Rossi	ITA	Movistar Yamaha MotoGP	YAMAHA	Q2	1'46.705	0.564	0.179
5	Scott Redding**	GBR	OCTO Pramac Racing	DUCATI	Q2	1'47.574	1.433	0.869
6	Jonas Folger	GER	Monster Yamaha Tech 3	YAMAHA	Q2	1'47.663	1.522	0.089
7	Alvaro Bautista	SPA	Pull&Bear Aspar Team	DUCATI	Q2	1'47.812	1.671	0.149
8	Cal Crutchlow	GBR	LCR Honda	HONDA	Q2	1'48.042	1.901	0.230
9	Andrea Dovizioso	ITA	Ducati Team	DUCATI	Q2	1'48.079	1.938	0.037
10	Sam Lowes**	GBR	Aprilia Racing Team Gresini	APRILIA	Q2	1'48.128	1.987	0.049
11	Maverick Viñales	SPA	Movistar Yamaha MotoGP	YAMAHA	Q2	1'48.266	2.125	0.138
12	Dani Pedrosa	SPA	Repsol Honda Team	HONDA	Q2	1'49.623	3.482	1.357
13	Jack Miller	AUS	EG 0,0 Marc VDS	HONDA	Q1	1'47.217	*0.291	0.026
14	Loris Baz	FRA	Reale Avintia Racing	DUCATI	Q1	1'47.234	*0.308	0.017
15	Aleix Espargaro	SPA	Aprilia Racing Team Gresini	APRILIA	Q1	1'47.277	*0.351	0.043
16	Andrea Iannone	ITA	Team SUZUKI ECSTAR	SUZUKI	Q1	1'47.649	*0.723	0.372
17	Alex Rins	SPA	Team SUZUKI ECSTAR	SUZUKI	Q1	1'47.804	*0.878	0.155
18	Karel Abraham	CZE	Pull&Bear Aspar Team	DUCATI	Q1	1'47.947	*1.021	0.143
19	Pol Espargaro	SPA	Red Bull KTM Factory Racing	KTM	Q1	1'47.957	*1.031	0.010
20	Hector Barbera	SPA	Reale Avintia Racing	DUCATI	Q1	1'48.080	*1.154	0.123
21	Jorge Lorenzo	SPA	Ducati Team	DUCATI	Q1	1'48.219	*1.293	0.139
22	Bradley Smith	GBR	Red Bull KTM Factory Racing	KTM	Q1	1'48.448	*1.522	0.229
23	Tito Rabat	SPA	EG 0,0 Marc VDS	HONDA	Q1	1'48.700	*1.774	0.252

Gap to the fastest rider in the Q1 session
**Went forward from Q1 to Q2*

1 | VALENTINO ROSSI
A tenth win at Assen and under the trickiest conditions. Armed with a new/old chassis, Valentino was quick from FP1, and tough bordering on masterful in the race. He had to deal with Zarco, Marquez and Petrucci before collecting his 115th GP win. It also showed he is a genuine championship contender.

2 | DANILO PETRUCCI
Just missed pole; just missed the win, and felt aggrieved on both counts. Pole was his mistake, but he was baulked on the last lap by Rins and lost contact with Rossi. He may not have won but he would have had a chance to try.

3 | MARC MARQUEZ
Very happy to have got on the podium at a track where he thought he might struggle. Decided against risking too much for the win after the rain but was more than happy to fight Crutchlow and Dovizioso at the end.

4 | CAL CRUTCHLOW
Pressed hard when the rain came and got up to third, only to be repassed by Marquez on the fast run back to the final corner. felt that he showed his hand too early.

5 | ANDREA DOVIZIOSO
A complicated race that saw him struggle at the start then close a gap to the leaders as the rain came. He decided not to take too many risks and was rewarded with the championship lead for the first time in his MotoGP career.

6 | JACK MILLER
A good result from 13th on the grid, especially as he was hung out to dry first time round the right-handers that start the lap. Fought with fellow Honda riders Pedrosa and Crutchlow and when the rain came moved forward but didn't risk too much.

7 | KAREL ABRAHAMS
Equalled his best ever MotoGP finish with a brave race. In the points when the rain came but ignored it and pushed hard. Took two places in one go at the end of the last lap.

8 | LORIS BAZ
In trouble from the start but when the rain came knew he had to push to keep heat in the tyres. Decided not to pit and repassed Iannone on last lap but was mugged by Abraham.

9 | ANDREA IANNONE
A much more positive race, at least in the early stages before tyre degradation again drastically altered the Suzuki's behaviour. The team were happier than they've been for a while.

10 | ALEIX ESPARGARO
Really fast in the dry and looking to have the potential for a top-six finish at least. Lost a little confidence when the rain came.

11 | POL ESPARGARO
KTM's best result so far, thanks to staying out and not changing bikes when the rain started to fall. Helped by the choice of soft tyres, but a great race.

RACE LAP CHART

‑‑‑‑‑ Dashed line: Lapped rider

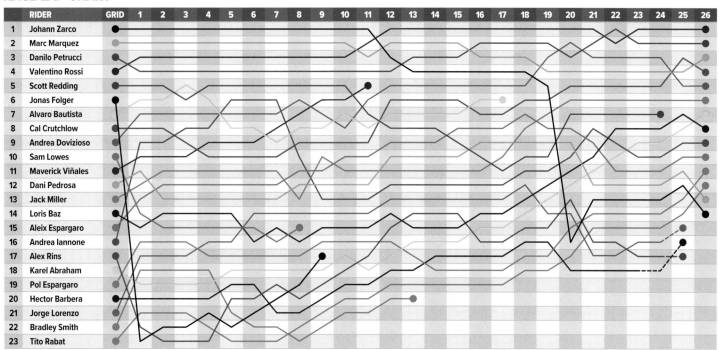

	RIDER	GRID	1	2	3	4	5	6	7	8	9	10	11	12	13	14	15	16	17	18	19	20	21	22	23	24	25	26
1	Johann Zarco																												
2	Marc Marquez																												
3	Danilo Petrucci																												
4	Valentino Rossi																												
5	Scott Redding																												
6	Jonas Folger																												
7	Alvaro Bautista																												
8	Cal Crutchlow																												
9	Andrea Dovizioso																												
10	Sam Lowes																												
11	Maverick Viñales																												
12	Dani Pedrosa																												
13	Jack Miller																												
14	Loris Baz																												
15	Aleix Espargaro																												
16	Andrea Iannone																												
17	Alex Rins																												
18	Karel Abraham																												
19	Pol Espargaro																												
20	Hector Barbera																												
21	Jorge Lorenzo																												
22	Bradley Smith																												
23	Tito Rabat																												

RACE CLASSIFICATION AFTER 26 LAPS = 118.092 KM

	RIDER	NAT	TEAM	MACHINE	TIME	+ GAP	TYRES
1	Valentino Rossi	ITA	Movistar Yamaha MotoGP	YAMAHA	41'41.149		M/H
2	Danilo Petrucci	ITA	OCTO Pramac Racing	DUCATI	41'41.212	0.063	M/M
3	Marc Marquez	SPA	Repsol Honda Team	HONDA	41'46.350	5.201	M/M
4	Cal Crutchlow	GBR	LCR Honda	HONDA	41'46.392	5.243	M/M
5	Andrea Dovizioso	ITA	Ducati Team	DUCATI	41'46.476	5.327	M/M
6	Jack Miller	AUS	EG 0,0 Marc VDS	HONDA	42'04.539	23.390	M/M
7	Karel Abraham	CZE	Pull&Bear Aspar Team	DUCATI	42'18.131	36.982	M/M
8	Loris Baz	FRA	Reale Avintia Racing	DUCATI	42'18.207	37.058	M/M
9	Andrea Iannone	ITA	Team SUZUKI ECSTAR	SUZUKI	42'18.315	37.166	M/H
10	Aleix Espargaro	SPA	Aprilia Racing Team Gresini	APRILIA	42'43.078	61.929	M/M
11	Pol Espargaro	SPA	Red Bull KTM Factory Racing	KTM	42'50.533	69.384	S/S
12	Tito Rabat	SPA	EG 0,0 Marc VDS	HONDA	42'51.270	70.121	M/M
13	Dani Pedrosa	SPA	Repsol Honda Team	HONDA	42'51.493	70.344	M/M
14	Johann Zarco	FRA	Monster Yamaha Tech 3	YAMAHA	43'16.804	95.655	S/S
15	Jorge Lorenzo	SPA	Ducati Team	DUCATI	41'44.184	1 lap	M/M
16	Hector Barbera	SPA	Reale Avintia Racing	DUCATI	41'56.943	1 lap	M/S
17	Alex Rins	SPA	Team SUZUKI ECSTAR	SUZUKI	42'01.174	1 lap	M/H
NC	Scott Redding	GBR	OCTO Pramac Racing	DUCATI	38'59.934	2 laps	M/M
NC	Alvaro Bautista	SPA	Pull&Bear Aspar Team	DUCATI	27'07.172	9 laps	M/M
NC	Bradley Smith	GBR	Red Bull KTM Factory Racing	KTM	21'10.245	13 laps	M/H
NC	Maverick Viñales	SPA	Movistar Yamaha MotoGP	YAMAHA	17'34.224	15 laps	M/H
NC	Jonas Folger	GER	Monster Yamaha Tech 3	YAMAHA	14'34.142	17 laps	M/M
NC	Sam Lowes	GBR	Aprilia Racing Team Gresini	APRILIA	12'56.939	18 laps	S/S

CHAMPIONSHIP STANDINGS

	RIDER	NAT	TEAM	POINTS
1	Andrea Dovizioso	ITA	Ducati Team	115
2	Maverick Viñales	SPA	Movistar Yamaha MotoGP	111
3	Valentino Rossi	ITA	Movistar Yamaha MotoGP	108
4	Marc Marquez	SPA	Repsol Honda Team	104
5	Dani Pedrosa	SPA	Repsol Honda Team	87
6	Johann Zarco	FRA	Monster Yamaha Tech 3	77
7	Danilo Petrucci	ITA	OCTO Pramac Racing	62
8	Jorge Lorenzo	SPA	Ducati Team	60
9	Cal Crutchlow	GBR	LCR Honda	58
10	Jonas Folger	GER	Monster Yamaha Tech 3	51
11	Jack Miller	AUS	EG 0,0 Marc VDS	40
12	Alvaro Bautista	SPA	Pull&Bear Aspar Team	34
13	Scott Redding	GBR	OCTO Pramac Racing	33
14	Loris Baz	FRA	Reale Avintia Racing	31
15	Andrea Iannone	ITA	Team SUZUKI ECSTAR	28
16	Aleix Espargaro	SPA	Aprilia Racing Team Gresini	23
17	Tito Rabat	SPA	EG 0,0 Marc VDS	23
18	Hector Barbera	SPA	Reale Avintia Racing	21
19	Karel Abraham	CZE	Pull&Bear Aspar Team	20
20	Pol Espargaro	SPA	Red Bull KTM Factory Racing	11
21	Alex Rins	SPA	Team SUZUKI ECSTAR	7
22	Michele Pirro	ITA	Ducati Team	7
23	Bradley Smith	GBR	Red Bull KTM Factory Racing	6
24	Sam Lowes	GBR	Aprilia Racing Team Gresini	2
25	Sylvain Guintoli	FRA	Team SUZUKI ECSTAR	1

12 | TITO RABAT
A controlled ride from last on the grid to another points-scoring finish. Stayed out when it rained and was rewarded for his bravery.

13 | DANI PEDROSA
A horrible weekend in which he never got enough heat in the tyres, especially when the rain came. Managed to find one positive: that he'd only lost one point on the championship leader.

14 | JOHANN ZARCO
Just hanging on to the leaders when the rains came, having led the early stages. Gambled on the rain getting heavier, as it had every other time in the weekend. He was wrong, but his soft slicks were worn out, so he had no choice.

15 | JORGE LORENZO
Haunted by the ghosts of his past troubles at Assen. Made some progress in the race after awful qualifying but gambled on changing bikes.

16 | HECTOR BARBERA
Habitually a late changer in flag-to-flag races but this time he saw Zarco go in and followed, which turned out to be a mistake.

17 | ALEX RINS
His first experience of wet tarmac and a flag-to-flag race and a solid return from injury, at least until it rained. Early into the pits to swap bikes and then found himself in Petrucci's way on final lap, for which Alex apologised.

DID NOT FINISH

SCOTT REDDING
Good qualifying followed by a good start that suggested he could join the leaders. But he stayed out and was a stunning seventh when he fell on the last lap, having set the fastest lap.

ALVARO BAUTISTA
Crashed out at Turn 5 when in sixth place just before the rains came. Lost the front and not sure why.

BRADLEY SMITH
Raced despite a mangled little finger on his left hand, a legacy of Barcelona. Crashed again in the race when he ran wide at Turn 7.

MAVERICK VIÑALES
Started from 11th and was forcing his way to the front, where he was expecting to be, when he crashed at the chicane. A victim of his bad qualifying.

JONAS FOLGER
Ended his run of finishing every race by crashing at the first corner while trying to make up for an off-track excursion that put him to the back of the field.

SAM LOWES
Brilliant in qualifying despite some destabilising talk from the team. Crashed while chasing Lorenzo, but felt he'd made a big step forward.

NORMALITY INTRUDES

Marc Marquez wins again in Germany, Folger gets his first podium.

Even in this season of total unpredictability some things remain constant. One of those is that Marc Marquez will win from pole position at the Sachsenring as he has done every year since 2010 when he was on a 125. Sure enough he did it again and, for good measure, went to the top of the championship for the first time this year. The fact that this was only his second win of the year shows how topsy-turvy the first half of the season has been. Marquez is the fourth man to lead the points table, after Viñales, Rossi and Dovizioso, and this despite the fact he has crashed out of two races. Remarkably, Maverick Viñales, only four points adrift, has also crashed twice during races. Third-and fourth-place men, Andrea Dovizioso and Valentino Rossi, have both crashed just the once. It is worth noting that the only one that was someone else's crash was Dovizioso's. In anything like a normal season, two crashes in nine races would put you out of championship contention. Not this year.

The Sachsenring surprise was that the man who gave Marquez the hardest time he's ever had in Germany was Jonas Folger. In the shadow of his teammate Johann Zarco for most of the time, the German's season had still been impressive by the normal rookie standards – he came to his home race tenth in the championship having scored points in every race except one. His weak point had been the early laps, a lack of confidence on new

tyres and a full tank. This time he had his mind made up for him by – who else? – Danilo Petrucci who elbowed Jonas onto the grass on the outside of Turn 2 on the run down to the Omega on Lap 1. Jonas managed to fit himself back into the pack without having what seemed like the inevitable accident and finished the lap in fourth. Two laps later he was third, and another two later he was second. Next time round he outbraked leader Marc Marquez at the bottom of the long, fast downhill straight and made it look ludicrously easy.

Everyone else appeared to be in various degrees of tyre trouble, a situation brought about by, yet again, very mixed weather on Friday and Saturday plus new tarmac which Michelin had been prevented from organising a test on. Not that anyone was complaining about the resurfacing, quite the reverse, the grip in the wet was exceptional and most of the bumps had been eliminated. However, the very nature of the circuit means that the left side of the tyres have to cope with severe stresses and a lot of riders were affected by sudden tyre drop.

Again, it was the satellite Yamahas which impressed. While Folger was fighting for the lead, Johann Zarco was carving through the field. Both factory men were using the new chassis first seen at the Barcelona test. Valentino Rossi was so keen on it that in practice he lost valuable time getting it back to the pits after the motor cut out rather than get a lift back for his second bike, which was still equipped with the original frame. Maverick Viñales still seemed less sure about any improvements and wouldn't (or, more likely, was told not to) answer any direct questions on the subject. However, both men improved on sketchy qualifying to finish fourth and fifth with Viñales winning the internecine struggle.

ABOVE, LEFT-RIGHT *Andrea Dovizioso couldn't make the soft rear tyre last; Jonas Folger contemplates his home race from the middle of the second row; Bautista takes advantage of Lorenzo and Crutchlow's tyre woes*

MAIN *The focus of the race, the rare sight of a German towards the front of the German GP*

RIGHT *For once, Johann Zarco was eclipsed by his teammate*

Jonas Folger led for five laps before Marquez came back past but to the surprise of most observers he did not pull away. The gap rarely crept above a quarter of a second over the next dozen laps but more than once Folger made a mistake on the brakes at the first corner and ran deep, he quickly got back up to Marquez's back wheel but the effort finished his tyres off. Folger only really lost touch over the final couple of laps but he was well clear of

'I WISH TO DEDICATE THIS WIN TO NICKY [HAYDEN] AND HIS FAMILY. I HAD PROMISED THIS TO MYSELF AFTER HIS INCIDENT BECAUSE WE HAD SOME VERY GOOD MOMENTS TOGETHER'

MARC MARQUEZ

HALF-TERM REPORT

In the 69-year history of the World Championship, there hasn't been an opening half as close as this year, as the following statistics clearly show:

Just ten points cover the top four in the MotoGP Championship classification. This is the smallest points spread ever covering the top four riders in the premier-class championship after the first nine races of the year.

Dani Pedrosa, in fifth place in the championship, is just 26 points

third-placed Dani Pedrosa who'd had a lonely race. In parc fermé Marquez congratulated Folger by feigning outrage at the pressure he'd been put under and shoving the German a few times. It was undoubtedly the toughest fight of his eight wins at the Sachsenring but Marc seemed even more surprised by the fact he was on top of the championship having been 37 points adrift three races previously.

The factory Yamahas and Ducatis followed along without really making an impression on the race, Alvaro Bautista in among them in sixth place was the standout result from the customer teams. The final race before the Summer break also showed how the KTM project was progressing. Both riders scored points, Espargaro went direct to second qualifying and was only just over 30 seconds adrift of the winner. The factory test rider, Mika Kallio, also impressed as a wild card on his favourite track. Given the bike's weak point is supposed to be turning in long corners, this was another impressive showing and the best indication of the progress was that, honestly, no-one was really surprised by their performance.

So what had the first half of the 2017 season taught us? Frankly, nothing. Making any sort of prediction until at least a couple of sessions had run was an exercise in futility as each manufacturer had no idea if their base setting would work at any given track with the new Michelins. Four riders on three different makes of motorcycle ended part one of the '17 season separated by just ten points after nine races. The paddock went off on its longer than usual Summer break well aware they would effectively be starting again when they reconvened at Brno.

MAIN | *Marquez maintained his 100% record at the Sachsenring - just*

LEFT, TOP-BOTTOM | *Bradley Smith is shadowed by KTM test rider Mika Kallio, the story of the second half of his season; Valentino Rossi didn't have a bad weekend, but it wasn't great either; Dani Pedrosa rode to a solid if unspectacular third place*

behind teammate Marc Marquez – the closest top five ever in the premier class after the first nine races of the year.

There have been five different winners in the first nine MotoGP races of the year, and ten different riders representing five different nations have stood on the podium.

Four different riders have led the championship standings in the opening half of the season: Maverick Viñales, Valentino Rossi, Andrea Dovizioso and Marc Marquez.

All 23 riders in the full-time MotoGP entry list have scored World Championship points during 2017 and 17 of them have had at least one finish in the top eight.

Eleven different riders have qualified on the front row of the grid during the first half of 2017.

Following the German Grand Prix, Marc Marquez leads the MotoGP championship standings with 129 points. This is the lowest points total for a rider leading the championship after the opening nine races of the year since the current points scoring system was introduced in 1993; the previous lowest was 2000 when Kenny Roberts Jnr had 145 points after nine races.

9 | GERMANY

RACE RESULTS

WINNER | MARC MARQUEZ

CIRCUIT LENGTH | 3.7 KM | 2.28 MILES

NO. OF LAPS | 30

RACE DISTANCE | 110.1 KM | 68.4 MILES

CIRCUIT RECORD LAP | 1'21.530 | 162.0 KM/H
MARC MARQUEZ (2015)

CIRCUIT BEST LAP | 1'20.336 | 164.5 KM/H
MARC MARQUEZ (2015)

RACE CONDITION | DRY

AIR | 18°C

HUMIDITY | 65%

GROUND | 26°C

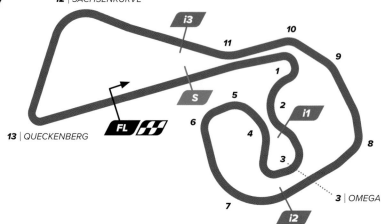

Sectors
Speed Trap
Finish Line

12 | SACHSENKURVE
13 | QUECKENBERG
3 | OMEGA

TISSOT | MotoGP
SWISS WATCHES SINCE 1853
OFFICIAL TIMEKEEPER

MICHELIN | MotoGP
OFFICIAL MotoGP™ CLASS TYRE

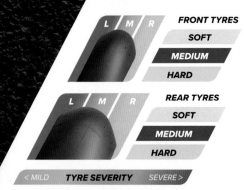

FRONT TYRES
SOFT
MEDIUM
HARD

REAR TYRES
SOFT
MEDIUM
HARD

< MILD   **TYRE SEVERITY**   SEVERE >

QUALIFYING RESULTS

	RIDER	NAT	TEAM	MACHINE	QP/TIME	GAP 1ST/PREV	
1	Marc Marquez	SPA	Repsol Honda Team	HONDA	Q2 1'27.302		
2	Danilo Petrucci**	ITA	OCTO Pramac Racing	DUCATI	Q2 1'27.462	0.160	0.160
3	Dani Pedrosa	SPA	Repsol Honda Team	HONDA	Q2 1'27.949	0.647	0.487
4	Cal Crutchlow	GBR	LCR Honda	HONDA	Q2 1'28.089	0.787	0.140
5	Jonas Folger	GER	Monster Yamaha Tech 3	YAMAHA	Q2 1'28.210	0.908	0.121
6	Jorge Lorenzo	SPA	Ducati Team	DUCATI	Q2 1'28.383	1.081	0.173
7	Pol Espargaro**	SPA	Red Bull KTM Factory Racing	KTM	Q2 1'28.402	1.100	0.019
8	Aleix Espargaro	SPA	Aprilia Racing Team Gresini	APRILIA	Q2 1'28.526	1.224	0.124
9	Valentino Rossi	ITA	Movistar Yamaha MotoGP	YAMAHA	Q2 1'28.669	1.367	0.143
10	Andrea Dovizioso	ITA	Ducati Team	DUCATI	Q2 1'28.703	1.401	0.034
11	Maverick Viñales	SPA	Movistar Yamaha MotoGP	YAMAHA	Q2 1'28.823	1.521	0.120
12	Alvaro Bautista	SPA	Pull&Bear Aspar Team	DUCATI	Q2 1'28.968	1.666	0.145
13	Jack Miller	AUS	EG 0,0 Marc VDS	HONDA	Q1 1'27.967	*0.279	0.272
14	Loris Baz	FRA	Reale Avintia Racing	DUCATI	Q1 1'27.979	*0.291	0.012
15	Bradley Smith	GBR	Red Bull KTM Factory Racing	KTM	Q1 1'28.015	*0.327	0.036
16	Andrea Iannone	ITA	Team SUZUKI ECSTAR	SUZUKI	Q1 1'28.103	*0.415	0.088
17	Mika Kallio	FIN	Red Bull KTM Factory Racing	KTM	Q1 1'28.285	*0.597	0.182
18	Hector Barbera	SPA	Reale Avintia Racing	DUCATI	Q1 1'28.404	*0.716	0.119
19	Johann Zarco	FRA	Monster Yamaha Tech 3	YAMAHA	Q1 1'28.444	*0.756	0.040
20	Karel Abraham	CZE	Pull&Bear Aspar Team	DUCATI	Q1 1'28.625	*0.937	0.181
21	Sam Lowes	GBR	Aprilia Racing Team Gresini	APRILIA	Q1 1'28.659	*0.971	0.034
22	Alex Rins	SPA	Team SUZUKI ECSTAR	SUZUKI	Q1 1'29.504	*1.816	0.845
23	Scott Redding	GBR	OCTO Pramac Racing	DUCATI	Q1 1'29.578	*1.890	0.074
24	Tito Rabat	SPA	EG 0,0 Marc VDS	HONDA	Q1 1'30.028	*2.340	0.450

*Gap with the fastest rider in the Q1 session
** Went forward from Q1 to Q2

1 | MARC MARQUEZ
His sixth win in a row here, eighth counting all classes, and his most difficult. Chased all the way by Folger, who led for five laps, and pushed Marc all the way. Almost surprised to find himself leading the championship. Dedicated the win to Nicky Hayden's family.

2 | JONAS FOLGER
Equalled his teammate's achievement with a home-race rostrum – to the delight of the crowd. Survived a barge from Petrucci going down to the Omega

first time round then took the lead on lap six and held it for five laps. Only lost touch with Marquez in final three laps.

3 | DANI PEDROSA
Had no problems staying with Marquez in early laps but when Folger overtook started to develop wheelspin problems and decided to settle for a podium finish.

4 | MAVERICK VIÑALES
Like his teammate couldn't work out whether he'd had a good GP or not. His progress through the field from

11th on the grid was impressive. Took a few laps to assess the situation then moved forwards quickly. Passed Dovizioso and Rossi in very quick succession.

5 | VALENTINO ROSSI
Not a weekend to get excited about, Valentino's minimum requirement is to fight for the podium. However, there was plenty to be happy about – notably the fact he is only ten points behind the championship leader Marquez.

6 | ALVARO BAUTISTA
Another impressive charge through the field to within sniffing distance of a podium. From 14th on the first lap to a superb sixth, which is where Alvaro feels he should be every race.

7 | ALEIX ESPARGARO
Had to press harder than he wanted to make passes which stressed the front tyre, but still an impressive race in which he ran with some of the championship contenders. The bike again seemed to preserve its tyres well.

8 | ANDREA DOVIZIOSO
Up to fourth by Lap 18 but then suffered from the performance of his soft rear tyre dropping severely. Happy to get a race that the Ducatis never enjoy out of the way.

9 | JOHANN ZARCO
A remarkable recovery from 19th on the grid, almost undeservedly overshadowed by his teammate's race. Made an astonishing ten overtaking moves and a little disappointed not to catch the two in front of him.

10 | CAL CRUTCHLOW
Disappointed after stellar qualifying. His problem was high front-tyre pressure.

11 | JORGE LORENZO
Only happy with the first few laps. Then started spinning the rear in all the lefts but was hanging on to ninth place when he got serious spinning on acceleration as well and lost two places.

RACE LAP CHART

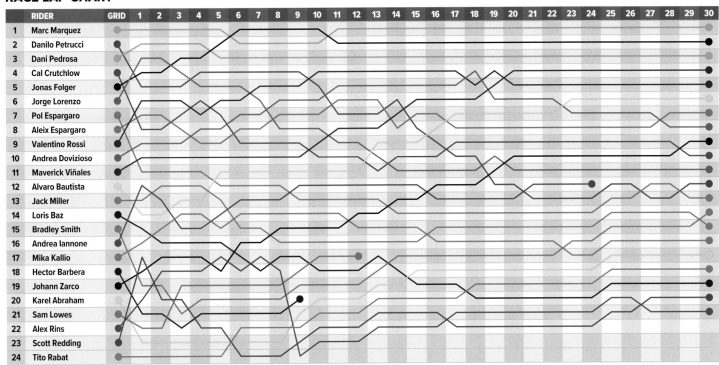

	RIDER	GRID	1	2	3	4	5	6	7	8	9	10	11	12	13	14	15	16	17	18	19	20	21	22	23	24	25	26	27	28	29	30
1	Marc Marquez																															
2	Danilo Petrucci																															
3	Dani Pedrosa																															
4	Cal Crutchlow																															
5	Jonas Folger																															
6	Jorge Lorenzo																															
7	Pol Espargaro																															
8	Aleix Espargaro																															
9	Valentino Rossi																															
10	Andrea Dovizioso																															
11	Maverick Viñales																															
12	Alvaro Bautista																															
13	Jack Miller																															
14	Loris Baz																															
15	Bradley Smith																															
16	Andrea Iannone																															
17	Mika Kallio																															
18	Hector Barbera																															
19	Johann Zarco																															
20	Karel Abraham																															
21	Sam Lowes																															
22	Alex Rins																															
23	Scott Redding																															
24	Tito Rabat																															

RACE CLASSIFICATION AFTER 30 LAPS = 110.13 KM

	RIDER	NAT	TEAM	MACHINE	TIME	+ GAP	TYRES
1	Marc Marquez	SPA	Repsol Honda Team	HONDA	40'59.525		MB/MB
2	Jonas Folger	GER	Monster Yamaha Tech 3	YAMAHA	41'02.835	3.310	MB/MB
3	Dani Pedrosa	SPA	Repsol Honda Team	HONDA	41'11.071	11.546	MB/MB
4	Maverick Viñales	SPA	Movistar Yamaha MotoGP	YAMAHA	41'13.778	14.253	MB/MB
5	Valentino Rossi	ITA	Movistar Yamaha MotoGP	YAMAHA	41'14.505	14.980	MB/MB
6	Alvaro Bautista	SPA	Pull&Bear Aspar Team	DUCATI	41'16.059	16.534	MB/MB
7	Aleix Espargaro	SPA	Aprilia Racing Team Gresini	APRILIA	41'19.261	19.736	MB/MB
8	Andrea Dovizioso	ITA	Ducati Team	DUCATI	41'19.713	20.188	MB/SA
9	Johann Zarco	FRA	Monster Yamaha Tech 3	YAMAHA	41'20.663	21.138	MB/HC
10	Cal Crutchlow	GBR	LCR Honda	HONDA	41'23.735	24.210	MB/HC
11	Jorge Lorenzo	SPA	Ducati Team	DUCATI	41'25.184	25.659	SA/SA
12	Danilo Petrucci	ITA	OCTO Pramac Racing	DUCATI	41'31.065	31.540	MB/MB
13	Pol Espargaro	SPA	Red Bull KTM Factory Racing	KTM	41'31.704	32.179	MB/MB
14	Bradley Smith	GBR	Red Bull KTM Factory Racing	KTM	41'35.978	36.453	MB/MB
15	Jack Miller	AUS	EG 0,0 Marc VDS	HONDA	41'37.296	37.771	MB/MB
16	Mika Kallio	FIN	Red Bull KTM Factory Racing	KTM	41'37.377	37.852	MB/HC
17	Karel Abraham	CZE	Pull&Bear Aspar Team	DUCATI	41'38.848	39.323	SA/SA
18	Tito Rabat	SPA	EG 0,0 Marc VDS	HONDA	41'40.715	41.190	MB/MB
19	Loris Baz	FRA	Reale Avintia Racing	DUCATI	41'59.375	59.850	MB/MB
20	Scott Redding	GBR	OCTO Pramac Racing	DUCATI	42'01.189	61.664	MB/MB
21	Alex Rins	SPA	Team SUZUKI ECSTAR	SUZUKI	42'01.220	61.695	MB/MB
NC	Andrea Iannone	ITA	Team SUZUKI ECSTAR	SUZUKI	33'06.105	6 laps	MB/MB
NC	Sam Lowes	GBR	Aprilia Racing Team Gresini	APRILIA	16'39.370	18 laps	MB/MB
DSQ	Hector Barbera	SPA	Reale Avintia Racing	DUCATI			SA/MB

Michelin came to Germany with the option of A, B, C & D specification tyres
***FRONT** : Soft-A / Medium-B / Medium-C / Hard-D   **REAR** : Soft-A / Medium-B / Hard-C / Hard-D*

CHAMPIONSHIP STANDINGS

	RIDER	NAT	TEAM	POINTS
1	Marc Marquez	SPA	Repsol Honda Team	129
2	Maverick Viñales	SPA	Movistar Yamaha MotoGP	124
3	Andrea Dovizioso	ITA	Ducati Team	123
4	Valentino Rossi	ITA	Movistar Yamaha MotoGP	119
5	Dani Pedrosa	SPA	Repsol Honda Team	103
6	Johann Zarco	FRA	Monster Yamaha Tech 3	84
7	Jonas Folger	GER	Monster Yamaha Tech 3	71
8	Danilo Petrucci	ITA	OCTO Pramac Racing	66
9	Jorge Lorenzo	SPA	Ducati Team	65
10	Cal Crutchlow	GBR	LCR Honda	64
11	Alvaro Bautista	SPA	Pull&Bear Aspar Team	44
12	Jack Miller	AUS	EG 0,0 Marc VDS	41
13	Scott Redding	GBR	OCTO Pramac Racing	33
14	Aleix Espargaro	SPA	Aprilia Racing Team Gresini	32
15	Loris Baz	FRA	Reale Avintia Racing	31
16	Andrea Iannone	ITA	Team SUZUKI ECSTAR	28
17	Tito Rabat	SPA	EG 0,0 Marc VDS	23
18	Hector Barbera	SPA	Reale Avintia Racing	21
19	Karel Abraham	CZE	Pull&Bear Aspar Team	20
20	Pol Espargaro	SPA	Red Bull KTM Factory Racing	14
21	Bradley Smith	GBR	Red Bull KTM Factory Racing	8
22	Alex Rins	SPA	Team SUZUKI ECSTAR	7
23	Michele Pirro	ITA	Ducati Team	7
24	Sam Lowes	GBR	Aprilia Racing Team Gresini	2
25	Sylvain Guintoli	FRA	Team SUZUKI ECSTAR	1

12 | DANILO PETRUCCI
Started from second on the grid but could only run the leaders' pace for fewer than ten laps. Like many others, he then ran into serious rear-tyre grip problems.

13 | POL ESPARGARO
Started from seventh, KTM's best grid position so far on the bike's first visit to the track. Only lost out to Petrucci when his front tyre dropped in the last couple of laps.

14 | BRADLEY SMITH
Raced with his finger still severely injured. Not happy with his performance over first ten laps but he and the team were very happy with their performance over the meeting.

15 | JACK MILLER
Unable to run the pace he had in practice when, after four or five laps, the rear started to spin on both sides of the tyre. "It was like it had already done 30 laps," he said.

16 | MIKA KALLIO
KTM's test rider entered as a wild card and did a good job of keeping the regular team riders on their toes. Set KTM's best lap time of the race.

17 | KAREL ABRAHAM
Never happy, had problems all through practice and not combative in the opening laps. The only plus-point was setting best lap times of the weekend at end of race.

18 | TITO RABAT
Like his teammate lost all rear grip after five laps. Switching maps

helped but he couldn't run the pace he did in FP3.

19 | LORIS BAZ
After ten laps rear tyre degradation was so high he felt like he was using a wet. Disappointed, headed to summer break for arm-pump surgery.

20 | SCOTT REDDING
The worst race of his entire career left Scott confused and upset. Started from the last row, charged past seven other riders on first lap but then had no grip, unlike in warm-up.

21 | ALEX RINS
Started well on his return to MotoGP after missing six races with injuries. Not surprisingly, dropped back when the tyre dropped.

DID NOT FINISH

ANDREA IANNONE
Team and rider were a lot happier than you would expect. Found some feel and some fight and after a cautious two or three laps was more

like his old self. No-one complained about his crash.

SAM LOWES
Crashed out of 17th place as he was making good progress towards points.

HECTOR BARBERA
Black-flagged after failing to come in for a ride-through penalty for a jump start.

COMEDY OF ERRORS

Marc Marquez is forced into an early bike change yet still destroys the field, Maverick Viñales top Yamaha.

It was, said Marc Marquez, a weekend to take risks and remember the genius of Angel Nieto, Spain's greatest motorcycle racer, who passed away after a traffic accident on the Thursday of the GP. Marc took a couple of big risks, both of which paid off and rewarded him in ways he couldn't have imagined. Brno is a track that Marquez does not look forward to and where he plans for damage limitation. This time he came away as winner and increased his championship lead.

First he gambled on the grid after a sighting lap on a rapidly drying track. The medium-compound wet rear tyre did not feel good so he swapped to the soft, thinking he'd get five laps out of it and pit early to change bikes. He pitted early alright, very early indeed. Marc had completely fried the rear tyre by the end of the first lap, so at the end of the second lap, during which he slid down the field, Marc dived into pitlane. His second bike was waiting with a fully dry set up, and after he'd survived a tricky out lap and the bike changes had shaken out Marc found himself leading by nearly 20 seconds. Job done.

Marquez did not come into the pits alone, he was followed in by both KTMs, Jack Miller and Jonas Folger. How did he gain 20 seconds on them in five laps? Simply because the other teams weren't ready, they were still altering the second bike to a dry set up.

MAIN Treaded tyres all round at the start of the race, it was surprising no-one changed after the sighting lap

BELOW, LEFT-RIGHT | *Jonas Folger could have been on the podium if his dry bike had been ready when he came in; Sam Lowes finished his first flag-to-flag race as he started it, in good spirits; Maverick Vinales salvaged his first podium in four races from unpromising beginnings*

RIGHT | *Jorge Lorenzo used Ducati's new aero bodywork and led the race from the start*

Tech 3 even sent Folger out to do another lap on his wet bike. IRTA always calculate what the equivalent time of ride-through penalty is in case one is handed out on the last three laps of a race. In the case of Brno it is 28 seconds, so it is easy to calculate where the German might have finished if his bike had been ready.

Why wasn't it? Normal practice is to have the second bike set up identical to the first in case of a problem on the grid or sighting lap. Once the race has started the second bike is then converted. This takes a few minutes: wheels need to be changed, as do suspension settings, and maybe brakes. Clearly, the Repsol Honda team either dispensed with the insurance policy of the identical bike or simply worked faster than the opposition. Can you remember a spare bike being needed at the start of a race? All the men who pitted with Marquez had to wait for their bikes, and they weren't the only ones. Given the conditions, it was surprising that no-one came up pit lane at the end of the sighting lap to risk starting on slicks. Sam Lowes said he would have started a Moto2 race on slicks in the same conditions but doesn't yet have the clout within Aprilia to make that sort of decision.

Even some of those who came in at the end of Lap 4 had to wait for their bikes. Jorge Lorenzo, who led the first three laps on the Ducati with its new aero fairing, was called in via the new dashboard messaging system just in time for him to nip in. Unfortunately, the team had intended to keep him out for another lap and Jorge had to hang around. Lorenzo was one of several men who had a much better weekend than the results would lead you to believe. Two more, Aleix Espargaro and Andrea Iannone, were involved in an incident that will likely have repercussions.

Aleix was on his second bike and ready to go as Iannone was coming in. Either he didn't look or the Italian was obscured by Scott Redding, but Iannone had to brake to avoid hitting Espargaro as he left. Iannone fell and for good measure knocked his teammate's bike over. Loris Baz also threw his Ducati at a mechanic. Espargaro was required to drop three places as penalty for an unsafe release. The riders have always been ambivalent about bike change procedure, Dani Pedrosa has for a while

SHIP TO SHORE

This should have been the first race where MotoGP's dashboard messaging system proved its worth. Teams had been experimenting with the virtual pit board before the Summer break, but the system was only approved for race use by the Grand Prix Commission at the German GP. Theoretically, teams could now communicate with their rider at any time using a set menu of approved messages. However, teams had to have their systems approved by Race Direction before use, proving among other things that all messages could be read by Race Direction. Surprisingly, only Ducati had this approval by the Czech GP. Yamaha were only working on it while Honda didn't even have it in their to-do schedule for this year, preferring to wait until it is compulsory in 2018 for MotoGP and Moto3; Moto2 will get it in 2019 when the class gets its new engine and updated electronics.

This is the first time that any form of direct communication between the pits and their bike has been allowed in motorcycle racing. Kenny Roberts' team were allowed to experiment with ship-to-shore radio and came to the conclusion that it could be useful in practice and qualifying but not in a race. However, that

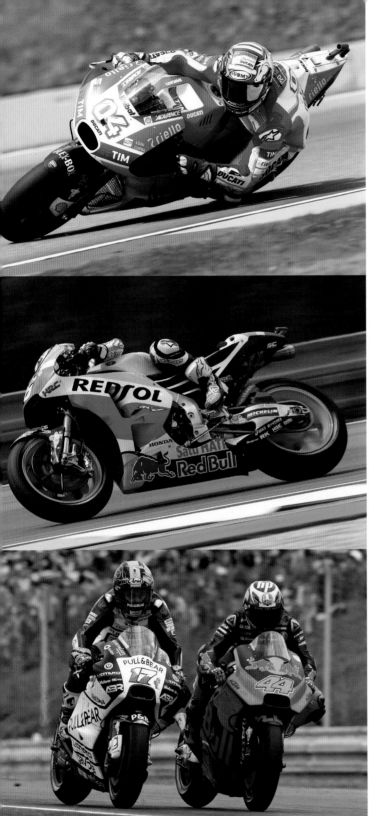

been advocating the World Superbike rule whereby the bike is stationary for a mandatory 30 seconds thus taking the heat out of the situation. Aleix Espargaro among others said he will also be lobbying for that rule.

As usual, Valentino Rossi again failed to get on the podium of a flag-to-flag race. This time, though, he shared the blame with his team. He was in the big group that came in at the end of the fourth lap and included the leading group of Rossi himself plus Dovizioso and Lorenzo. The timing, which Valentino called at least a lap too late, put him back on track in 13th nearly 30 seconds in arrears of Marquez. Rossi's ride through the field, with Dovi not far behind, was impressive. However, the three men who beat him were all championship challengers and one of them was his teammate Viñales who, up until the race, was having a bad weekend. If Aleix Espargaro had put the new Aprilia motor in his dry bike he might have had an even better time. His brother was delighted to give KTM their best finish yet, and even Suzuki were happy with what Iannone had done with new parts before the pitlane tangle. It should be noted that Yamaha were not yet using the dashboard messaging system, and neither were Honda. Ducati had it and still managed to mess up. Satellite Ducati teams and Aprilia also had it. Honda had also tested at Brno in July, which certainly helped them but they were also the only factory that reacted to the changing situation.

So three Spaniards, World Champions all, went to the podium to salute the memory of Angel Nieto, the man who started it all and who one national newspaper described as "the inventor of Spanish motorcycling." Some legacy.

LEFT, TOP-BOTTOM | *Andrea Dovizioso shadowed Rossi to a late bike change and an impressive ride through the field; Dani Pedrosa was fast wet and dry; Pol Espargaro passes Karel Abraham on his way to KTM's first top-ten finish*

was before the era of flag-to-flag races.

Yamaha's lack of urgency was a little surprising given Valentino Rossi was one of the strongest voices in favour of the virtual pit board when it was discussed by the Safety Commission. Not every rider was in favour, in fact a couple were vehemently against. Valentino hoped it might make a small but vital difference in how his team dealt with bike changes in flag-to-flag races. Not that it helped Ducati in the race, they managed to bring Jorge Lorenzo in a lap early, and Repsol Honda proved to be the only team to get their tactics completely right, all without the benefit of the virtual pit board.

10 | CZECH REPUBLIC

RACE RESULTS

WINNER MARC MARQUEZ

CIRCUIT LENGTH 5.4 KM | 3.36 MILES

NO. OF LAPS 22

RACE DISTANCE 118.9 KM | 73.9 MILES

CIRCUIT RECORD LAP 1'56.027 | 167.6 KM/H
DANI PEDROSA (2014)

CIRCUIT BEST LAP 1'54.596 | 169.7 KM/H
MARC MARQUEZ (2016)

RACE CONDITION WET

AIR 21°C

HUMIDITY 70%

GROUND 24°C

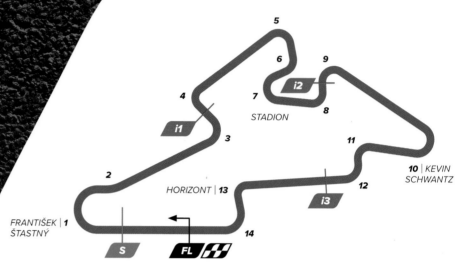

Sectors
Speed Trap
Finish Line

10 | KEVIN SCHWANTZ

STADION

HORIZONT | 13

FRANTIŠEK | 1
ŠTASTNÝ

TISSOT SWISS WATCHES SINCE 1853 | motoGP
OFFICIAL TIMEKEEPER

MICHELIN | motoGP
OFFICIAL MotoGP™ CLASS TYRE

RAIN FRONT TYRES
SOFT
MEDIUM

RAIN REAR TYRES
SOFT
MEDIUM

< MILD   **TYRE SEVERITY**   SEVERE >

QUALIFYING RESULTS

	RIDER	NAT	TEAM	MACHINE	QP/TIME	GAP 1ST/PREV	
1	Marc Marquez	SPA	Repsol Honda Team	HONDA	Q2 1'54.981		
2	Valentino Rossi	ITA	Movistar Yamaha MotoGP	YAMAHA	Q2 1'55.073	0.092	0.092
3	Dani Pedrosa	SPA	Repsol Honda Team	HONDA	Q2 1'55.119	0.138	0.046
4	Andrea Dovizioso	ITA	Ducati Team	DUCATI	Q2 1'55.441	0.460	0.322
5	Cal Crutchlow	GBR	LCR Honda	HONDA	Q2 1'55.489	0.508	0.048
6	Jorge Lorenzo	SPA	Ducati Team	DUCATI	Q2 1'55.552	0.571	0.063
7	Maverick Viñales	SPA	Movistar Yamaha MotoGP	YAMAHA	Q2 1'55.663	0.682	0.111
8	Danilo Petrucci**	ITA	OCTO Pramac Racing	DUCATI	Q2 1'55.738	0.757	0.075
9	Alvaro Bautista**	SPA	Pull&Bear Aspar Team	DUCATI	Q2 1'56.027	1.046	0.289
10	Johann Zarco	FRA	Monster Yamaha Tech	YAMAHA	Q2 1'56.075	1.094	0.048
11	Aleix Espargaro	SPA	Aprilia Racing Team Gresini	APRILIA	Q2 1'56.355	1.374	0.280
12	Loris Baz	FRA	Reale Avintia Racing	DUCATI	Q2 1'56.624	1.643	0.269
13	Alex Rins	SPA	Team SUZUKI ECSTAR	SUZUKI	Q1 1'56.460	*0.240	0.006
14	Jonas Folger	GER	Monster Yamaha Tech 3	YAMAHA	Q1 1'56.540	*0.320	0.080
15	Jack Miller	AUS	EG 0,0 Marc VDS	HONDA	Q1 1'56.543	*0.323	0.003
16	Hector Barbera	SPA	Reale Avintia Racing	DUCATI	Q1 1'56.685	*0.465	0.142
17	Karel Abraham	CZE	Pull&Bear Aspar Team	DUCATI	Q1 1'56.786	*0.566	0.101
18	Pol Espargaro	SPA	Red Bull KTM Factory Racing	KTM	Q1 1'57.034	*0.814	0.248
19	Bradley Smith	GBR	Red Bull KTM Factory Racing	KTM	Q1 1'57.042	*0.822	0.008
20	Andrea Iannone	ITA	Team SUZUKI ECSTAR	SUZUKI	Q1 1'57.245	*1.025	0.203
21	Tito Rabat	SPA	EG 0,0 Marc VDS	HONDA	Q1 1'57.288	*1.068	0.043
22	Sam Lowes	GBR	Aprilia Racing Team Gresini	APRILIA	Q1 1'57.465	*1.245	0.177
23	Scott Redding	GBR	OCTO Pramac Racing	DUCATI	Q1 1'57.517	*1.297	0.052

*Gap with the fastest rider in the Q1 session
** Went forward from Q1 to Q2

1 | MARC MARQUEZ
Bad tyre choice sent him in to change bikes at the end of the second lap. He survived a fraught out lap then found himself 20 seconds ahead when the rest had pitted. Twenty-five points and an increased championship lead on a track that he usually suffers on.

2 | DANI PEDROSA
Changed bike on the fourth lap and found himself just over 20 seconds behind Marquez, which is where he stayed. Very impressive in both wet and dry practice.

3 | MAVERICK VIÑALES
Started from seventh on the grid, pitted after the fourth lap with most of the other championship contenders. Only really happy after the race, when he declared finishing third on a bad weekend a very good result.

4 | VALENTINO ROSSI
Led the first, wet part of the race but as is his habit delayed his bike change by at least one lap more than optimum. Yet to get on the podium in a flag-to-flag race.

5 | CAL CRUTCHLOW
A brave ride after a big practice crash. Aiming for the podium but although he pitted the same time as Pedrosa Cal spent ten laps getting past Petrucci, which let Pedrosa escape. Viñales went past in those ten laps and Rossi got him on the last lap.

6 | ANDREA DOVIZIOSO
Should have been better. Impressive in practice on a track neither he or the Ducati have liked. Racing for the lead with Rossi and , like Vale, changed bikes too late then

mounted an impressive charge through the field.

7 | DANILO PETRUCCI
In a podium position at two-thirds distance but, as is his wont, he wore the rear tyre out and couldn't defend either top Ducati or top independent position. Behind the drama, this was a good weekend.

8 | ALEIX ESPARGARO
Used his only new engine in the dry bike. Going very well but had to drop three places for an unsafe release after his bike change. Behind the drama, this was a good weekend.

10 | POL ESPARGARO
KTM's first top-ten finish, and but for a trip through a gravel trap on the second bike it might have been even better. Thought they'd struggle but benefitted from work done at an Aragon test.

10 | JONAS FOLGER
Followed Marquez in but his bike wasn't ready; had to do another lap. That ride-through penalty was reckoned to cost him 28 seconds. Take that off his race time and Jonas would have been second.

11 | ALEX RINS
His bike was knocked over in Iannone's pit-lane crash, meaning Alex had to ride with bent handlebars. Only lost tenth on the last lap and missed Q2 by 0.006sec. Impressive.

12 | JOHANN ZARCO
A typically eccentric decision to come in a lap after anyone else. He was running with leaders Rossi and Dovizioso when they came in but continued for another two laps. That put him 16th when he exited the pits. If he'd pitted even one lap

RACE LAP CHART

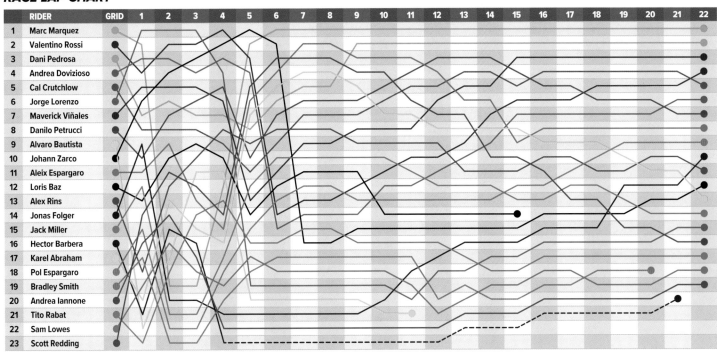

----- Dashed line: Lapped rider

	RIDER	GRID	1	2	3	4	5	6	7	8	9	10	11	12	13	14	15	16	17	18	19	20	21	22
1	Marc Marquez																								
2	Valentino Rossi																								
3	Dani Pedrosa																								
4	Andrea Dovizioso																								
5	Cal Crutchlow																								
6	Jorge Lorenzo																								
7	Maverick Viñales																								
8	Danilo Petrucci																								
9	Alvaro Bautista																								
10	Johann Zarco																								
11	Aleix Espargaro																								
12	Loris Baz																								
13	Alex Rins																								
14	Jonas Folger																								
15	Jack Miller																								
16	Hector Barbera																								
17	Karel Abraham																								
18	Pol Espargaro																								
19	Bradley Smith																								
20	Andrea Iannone																								
21	Tito Rabat																								
22	Sam Lowes																								
23	Scott Redding																								

RACE CLASSIFICATION AFTER 22 LAPS = 118.866 KM

	RIDER	NAT	TEAM	MACHINE	TIME	+ GAP	TYRES
1	Marc Marquez	SPA	Repsol Honda Team	HONDA	44'15.974		RM/RS
2	Dani Pedrosa	SPA	Repsol Honda Team	HONDA	44'28.412	12.438	RM/RM
3	Maverick Viñales	SPA	Movistar Yamaha MotoGP	YAMAHA	44'34.109	18.135	RM/RM
4	Valentino Rossi	ITA	Movistar Yamaha MotoGP	YAMAHA	44'36.440	20.466	RM/RM
5	Cal Crutchlow	GBR	LCR Honda	HONDA	44'36.866	20.892	RM/RM
6	Andrea Dovizioso	ITA	Ducati Team	DUCATI	44'39.233	23.259	RM/RM
7	Danilo Petrucci	ITA	OCTO Pramac Racing	DUCATI	44'40.053	24.079	RM/RM
8	Aleix Espargaro	SPA	Aprilia Racing Team Gresini	APRILIA	44'46.533	30.559	RM/RM
9	Pol Espargaro	SPA	Red Bull KTM Factory Racing	KTM	44'46.728	30.754	RM/RM
10	Jonas Folger	GER	Monster Yamaha Tech 3	YAMAHA	44'49.210	33.236	RM/RM
11	Alex Rins	SPA	Team SUZUKI ECSTAR	SUZUKI	44'49.264	33.290	RM/RM
12	Johann Zarco	FRA	Monster Yamaha Tech	YAMAHA	44'50.569	34.595	RM/RM
13	Karel Abraham	CZE	Pull&Bear Aspar Team	DUCATI	44'50.671	34.697	RS/RM
14	Jack Miller	AUS	EG 0,0 Marc VDS	HONDA	44'54.036	38.062	RS/RM
15	Jorge Lorenzo	SPA	Ducati Team	DUCATI	44'56.074	40.100	RM/RM
16	Scott Redding	GBR	OCTO Pramac Racing	DUCATI	45'00.350	44.376	RM/RM
17	Tito Rabat	SPA	EG 0,0 Marc VDS	HONDA	45'01.428	45.454	RM/RM
18	Sam Lowes	GBR	Aprilia Racing Team Gresini	APRILIA	45'09.950	53.976	RM/RM
19	Andrea Iannone	ITA	Team SUZUKI ECSTAR	SUZUKI	45'39.320	83.346	RM/RM
20	Hector Barbera	SPA	Reale Avintia Racing	DUCATI	45'39.631	1 lap	RM/RM
NC	Bradley Smith	GBR	Red Bull KTM Factory Racing	KTM	41'10.379	2 laps	RM/RM
NC	Loris Baz	FRA	Reale Avintia Racing	DUCATI	31'01.736	7 laps	RM/RM
NC	Alvaro Bautista	SPA	Pull&Bear Aspar Team	DUCATI	25'15.031	10 laps	RS/RM

*Michelin wet tyre options
FRONT : Rain Soft / Rain Medium   **REAR** : Rain Soft / Rain Medium

CHAMPIONSHIP STANDINGS

	RIDER	NAT	TEAM	POINTS
1	Marc Marquez	SPA	Repsol Honda Team	154
2	Maverick Viñales	SPA	Movistar Yamaha MotoGP	140
3	Andrea Dovizioso	ITA	Ducati Team	133
4	Valentino Rossi	ITA	Movistar Yamaha MotoGP	132
5	Dani Pedrosa	SPA	Repsol Honda Team	123
6	Johann Zarco	FRA	Monster Yamaha Tech 3	88
7	Jonas Folger	GER	Monster Yamaha Tech 3	77
8	Danilo Petrucci	ITA	OCTO Pramac Racing	75
9	Cal Crutchlow	GBR	LCR Honda	75
10	Jorge Lorenzo	SPA	Ducati Team	66
11	Alvaro Bautista	SPA	Pull&Bear Aspar Team	44
12	Jack Miller	AUS	EG 0,0 Marc VDS	43
13	Aleix Espargaro	SPA	Aprilia Racing Team Gresini	40
14	Scott Redding	GBR	OCTO Pramac Racing	33
15	Loris Baz	FRA	Reale Avintia Racing	31
16	Andrea Iannone	ITA	Team SUZUKI ECSTAR	28
17	Karel Abraham	CZE	Pull&Bear Aspar Team	23
18	Tito Rabat	SPA	EG 0,0 Marc VDS	23
19	Pol Espargaro	SPA	Red Bull KTM Factory Racing	21
20	Hector Barbera	SPA	Reale Avintia Racing	21
21	Alex Rins	SPA	Team SUZUKI ECSTAR	12
22	Bradley Smith	GBR	Red Bull KTM Factory Racing	8
23	Michele Pirro	ITA	Ducati Team	7
24	Sam Lowes	GBR	Aprilia Racing Team Gresini	2
25	Sylvain Guintoli	FRA	Team SUZUKI ECSTAR	1

earlier he'd have been fighting for the top six.

13 | KAREL ABRAHAM
Impressive in wet and dry but his wet bike suffered a broken exhaust and he lost power.

14 | JACK MILLER
Changed bikes at the same time as Marquez but had to wait ten seconds for his bike. Lacking rear grip on dry bike and couldn't match practice times.

15 | JORGE LORENZO
Used Ducati's new aero fairing and led the race until he went in to change bikes. Unfortunately the on-board message was sent too early and he had to wait over ten seconds for his dry bike. Should have been well inside the top ten.

16 | SCOTT REDDING
A much better race than it looks. Awful qualifying but made up ten places in two laps before pitting early. However, a hole in his exhaust meant he couldn't compete when he switched map for more power.

17 | TITO RABAT
Like his teammate had rear grip problems on Sunday that weren't apparent before.

18 | SAM LOWES
Got the same updates as his teammate, which were all on the wet bike. Pleased with the new parts – and to finish his first flag-to-flag race.

19 | ANDREA IANNONE
New parts from Japan looked to have improved his situation, and his early pace made up for problems in

qualifying. Came in early but crashed in pits avoiding Aleix Espargaro. Not only did he hit his head and leg, the bike wasn't ready. A good weekend in heavy disguise.

20 | HECTOR BARBERA
Had to make a second pit stop because of a problem with his second bike, which ruled out any chance of scoring points.

DID NOT FINISH

BRADLEY SMITH
Came in with Marquez but had to wait for his bike. That put Bradley outside the points and an engine issue forced his retirement a couple of laps from the flag.

LORIS BAZ
Went straight to Q2 but had a difficult race. Had to wait for his second bike then hit a mechanic when he came in. Took a few laps to regain his composure then fell when chasing Miller.

ALVARO BAUTISTA
A variety of brake and clutch problems led to him crashing the second bike.

CLIMBING THE MOUNTAIN

Andrea Dovizioso wins a race-long duel with Marc Marquez and is revealed as a genuine championship contender, Dani Pedrosa a distant third.

Twelve months previously at the Red Bull Ring, Andrea Dovizioso made the wrong tyre choice and lost the Austrian GP to his teammate. This time he got every decision right and won his third race of the year to go back to second in the championship. First, he had the new aero fairing fitted to both bikes from the start. Secondly, he used a medium tyre for qualifying and a soft for the race. Thirdly, he managed to think clearly under race-long attack from Marc Marquez. Finally, he avoided a kamikaze last corner move that could easily have taken both riders down.

Ducati's superiority from the first race on this version of the track was still there, but much diminished. The red bikes could still pass the opposition in a straight line, but only just. Honda had clearly improved massively, as the presence of both factory riders on the podium shows. In 2016 they were well over ten seconds back in fifth and seventh, this time it was the Yamahas that suffered. Maverick Viñales and Valentino Rossi were among many riders who found their rear tyre performance dropping off steeply. Both men also ran wide, very wide, at Turn 1 and lost any chance of dealing with the man in front of them - Johann Zarco, who again embarrassed the factory men. In fact, Viñales and Rossi saw their title chances dented not just by Zarco but also by Jorge Lorenzo who led the first 11 laps and finished in fourth.

MAIN Jorge Lorenzo led the first third of the race but hit fuel and tyre issues

This was one of the best races of the season, one of the best of recent years, a battle between the two men emerging as championship favourites with no major issues favouring either man. It was also a wonderful contrast in styles. The thoughtful, calculating Dovizioso, a man with a plan and executing it to the letter, versus Marc Marquez, who was the Marc Marquez of old. He lost out to the Ducati on the major acceleration points, all of them, but was massively quick in the middle of the track, specifically the left handers, where he could take nearly half a second back in one sector. Once the pair had dealt with Lorenzo and repulsed a late challenge from Pedrosa it was obvious it was going to be a last lap showdown. The pair were only ever 0.3sec apart, for the last 12 laps never more than 0.2, and usually seperated by around a tenth of a second. The gap was smaller than that as they started the last lap, and as expected Dovizioso stretched the lead all the way round to the left handers. Going into Turn 6 it looked as if Dovi had the job done, but going into Turn 8 Marquez was right on him. A perfect line around the next corner, the penultimate one, kept Marquez at bay. Only one corner left, and one that is the definition of 'one line.' Now it is important to bear in mind that the only attempted overtake at this final corner we've seen ended with Danilo Petrucci torpedoing Eugene Laverty and getting sanctioned. This, of course, did not deter Marquez, he said he wouldn't have been able to sleep if he hadn't tried.

BELOW, LEFT-RIGHT | *Loris Baz expresses his opinion of Andrea Iannone's riding; Scott Redding announce he will be an Aprilia rider in 2018; Dani Pedrosa got faster through he weekend but ran out of tyre charging up to the leaders*

RIGHT | *Andrea Dovizioso raced with the aero fairing for the first time*

And he tried. He went flying up the inside and straight across Dovizioso's nose. Dovi had heard Marc get on the throttle early and knew what was happening, he picked the bike up and was able to dive inside Marc who was heading onto the painted curbs on full lean with his rear wheel way out of line.

Andrea's view of proceedings was pretty clear from the dismissive flick of the left hand he aimed at Marc as he crossed the line. And when Marc, bubbly and enthusiastic as ever, went to shake his hand another curt gesture suggested he kept on going.

Andrea later said the first gesture was half 'ha ha, I out-thought you,' and half a strong suggestion that Marc go away. Then, when Marc giggled about touching his front to Dovi's rear tyre on the

'IT WAS A CRAZY RACE, AND IN PARTICULAR THE FINAL CURVE OF THE LAST LAP, BUT I MANAGED TO REMAIN CLEAR HEADED'
ANDREA DOVIZIOSO

SLIPPERY SLOPES

There is no doubt that the Austrian GP is a great event and the facilities at the Red Bull Ring are almost unmatched. However, in its first year riders noted that the Armco was a little too close in a couple of places and there was some concern when it was noted that nothing had been changed for this year.

Of more concern this year was a new problem that appeared in Moto2 Free Practice on Friday when 11 riders crashed on the brakes, most at Turn 1 and some at Turn 3. The problem was thought to be rubber ground into the surface by cars under hard braking on a circuit that gets a lot of use. Industrial cleaning trucks were brought in and worked overnight, but thankfully Sunday was dry.

run to Turn 3 at about 190mph, Dovi put his hand to his face and slowly shook his head. Even the most experienced, ex-World Champions sometimes find Marc difficult to cope with.

There may also have been some head shaking in the KTM garage. Mika Kallio, the factory test rider, entered as a wild card for the second time this year and finished tenth. Not the factory's best position so far but definitely the closest a KTM has been to the winner. While it is true that the circuit plays to the bike's strengths and that Pol Espargaro was eliminated through no fault of his own, the Finn backed up his remarks in Germany about intending to return to MotoGP full time. With a Finnish Grand Prix on the calendar for 2019, he might find himself a wanted man.

Some wet-weather problems apart, Austria hosted a wonderful race, one of those great head-to-head confrontations that live long in the memory. It also brought the strengths of each bike into sharp focus. Ducati are still the leaders in aerodynamics, Honda have improved to the extent that they might now be the best all rounders, and Yamaha cannot control rear-tyre wear no matter which chassis they use. Some frantic testing was scheduled before the next round, any benefits may very well affect the Yamaha riders' chances of getting to the end of the season still in contention for the title.

Things are still close though. Just 35 points cover the top five although Marquez managed to extend his championship lead by two points, but the second-place man is now Dovi not Maverick. Andrea is also only the third rider, after Loris Capirossi and Casey Stoner, to win three races in a season on a Ducati. Not bad company. He has the air of a man whose time has come.

MAIN | *A rare treat - the two best in the world, the men disputing the title, go head to head*

LEFT, TOP-BOTTOM | *Test rider Mika Kallio finished closer to the winner than any KTM had done before; Andrea Dovizioso stood on the top box for the third time this season*

Nevertheless, more than a few riders, including Loris Baz, Danilo Petrucci, Jonas Folger, and a very vocal Aleix Espargaro said they would think very hard before riding if it rained. It wasn't just the braking areas but the proximity of the Armco in critical areas that together caused the concern.

The Safety Commission that meets on Friday evenings is an informal grouping that advises Dorna CEO Carmelo Ezpeleta on issues of concern. Decisions are made by Franco Uncini and Loris Capirossi, the Grand Prix Safety Officer and Dorna's Safety Advisor, respectively. They oversaw the overnight cleaning and will no doubt have a view on what needs to be done.

Expect clearer information on modifications and improvements for the 2018 event.

Sectors
Speed Trap
Finish Line

RACE RESULTS

WINNER | ANDREA DOVIZIOSO

CIRCUIT LENGTH | 4.3 KM | 2.68 MILES

NO. OF LAPS | 28

RACE DISTANCE | 120.9 KM | 75.0 MILES

CIRCUIT RECORD LAP | 1'24.312 | 184.3 KM/H
JOHANN ZARCO (2017)

CIRCUIT BEST LAP | 1'23.142 | 186.9 KM/H
ANDREA IANNONE (2016)

RACE CONDITION | DRY

AIR | 23°C

HUMIDITY | 46%

GROUND | 30°C

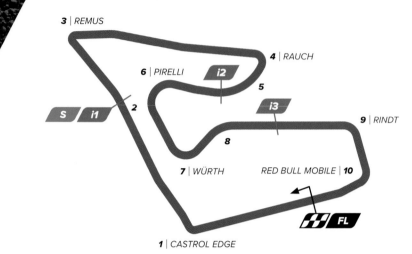

3 | REMUS
4 | RAUCH
6 | PIRELLI i2
5
S i1 2 i3
9 | RINDT
8
7 | WÜRTH   RED BULL MOBILE | 10
FL
1 | CASTROL EDGE

TISSOT — SWISS WATCHES SINCE 1853
OFFICIAL TIMEKEEPER

MICHELIN
OFFICIAL MotoGP™ CLASS TYRE

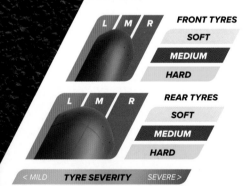

FRONT TYRES
SOFT
MEDIUM
HARD

REAR TYRES
SOFT
MEDIUM
HARD

< MILD   **TYRE SEVERITY**   SEVERE >

QUALIFYING RESULTS

	RIDER	NAT	TEAM	MACHINE	QP/TIME	GAP 1ST/PREV	
1	Marc Marquez	SPA	Repsol Honda Team	HONDA	Q2 1'23.235		
2	Andrea Dovizioso	ITA	Ducati Team	DUCATI	Q2 1'23.379	0.144	0.144
3	Jorge Lorenzo	SPA	Ducati Team	DUCATI	Q2 1'23.621	0.386	0.242
4	Maverick Viñales	SPA	Movistar Yamaha MotoGP	YAMAHA	Q2 1'23.754	0.519	0.133
5	Danilo Petrucci**	ITA	OCTO Pramac Racing	DUCATI	Q2 1'23.780	0.545	0.026
6	Johann Zarco	FRA	Monster Yamaha Tech 3	YAMAHA	Q2 1'23.879	0.644	0.099
7	Valentino Rossi	ITA	Movistar Yamaha MotoGP	YAMAHA	Q2 1'23.982	0.747	0.103
8	Dani Pedrosa**	SPA	Repsol Honda Team	HONDA	Q2 1'23.985	0.750	0.003
9	Cal Crutchlow	GBR	LCR Honda	HONDA	Q2 1'24.024	0.789	0.039
10	Andrea Iannone	ITA	Team SUZUKI ECSTAR	SUZUKI	Q2 1'24.185	0.950	0.161
11	Karel Abraham	CZE	Pull&Bear Aspar Team	DUCATI	Q2 1'24.220	0.985	0.035
12	Loris Baz	FRA	Reale Avintia Racing	DUCATI	Q2 1'24.483	1.248	0.263
13	Jonas Folger	GER	Monster Yamaha Tech 3	YAMAHA	Q1 1'24.015	*0.261	0.166
14	Hector Barbera	SPA	Reale Avintia Racing	DUCATI	Q1 1'24.036	*0.282	0.021
15	Scott Redding	GBR	OCTO Pramac Racing	DUCATI	Q1 1'24.037	*0.283	0.001
16	Pol Espargaro	SPA	Red Bull KTM Factory Racing	KTM	Q1 1'24.101	*0.347	0.064
17	Alvaro Bautista	SPA	Pull&Bear Aspar Team	DUCATI	Q1 1'24.202	*0.448	0.101
18	Mika Kallio	FIN	Red Bull KTM Factory Racing	KTM	Q1 1'24.261	*0.507	0.059
19	Jack Miller	AUS	EG 0,0 Marc VDS	HONDA	Q1 1'24.321	*0.567	0.060
20	Aleix Espargaro	SPA	Aprilia Racing Team Gresini	APRILIA	Q1 1'24.447	*0.693	0.126
21	Alex Rins	SPA	Team SUZUKI ECSTAR	SUZUKI	Q1 1'24.448	*0.694	0.001
22	Bradley Smith	GBR	Red Bull KTM Factory Racing	KTM	Q1 1'24.530	*0.776	0.082
23	Sam Lowes	GBR	Aprilia Racing Team Gresini	APRILIA	Q1 1'24.852	*1.098	0.322
24	Tito Rabat	SPA	EG 0,0 Marc VDS	HONDA	Q1 1'24.900	*1.146	0.048

* Gap with the fastest rider in the Q1 session
** Went forward from Q1 to Q2

1 | ANDREA DOVIZIOSO
Had a plan and executed it perfectly, both in qualifying and the race. Used the soft rear and conserved his resources. Duelled with Marquez at his most aggressive, holding off a scary last-corner attack.

2 | MARC MARQUEZ
Second, but started from pole and extended his championship lead by two points. The Honda was much better than 12 months earlier and he took advantage, particularly in the lefthanders. Out-thought by Dovizioso on last lap.

3 | DANI PEDROSA
Had to go through Q1 but rode very cleverly, conserving fuel and tyre in the opening laps. Increased his pace rapidly but was spinning the rear tyre too much to challenge when he caught the two leaders.

4 | JORGE LORENZO
Led 11 laps but had to select the most fuel-efficient ignition map after just three, and then hit trouble with the right side of the rear tyre. Finished with a few millilitres of fuel in the tank. Not happy with fourth but delighted to be so close to the winner.

5 | JOHANN ZARCO
Top Yamaha. Said he couldn't really push to overtake after the fifth lap. Used soft tyres, unlike the factory men but passed and stayed ahead of them. Set a new lap record on Lap 6.

6 | MAVERICK VIÑALES
Both factory Yamahas lost rear tyre grip early in the race, and both ran on at Turn 1, losing touch with the leaders. Still refusing to answer questions about which chassis he is using.

7 | VALENTINO ROSSI
Lost rear-tyre performance after about a dozen laps and also made a mistake on the brakes at the first corner. A rather worrying weekend for the factory Yamaha team and for both riders' championship.

8 | ALVARO BAUTISTA
In trouble with rear grip after warm-up so reverted to his Friday set-up and despite qualifying down in 17th rode through the field. Lapping as fast as the second group but too far back to challenge them.

9 | LORIS BAZ
Brilliant qualifying, he went direct to Q1, and his best race in MotoGP. Nearly hit on the grid, then held up by Iannone then unable to defend against Bautista. Under 20 seconds behind the winner.

10 | MIKA KALLIO
Not KTM's best finishing position but under 20 seconds from the winner was the closest of the season. The factory test rider forcibly reminded everyone that he wants to race full-time again.

11 | ANDREA IANNONE
Like many others, suffered from rear-tyre drop off. Although the finishing position doesn't look too good, he was pleased with the potential the bike was now showing and the effort from the factory.

12 | SCOTT REDDING
Happier than expected because he made progress each day. And maybe because he'd signed with Aprilia for the 2018 season.

RACE LAP CHART

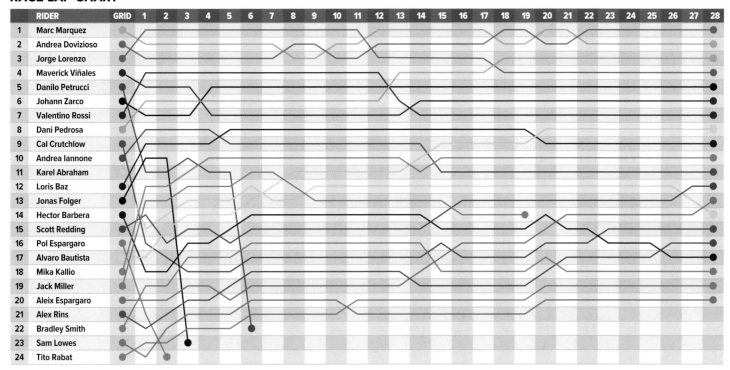

	RIDER	GRID	1	2	3	4	5	6	7	8	9	10	11	12	13	14	15	16	17	18	19	20	21	22	23	24	25	26	27	28
1	Marc Marquez																													
2	Andrea Dovizioso																													
3	Jorge Lorenzo																													
4	Maverick Viñales																													
5	Danilo Petrucci																													
6	Johann Zarco																													
7	Valentino Rossi																													
8	Dani Pedrosa																													
9	Cal Crutchlow																													
10	Andrea Iannone																													
11	Karel Abraham																													
12	Loris Baz																													
13	Jonas Folger																													
14	Hector Barbera																													
15	Scott Redding																													
16	Pol Espargaro																													
17	Alvaro Bautista																													
18	Mika Kallio																													
19	Jack Miller																													
20	Aleix Espargaro																													
21	Alex Rins																													
22	Bradley Smith																													
23	Sam Lowes																													
24	Tito Rabat																													

RACE CLASSIFICATION AFTER 28 LAPS = 120.904 KM

	RIDER	NAT	TEAM	MACHINE	TIME	+ GAP	TYRES
1	Andrea Dovizioso	ITA	Ducati Team	DUCATI	39'43.323		M/S
2	Marc Marquez	SPA	Repsol Honda Team	HONDA	39'43.499	0.176	M/H
3	Dani Pedrosa	SPA	Repsol Honda Team	HONDA	39'45.984	2.661	M/H
4	Jorge Lorenzo	SPA	Ducati Team	DUCATI	39'49.986	6.663	M/S
5	Johann Zarco	FRA	Monster Yamaha Tech 3	YAMAHA	39'50.585	7.262	S/S
6	Maverick Viñales	SPA	Movistar Yamaha MotoGP	YAMAHA	39'50.770	7.447	M/H
7	Valentino Rossi	ITA	Movistar Yamaha MotoGP	YAMAHA	39'52.318	8.995	M/H
8	Alvaro Bautista	SPA	Pull&Bear Aspar Team	DUCATI	39'57.838	14.515	M/S
9	Loris Baz	FRA	Reale Avintia Racing	DUCATI	40'02.943	19.620	S/M
10	Mika Kallio	FIN	Red Bull KTM Factory Racing	KTM	40'03.089	19.766	M/H
11	Andrea Iannone	ITA	Team SUZUKI ECSTAR	SUZUKI	40'03.424	20.101	M/H
12	Scott Redding	GBR	OCTO Pramac Racing	DUCATI	40'08.846	25.523	M/H
13	Aleix Espargaro	SPA	Aprilia Racing Team Gresini	APRILIA	40'10.023	26.700	M/H
14	Karel Abraham	CZE	Pull&Bear Aspar Team	DUCATI	40'10.644	27.321	M/S
15	Cal Crutchlow	GBR	LCR Honda	HONDA	40'11.419	28.096	H/H
16	Alex Rins	SPA	Team SUZUKI ECSTAR	SUZUKI	40'16.235	32.912	M/H
17	Hector Barbera	SPA	Reale Avintia Racing	DUCATI	40'17.435	34.112	S/S
18	Bradley Smith	GBR	Red Bull KTM Factory Racing	KTM	40'19.746	36.423	M/H
19	Tito Rabat	SPA	EG 0,0 Marc VDS	HONDA	40'25.727	42.404	M/M
20	Sam Lowes	GBR	Aprilia Racing Team Gresini	APRILIA	40'35.815	52.492	M/S
NC	Jack Miller	AUS	EG 0,0 Marc VDS	HONDA	27'14.577	9 laps	M/M
NC	Danilo Petrucci	ITA	OCTO Pramac Racing	DUCATI	8'52.492	22 laps	M/H
NC	Jonas Folger	GER	Monster Yamaha Tech 3	YAMAHA	4'51.263	25 laps	M/S
NC	Pol Espargaro	SPA	Red Bull KTM Factory Racing	KTM	3'38.834	26 laps	M/H

CHAMPIONSHIP STANDINGS

	RIDER	NAT	TEAM	POINTS
1	Marc Marquez	SPA	Repsol Honda Team	174
2	Andrea Dovizioso	ITA	Ducati Team	158
3	Maverick Viñales	SPA	Movistar Yamaha MotoGP	150
4	Valentino Rossi	ITA	Movistar Yamaha MotoGP	141
5	Dani Pedrosa	SPA	Repsol Honda Team	139
6	Johann Zarco	FRA	Monster Yamaha Tech 3	99
7	Jorge Lorenzo	SPA	Ducati Team	79
8	Jonas Folger	GER	Monster Yamaha Tech 3	77
9	Cal Crutchlow	GBR	LCR Honda	76
10	Danilo Petrucci	ITA	OCTO Pramac Racing	75
11	Alvaro Bautista	SPA	Pull&Bear Aspar Team	52
12	Aleix Espargaro	SPA	Aprilia Racing Team Gresini	43
13	Jack Miller	AUS	EG 0,0 Marc VDS	43
14	Loris Baz	FRA	Reale Avintia Racing	38
15	Scott Redding	GBR	OCTO Pramac Racing	37
16	Andrea Iannone	ITA	Team SUZUKI ECSTAR	33
17	Karel Abraham	CZE	Pull&Bear Aspar Team	25
18	Tito Rabat	SPA	EG 0,0 Marc VDS	23
19	Pol Espargaro	SPA	Red Bull KTM Factory Racing	21
20	Hector Barbera	SPA	Reale Avintia Racing	21
21	Alex Rins	SPA	Team SUZUKI ECSTAR	12
22	Bradley Smith	GBR	Red Bull KTM Factory Racing	8
23	Michele Pirro	ITA	Ducati Team	7
24	Mika Kallio	FIN	Red Bull KTM Factory Racing	6
25	Sam Lowes	GBR	Aprilia Racing Team Gresini	2
26	Sylvain Guintoli	FRA	Team SUZUKI ECSTAR	1

13 | ALEIX ESPARGARO
Got set up wrong for qualifying and tyre choice wrong for race day. Near last at the start followed by a very decent ride to midfield from 20th place.

14 | KAREL ABRAHAM
Had a great weekend up to the last couple of laps, when his rear tyre was completely worn and he lost two places. Also had to avoid the coming together on the grid.

15 | CAL CRUTCHLOW
Hampered by Petrucci at the start then ran off track more than once. His hard front tyre came in towards the end of the race, but it was too late for more than one point.

16 | ALEX RINS
In a group when he was punted off-track. Then used up the rear tyre making up a couple of places.

17 | HECTOR BARBERA
Had tyre problems for the first time all weekend, probably because of the elevated temperatures. Held up by a collision with Pol Espargaro on the grid.

18 | BRADLEY SMITH
His set up was wrong for the warmer temperatures and he ran off track. After that, it was a matter of getting it home.

19 | TITO RABAT
Forced wide on the first lap when Pol Espargaro found he'd lost his rear brake and couldn't get back to the group.

20 | SAM LOWES
The best start to a race since he joined Aprilia, with lap times close to his teammate. But tyre drop-off hit hard and lap times dropped considerably in the second half of the race.

DID NOT FINISH

JACK MILLER
Making progress on a track that he knew would be tough when he crashed. Thought he was overheating the rear in the final sector and pushed the front.

DANILO PETRUCCI
Lost control when he dropped the clutch off the start, side-swiped Pol Espargaro and impeded several others, including Cal Crutchlow. An engine warning light sent Danilo into the pits on Lap 5.

JONAS FOLGER
Lost brake pressure early on.

POL ESPARGARO
Put out after a starting-grid collision with Barbera left him with no rear brake.

OCTO BRITISH
GRAND PRIX

Silverstone 2017

DOVI'S DA BOMB

Andrea Dovizioso wins his fourth race and goes back to the top of the table, both Yamahas on the podium, Marquez blows his engine.

Andrea Dovizioso again demonstrated what we now knew; he is the coolest player out there. As he said himself, he wasn't the fastest but he played his cards most intelligently, using the strengths of the Ducati to hold off a late run from an equally clever Maverick Viñales.

Before the race, Valentino Rossi said the best he could hope for was the podium, meaning third place. It sounded like another piece of Rossi misdirection, especially after he qualified in second, the middle of the front row for his 300th GP - and you know how he likes the significant numbers. Then he got a stunning start and opened up a lead of over a second in just three laps. Unfortunately for Valentino, that was as good as it got. He was pursued by a gang of four: Marc Marquez, Maverick Viñales, Dovizioso and Cal Crutchlow. All had declared themselves concerned with tyre conservation; the Honda men as usual worried that the hard front wasn't hard enough, and the Yamaha men unsure of rear tyre wear rate despite a rumoured new chassis after a test at Misano. Alone among the leaders, Viñales was conserving a soft rear Michelin, the rest were on hard rubber.

Behind the leaders, Lorenzo hadn't made his usual lightning start but was lapping in times comparable to the leaders while

MAIN | Silverstone again produced a great race, as fast circuits tend to

BELOW, LEFT-RIGHT | Alex Rins' black helmet paid respect to the victims of the Barcelona terrorist attack; As usual, Valentino Rossi was the main attraction of the Day of Champions auction; As usual, Cal Crutchlow gave the home fans something to shout about

Johann Zarco broke away from an entertaining dice and bridged the gap. Those two would fight to the flag. Unfortunately, Zarco's teammate Jonas Folger wasn't there, he started the weekend with Norovirus and ended it with a massive crash in warm up when he appeared to have no brakes at the end of the Hanger Straight. He was very lucky to avoid serious injury.

The group closed on Rossi by a few fractions of a second each lap without indulging in frantic dicing. Any move was smooth and calculated; Marquez had already deduced that Dovizioso was the man who had more in hand than the others, and when Dovi started to move forward Marc was in a hurry to shadow him. The Ducati man had moved smoothly up to second place when the crucial event of the race happened. Marquez's motor belched smoke as the leaders approached Stowe corner flat out in top gear. Once everyone was over the shock of a factory Honda breaking, it happens regularly as clockwork - once every ten years, realisation dawned that it wasn't just Marc's chances of a race win that had gone up in smoke but his championship lead as well. The question now was who could take most advantage of his misfortune?

Initially, it didn't appear likely to be Viñales, he'd been right behind Marquez and took evasive action when smoke appeared. It looked to be just enough to detach him from the duel for the win. Dovi was now right on Rossi's back wheel with Viñales struggling to make up lost ground. The gaps weren't large, this was a race played out in hundredths of a second, not tenths. Three laps from the flag, Dovi smoothly moved in front of Valentino as Maverick jumped away from Crutchlow. Valentino patently had no defence. It looked as if whatever chassis was being used hadn't completely solved the problem of rear tyre wear. His teammate, however, had enough grip left in his soft rear Michelin to mount a serious challenge for the win. Dovizioso was up to the challenge and for the fourth time this year used the acceleration and braking strengths of the Ducati to hold off the Yamaha. It was as good a race as you could hope to see, and a reminder that the big, fast tracks like Silverstone are most likely to produce great racing.

RIGHT | *Jorge Lorenzo finished closer to the winner than ever before on a Ducati*

'EVERY RACE WE WIN IS DIFFERENT FROM THE OTHERS, AND THIS MEANS THAT WE ARE REALLY STRONG AND CAN FIGHT FOR THE CHAMPIONSHIP'
ANDREA DOVIZIOSO

A TANGLED WEB

This year's British GP was not promoted by the Circuit of Wales (CoW), unlike the previous three, following a decision by Dorna to terminate their contract. This followed a decision by the Welsh government in late June not to underwrite the project to the tune of £210million and effectively ended any chance of the project progressing. So, after nearly six years politicking and spending over £9million of public money, the controversial idea of a circuit in the Welsh valleys was over.

The CoW did have a five-year contract, with an option for another five years, to promote the British GP so Dorna and the Silverstone circuit had to do some very rapid deals to get the show on. In previous years, CoW management contracted Silverstone to host the event and oversaw it. The 2017 race turned out to be a great event, maybe the one where motorcycle racing people finally felt welcome at a place that fans tend to regard, perhaps unfairly, as a car racing track. Two facts are incontrovertible, Silverstone provides fantastic racing and the riders regard it as a great challenge.

The event was greatly helped by good weather throughout the weekend and an enthusiastic, if slightly disappointing in terms of size, crowd. As well as an epic fight for the victory and Crutchlow's close fourth, there was plenty more for them to enjoy. Not least a return to some sort of form by Scott Redding who was a solid eighth. It was now confirmed that Scott would replace Sam Lowes at Aprilia in 2018 and that Sam would go back to Moto2 with the Interwetten team. The other Brit in MotoGP, Bradley Smith, was also having a mini-crisis. His form had dropped and his teammate, Pol Espargaro, had been seriously out-performing him. The KTM factory decided to change his crew chief as part of a process of elimination aimed at discovering the reasons for the slump. Neither Sam nor Bradley had a good race.

Andrea Dovizioso said after the race that he hadn't been the fastest, but "I was able to put my bike in the right place." More justification for team manager Davide Tardozzi christening him "Professor" Dovizioso. Would Viñales have caught him without the interruption from Marquez's motor? Probably. Would he have passed him? Totally different matter. As for the soft rear tyre, there was very little difference between it and the medium but Maverick and his team had decided very early in the weekend to use it.

While Dovi's fourth win of the year was seriously impressive, the crucial event of the British GP was Marc Marquez's engine failure. Just as it looked as if he was going to pull away from the pack Marc found himself nine points in arrears of Dovi with the top four covered by just 26 points, the closest the championship has ever been in its history at this point in a season. Some of the uncertainty is generated by the Michelins, which are still developing, but it must be noted that at Silverstone pole-position, race and lap records were all broken. Absolutely nothing to complain about there.

MAIN | *Valentino Rossi gave the crowd what they wanted, right up until three laps from home*

LEFT, TOP-BOTTOM | *Scott Redding had a decent home race; Bradley Smith did not have a good home race; Danilo Petrucci was lucky to walk away from a nasty crash initiated by Andrea Iannone*

The delicate sensibilities of some people aside, the demise of CoW effectively rendered the British GP homeless. A date was pencilled in to the 2018 calendar but no track was specified. There are only two tracks in the country that could conceivably host a MotoGP weekend; Silverstone and Donington Park - although the later would need a considerable amount of work. But as it has just been leased by Dr Jonathan Palmer's MotorSport Vision company, the organisation that has already turned around the fortunes of several other British tracks, the idea of a return to Donington is far from impossible.

RACE RESULTS

WINNER | ANDREA DOVIZIOSO

CIRCUIT LENGTH | 5.9 KM | 3.67 MILES

NO. OF LAPS | 20

RACE DISTANCE | 118.0 KM | 73.4 MILES

CIRCUIT RECORD LAP | 2'01.560 | 174.7 KM/H
MARC MARQUEZ (2017)

CIRCUIT BEST LAP | 1'59.941 | 177.0 KM/H
MARC MARQUEZ (2017)

RACE CONDITION | DRY

AIR | 25°C

HUMIDITY | 36%

GROUND | 40°C

TISSOT
SWISS WATCHES SINCE 1853 / MotoGP

OFFICIAL TIMEKEEPER

MICHELIN / MotoGP

OFFICIAL MotoGP™ CLASS TYRE

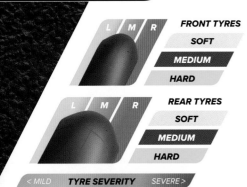

FRONT TYRES
SOFT
MEDIUM
HARD

REAR TYRES
SOFT
MEDIUM
HARD

< MILD | **TYRE SEVERITY** | SEVERE >

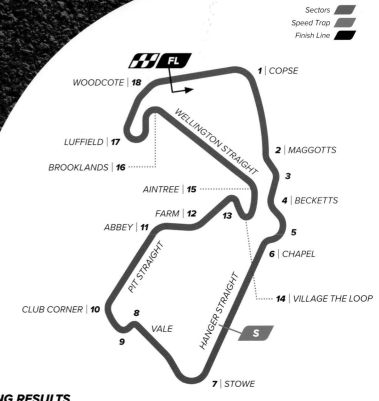

Sectors
Speed Trap
Finish Line

FL

WOODCOTE | 18
1 | COPSE
WELLINGTON STRAIGHT
LUFFIELD | 17
2 | MAGGOTTS
BROOKLANDS | 16
3
AINTREE | 15
4 | BECKETTS
FARM | 12 — 13
5
ABBEY | 11
6 | CHAPEL
PIT STRAIGHT
14 | VILLAGE THE LOOP
CLUB CORNER | 10
8
S
VALE
HANGER STRAIGHT
9
7 | STOWE

QUALIFYING RESULTS

	RIDER	NAT	TEAM	MACHINE	QP/TIME	GAP 1ST/PREV	
1	Marc Marquez	SPA	Repsol Honda Team	HONDA	Q2 1'59.941		
2	Valentino Rossi	ITA	Movistar Yamaha MotoGP	YAMAHA	Q2 2'00.025	0.084	0.084
3	Cal Crutchlow	GBR	LCR Honda	HONDA	Q2 2'00.106	0.165	0.081
4	Maverick Viñales	SPA	Movistar Yamaha MotoGP	YAMAHA	Q2 2'00.341	0.400	0.235
5	Jorge Lorenzo	SPA	Ducati Team	DUCATI	Q2 2'00.399	0.458	0.058
6	Andrea Dovizioso	ITA	Ducati Team	DUCATI	Q2 2'00.572	0.631	0.173
7	Dani Pedrosa**	SPA	Repsol Honda Team	HONDA	Q2 2'00.578	0.637	0.006
8	Johann Zarco	FRA	Monster Yamaha Tech 3	YAMAHA	Q2 2'00.622	0.681	0.044
9	Aleix Espargaro	SPA	Aprilia Racing Team Gresini	APRILIA	Q2 2'00.764	0.823	0.142
10	Jonas Folger**	GER	Monster Yamaha Tech 3	YAMAHA	Q2 2'00.829	0.888	0.065
11	Pol Espargaro	SPA	Red Bull KTM Factory Racing	KTM	Q2 2'01.378	1.437	0.549
12	Scott Redding	GBR	OCTO Pramac Racing	DUCATI	Q2 2'01.994	2.053	0.616
13	Alex Rins	SPA	Team SUZUKI ECSTAR	SUZUKI	Q1 2'01.285	*0.455	0.123
14	Alvaro Bautista	SPA	Pull&Bear Aspar Team	DUCATI	Q1 2'01.340	*0.510	0.055
15	Andrea Iannone	ITA	Team SUZUKI ECSTAR	SUZUKI	Q1 2'01.567	*0.737	0.227
16	Hector Barbera	SPA	Reale Avintia Racing	DUCATI	Q1 2'01.669	*0.839	0.102
17	Jack Miller	AUS	EG 0,0 Marc VDS	HONDA	Q1 2'01.672	*0.842	0.003
18	Danilo Petrucci	ITA	OCTO Pramac Racing	DUCATI	Q1 2'01.770	*0.940	0.098
19	Bradley Smith	GBR	Red Bull KTM Factory Racing	KTM	Q1 2'02.017	*1.187	0.247
20	Karel Abraham	CZE	Pull&Bear Aspar Team	DUCATI	Q1 2'02.037	*1.207	0.020
21	Loris Baz	FRA	Reale Avintia Racing	DUCATI	Q1 2'02.185	*1.355	0.148
22	Tito Rabat	SPA	EG 0,0 Marc VDS	HONDA	Q1 2'02.211	*1.381	0.026
23	Sam Lowes	GBR	Aprilia Racing Team Gresini	APRILIA	Q1 2'02.787	*1.957	0.576

*Gap with the fastest rider in the Q1 session
** Went forward from Q1 to Q2

1 ANDREA DOVIZIOSO
Another coolly executed win, his fourth of the year. He passed every other championship contender and fought off a last-lap charge from Viñales to go back to the top of the points table with a lead of nine points.

2 MAVERICK VIÑALES
Went with the soft rear tyre for the race, unlike any other factory rider. Like most fast men worked to conserve his tyres in the opening laps. Lost a few vital tenths when Marquez's engine blew up but was able to put in a stunning last lap to close down the winner.

3 VALENTINO ROSSI
Fast all weekend and led until three laps from the flag. Despite a test at Misano and a rumoured new chassis, still hit rear-tyre trouble late in the race and couldn't defend his lead.

4 CAL CRUTCHLOW
Disappointed not to be on the podium at least. As usual, the hard front tyre wasn't hard enough for the Honda and Cal had to use the rear hard to turn the bike in the second half of the race. A close fourth for much of the race but couldn't do anything about the men in front.

5 JORGE LORENZO
Started more cautiously than usual and made the rear tyre last. Finished just over three seconds behind the winner, the closest he's been this season. Another impressive race.

6 JOHANN ZARCO
Caught up with Pol Espargaro in the early stages then jumped across a gap to Lorenzo. Tyre wear made itself felt in the final laps and Johann couldn't make a decisive pass.

7 DANI PEDROSA
Improved lap times by a second on race day but still a weekend to forget. Dani has always found Silverstone's bumps difficult and this race was no exception.

8 SCOTT REDDING
Scott's best race for some time. Michelin persuaded him to use the medium tyre and his pace was both fast and constant through the race. Got over a bad Friday and enjoyed his home GP.

9 ALEX RINS
His most impressive race since returning from injury. Very fast at the start, able to comfortably maintain a top-ten position and then manage the worn rear tyre. Faster than his teammate again.

10 ALVARO BAUTISTA
The choice of a medium front tyre proved to be a mistake on the occasion of his 250th Grand Prix. Had to go into get-home mode early on.

11 POL ESPARGARO
A little slower than expected on race day when a combination of a hard rubber and the hot track caused the rear tyre to wear. Went directly to Q2 for the first time in the dry.

12 TITO RABAT
Not a bad race from the back of the grid, thanks to set up changes on Sunday morning plus a superb

RACE LAP CHART

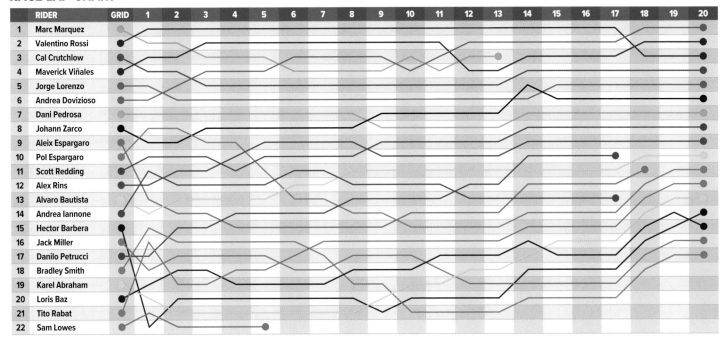

RIDER		GRID	1	2	3	4	5	6	7	8	9	10	11	12	13	14	15	16	17	18	19	20
1	Marc Marquez																						
2	Valentino Rossi																						
3	Cal Crutchlow																						
4	Maverick Viñales																						
5	Jorge Lorenzo																						
6	Andrea Dovizioso																						
7	Dani Pedrosa																						
8	Johann Zarco																						
9	Aleix Espargaro																						
10	Pol Espargaro																						
11	Scott Redding																						
12	Alex Rins																						
13	Alvaro Bautista																						
14	Andrea Iannone																						
15	Hector Barbera																						
16	Jack Miller																						
17	Danilo Petrucci																						
18	Bradley Smith																						
19	Karel Abraham																						
20	Loris Baz																						
21	Tito Rabat																						
22	Sam Lowes																						

RACE CLASSIFICATION AFTER 20 LAPS = 118 KM

	RIDER	NAT	TEAM	MACHINE	TIME	+ GAP	TYRES
1	Andrea Dovizioso	ITA	Ducati Team	DUCATI	40'45.496		H/H
2	Maverick Viñales	SPA	Movistar Yamaha MotoGP	YAMAHA	40'45.610	0.114	H/S
3	Valentino Rossi	ITA	Movistar Yamaha MotoGP	YAMAHA	40'46.245	0.749	H/H
4	Cal Crutchlow	GBR	LCR Honda	HONDA	40'47.175	1.679	H/H
5	Jorge Lorenzo	SPA	Ducati Team	DUCATI	40'49.004	3.508	H/H
6	Johann Zarco	FRA	Monster Yamaha Tech 3	YAMAHA	40'52.497	7.001	H/H
7	Dani Pedrosa	SPA	Repsol Honda Team	HONDA	40'56.440	10.944	H/H
8	Scott Redding	GBR	OCTO Pramac Racing	DUCATI	40'59.123	13.627	H/M
9	Alex Rins	SPA	Team SUZUKI ECSTAR	SUZUKI	41'01.157	15.661	H/H
10	Alvaro Bautista	SPA	Pull&Bear Aspar Team	DUCATI	41'10.775	25.279	M/S
11	Pol Espargaro	SPA	Red Bull KTM Factory Racing	KTM	41'15.832	30.336	H/H
12	Tito Rabat	SPA	EG 0,0 Marc VDS	HONDA	41'17.105	31.609	H/H
13	Karel Abraham	CZE	Pull&Bear Aspar Team	DUCATI	41'17.441	31.945	H/H
14	Hector Barbera	SPA	Reale Avintia Racing	DUCATI	41'19.063	33.567	S/S
15	Loris Baz	FRA	Reale Avintia Racing	DUCATI	41'19.397	33.901	M/S
16	Jack Miller	AUS	EG 0,0 Marc VDS	HONDA	41'28.508	43.012	H/H
17	Bradley Smith	GBR	Red Bull KTM Factory Racing	KTM	41'34.179	48.683	H/H
NC	Aleix Espargaro	SPA	Aprilia Racing Team Gresini	APRILIA	37'04.730	2 laps	H/H
NC	Danilo Petrucci	ITA	OCTO Pramac Racing	DUCATI	35'00.614	3 laps	H/H
NC	Andrea Iannone	ITA	Team SUZUKI ECSTAR	SUZUKI	35'01.018	3 laps	H/H
NC	Marc Marquez	SPA	Repsol Honda Team	HONDA	26'29.754	7 laps	H/H
NC	Sam Lowes	GBR	Aprilia Racing Team Gresini	APRILIA	10'25.948	15 laps	H/H
DNS	Jonas Folger	GER	Monster Yamaha Tech 3	YAMAHA			

CHAMPIONSHIP STANDINGS

	RIDER	NAT	TEAM	POINTS
1	Andrea Dovizioso	ITA	Ducati Team	183
2	Marc Marquez	SPA	Repsol Honda Team	174
3	Maverick Viñales	SPA	Movistar Yamaha MotoGP	170
4	Valentino Rossi	ITA	Movistar Yamaha MotoGP	157
5	Dani Pedrosa	SPA	Repsol Honda Team	148
6	Johann Zarco	FRA	Monster Yamaha Tech 3	109
7	Jorge Lorenzo	SPA	Ducati Team	90
8	Cal Crutchlow	GBR	LCR Honda	89
9	Jonas Folger	GER	Monster Yamaha Tech 3	77
10	Danilo Petrucci	ITA	OCTO Pramac Racing	75
11	Alvaro Bautista	SPA	Pull&Bear Aspar Team	58
12	Scott Redding	GBR	OCTO Pramac Racing	45
13	Aleix Espargaro	SPA	Aprilia Racing Team Gresini	43
14	Jack Miller	AUS	EG 0,0 Marc VDS	43
15	Loris Baz	FRA	Reale Avintia Racing	39
16	Andrea Iannone	ITA	Team SUZUKI ECSTAR	33
17	Karel Abraham	CZE	Pull&Bear Aspar Team	28
18	Tito Rabat	SPA	EG 0,0 Marc VDS	27
19	Pol Espargaro	SPA	Red Bull KTM Factory Racing	26
20	Hector Barbera	SPA	Reale Avintia Racing	23
21	Alex Rins	SPA	Team SUZUKI ECSTAR	19
22	Bradley Smith	GBR	Red Bull KTM Factory Racing	8
23	Michele Pirro	ITA	Ducati Team	7
24	Mika Kallio	FIN	Red Bull KTM Factory Racing	6
25	Sam Lowes	GBR	Aprilia Racing Team Gresini	2
26	Sylvain Guintoli	FRA	Team SUZUKI ECSTAR	1

start. Then picked off a few more to underline his recent form.

13 | KAREL ABRAHAM
Another impressive race after a disappointing practice and bad qualifying. Made progress despite the bike twice shaking its head on the fast straight and forcing the brake pads back.

14 | HECTOR BARBERA
Race compromised by the bike moving when he engaged gear on the start, so Hector stopped and

started again. Made some progress but could have been in top ten.

15 | LORIS BAZ
Gambled on the soft rear tyre and was fast in early laps. Paid the price in the final laps when he lost two places to fellow Ducati riders.

16 | JACK MILLER
Lost all rear grip on race day and not sure why. Thought it may have been the increase in track temperature.

17 | BRADLEY SMITH
Got a new crew chief in a bid to rediscover his form. Started the race really well but like his teammate the weather and a hard rear tyre produced problems.

DID NOT FINISH

SAM LOWES
Crashed at Turn 5 early on, although data showed very little difference from previous laps.

MARC MARQUEZ
Had already identified Dovizioso as the man to beat when his engine went at the end of the Hanger Straight on Lap 14 of the 20. Lost the championship lead.

ANDREA IANNONE
Very fast over the odd single lap but behind his teammate on race pace. Crashed out while in group fight near the finish and took out Petrucci.

DANILO PETRUCCI
In the big dice for places in the lower reaches of the top ten when Iannone crashed and brought Danilo down in a very nasty looking crash.

ALEIX ESPARGARO
Handicapped by damage to an intercostal muscle but on for a top-ten finish until another engine problem sent him into the pits just a couple of laps from the flag.

DID NOT START

JONAS FOLGER
Victim of a massive, high-speed crash in warm-up when he appeared to have brake failure at the end of the Hanger Straight. Taken to hospital for precautionary scans.

RISK ASSESSMENT

Marc Marquez rolls the dice on the last lap and wins, Danilo Petrucci is second again, Andrea Dovizioso content with third.

The Misano circuit has never been nice in the wet. No matter what resurfacing work has been done, it has always been utterly treacherous in the rain, treacherous enough to produce 80 crashes on race day. Only a dozen of them were in MotoGP, but this was a race which caused even Marc Marquez to err on the side of caution. The same could not be said of Jorge Lorenzo. Nor of Valentino Rossi, who put himself out of his home race by breaking his right leg in a slow-speed enduro training accident. Despite the weather and the local hero's absence, the crowds still turned out in force, if only to boo Marquez like a pantomime villain. He joined in the spirit of things by blowing the Rossi fan-club grandstand kisses from the back of a scooter after a warm-up crash.

Marquez duly won the race but not without some serious calculations based on the risk/reward equation. In any race on such a slippery surface, there are inevitably early crashes as someone weights the risk side of the equation, and this time that was Lorenzo. He shot into the lead from the second row and ripped out a big lead before losing concentration while changing the engine ignition map and flipping himself over the handlebars. It was yet another in the long line of hints that Jorge is going to deliver Ducati a victory sometime soon. The question now was what could championship leader Andrea Dovizioso do on a track where he had never stood on the podium and where, historically, Ducati had never enjoyed good fortune.

Once Lorenzo had left the stage, the lead was inherited by Danilo Petrucci who had pushed his way past Marquez just a lap earlier. Dovizioso was a close third but never found a way past the Honda. Just how hard was he having to ride to stay in touch? At three-quarters distance Dovi decided to minimise the risk and take a safe third place. In seven laps, his gap to the leader went from just over a second to just over ten seconds. Andrea was never in any danger of losing third place, such was the gap the leading trio had put on Maverick Viñales, He hadn't attacked simply because he couldn't. At no time during the weekend did he feel that he had any advantage at all in any department over any of his opponents. Under the circumstances Andrea did a good job of looking happy with the result.

The same could not be said of Danilo Petrucci. After leading the race for 20 of the 28 laps, up to and including the final one, he was the victim of the inevitable Marquez attack. And equally inevitably he was given no chance to respond. Marquez was just under half-a-second in arrears starting the last lap yet went past at the first corner, set the best first-sector time of the race and won the race by half-a-second having set the best second-and fourth-sector times as well on the last lap, which you won't be surprised to hear was the fastest of the race. Petrucci, pushing like hell for that elusive maiden win, did a 1min 48.296sec last lap as Marquez dropped his time to 1min 47.069sec, over half-a-second quicker than he'd gone before. Marc had most definitely been calculating the value of those five extra points and come to the conclusion that he couldn't afford effectively to hand them to Dovizioso and Viñales. It is worth noting that in Moto2 an hour earlier Thomas Luthi had come to precisely the opposite conclusion. Was it really a gamble? Marc thought so but, as in Assen 2016 when he finished a calculated second to Jack Miller, there was much pointing at his crash helmet to indicate he had again taken his crew's advice and thought about it.

In fact there was a lot of thinking going on. Andrea Dovizioso understood his hand was weak and played the cards accordingly. Maverick Viñales, on his third chassis of the year (he had two of the latest version thanks to his team mate's absence), was also

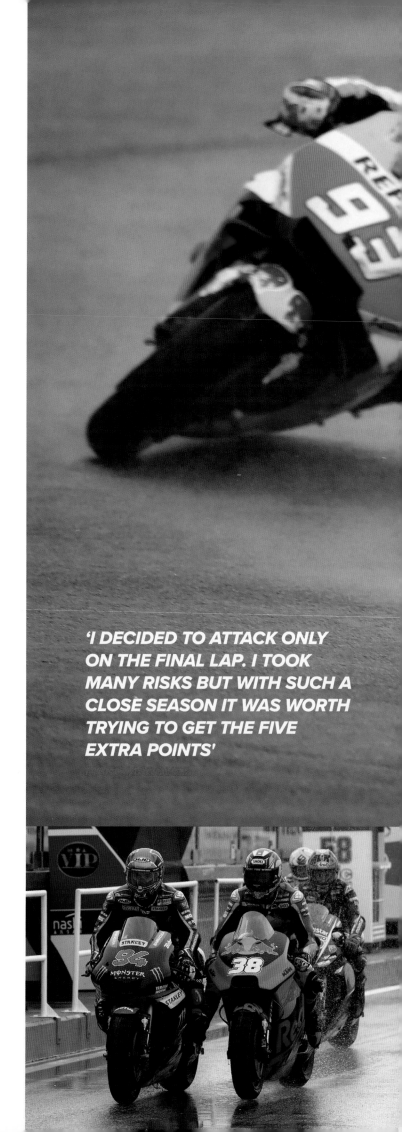

'I DECIDED TO ATTACK ONLY ON THE FINAL LAP. I TOOK MANY RISKS BUT WITH SUCH A CLOSE SEASON IT WAS WORTH TRYING TO GET THE FIVE EXTRA POINTS'

LEFT | *Maverick Viñales was fourth in his first wet race on a Yamaha and quite happy about it*

MAIN | *Danilo Petrucci is stalked by the implacable Marc Marquez, the inevitable happened at the start of the last lap*

BELOW, LEFT-RIGHT | *September on the Italian riviera?; Jack Miller shone in the wet as usual; Scott Redding had a good weekend, Jonas Folger didn't*

thinking and declared himself satisfied with fourth place in the wet despite the fact it put him 16 points behind the leading pair. In truth, it would have been most unreasonable to expect a better result given his experience with the Yamaha in any type of wet weather, never mind on the ice rink of Misano. The championship contender who really suffered was Dani Pedrosa, perhaps enough to put him out of reach of the title yet again. He simply could not get any heat in his tyres and only managed to claw his way into the points when conditions mellowed in the final laps. He cannot have had a worse race.

All that thinking put Marc back on top of the championship, albeit on a tie break level on points with Dovi. The weekend started with five men in contention for the title and while it is dangerous to make predictions in this of all seasons, it felt like two of them had been eliminated. Valentino Rossi's broken leg surely means that his already small chance has shrunk to vanishingly small, and Dani Pedrosa could not afford to find himself further adrift. Looking at the five races to come, it was tempting to wonder if it was really a two-horse race. Looking at what he did at Misano, it was tempting to think it was actually a one-horse race now, and that horse's name was Marc Marquez.

MAIN | Jorge Lorenzo led the first six laps before crashing spectacularly

ABOVE | Very local hero Valentino Rossi was missed by many

SLIPPERY WHEN WET

Race day's rash of crashes generated a lot of discussion about the Misano track surface and what should be done about it, but one wet-weather first escaped most people's notice. This was the first wet-weather win for a bike fitted with carbon brakes. Historically, carbon discs needed to be at such elevated temperatures, many hundreds of degrees Centigrade, to function that using them in the wet was simply impossible.

They were first used at Donington Park in 1988 to help Wayne Rainey to his first ever win, a dream debut if ever there was one. Manufacturer AP Lockheed said that their product saved nearly one-and-and-a-half kilograms over the standard steel discs, as a result of which Rainey said his 500 handled "like a 250" such was the effect of the reduction in mass of the gyroscope that is the front wheel assembly.

AP Lockheed had got the operating temperature down low enough to cope with sitting on the grid and even tried them that year in the wet in what was then Czechoslovakia, albeit with shrouds.

In the MotoGP era, Italian company Brembo have been the brake supplier of choice and advances in materials science have all but eliminated the old worries about operating temperature range. However, it was only last year that riders were happy to race with shrouded carbon discs in the wet, and for "riders" you could usually read Marc Marquez. Indeed, no-one else on the podium at Misano used carbon brakes, Petrucci and Dovizioso used steel. That is yet another indication of Marc's ability to adopt the high-risk strategy and make it work. Conditions at the start of the race were so bad he must have had difficulties keeping the rotors up to temperature, leading to the sort of brake instability riders dread. And all this on the slipperiest, most treacherous of surfaces.

13 | SAN MARINO

RACE RESULTS

Sectors
Speed Trap
Finish Line

WINNER | MARC MARQUEZ

CIRCUIT LENGTH | 4.2 KM | 2.63 MILES

NO. OF LAPS | 28

RACE DISTANCE | 118.3 KM | 73.6 MILES

CIRCUIT RECORD LAP | 1'32.979 | 163.6 KM/H
DANI PEDROSA (2016)

CIRCUIT BEST LAP | 1'31.868 | 165.6 KM/H
JORGE LORENZO (2016)

RACE CONDITION | WET

AIR | 18°C

HUMIDITY | 97%

GROUND | 19°C

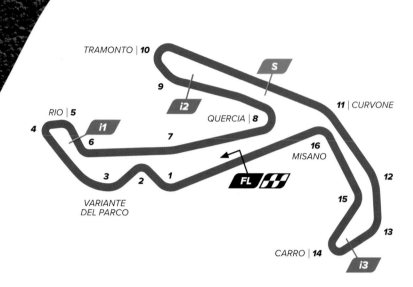

TISSOT
SWISS WATCHES SINCE 1853

OFFICIAL TIMEKEEPER

MICHELIN

OFFICIAL MotoGP™ CLASS TYRE

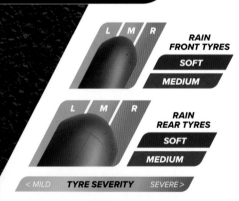

RAIN FRONT TYRES
SOFT
MEDIUM

RAIN REAR TYRES
SOFT
MEDIUM

< MILD   **TYRE SEVERITY**   SEVERE >

QUALIFYING RESULTS

	RIDER	NAT	TEAM	MACHINE		QP/TIME	GAP 1ST/PREV	
1	Maverick Viñales	SPA	Movistar Yamaha MotoGP	YAMAHA	Q2	1'32.439		
2	Andrea Dovizioso	ITA	Ducati Team	DUCATI	Q2	1'32.601	0.162	0.162
3	Marc Marquez	SPA	Repsol Honda Team	HONDA	Q2	1'32.636	0.197	0.035
4	Cal Crutchlow	GBR	LCR Honda	HONDA	Q2	1'32.768	0.329	0.132
5	Jorge Lorenzo	SPA	Ducati Team	DUCATI	Q2	1'32.792	0.353	0.024
6	Johann Zarco	FRA	Monster Yamaha Tech 3	YAMAHA	Q2	1'32.885	0.446	0.093
7	Dani Pedrosa	SPA	Repsol Honda Team	HONDA	Q2	1'32.992	0.553	0.107
8	Danilo Petrucci	ITA	OCTO Pramac Racing	DUCATI	Q2	1'32.997	0.558	0.005
9	Aleix Espargaro	SPA	Aprilia Racing Team Gresini	APRILIA	Q2	1'33.149	0.710	0.152
10	Alvaro Bautista**	SPA	Pull&Bear Aspar Team	DUCATI	Q2	1'33.417	0.978	0.268
11	Michele Pirro	ITA	Ducati Team	DUCATI	Q2	1'33.491	1.052	0.074
12	Karel Abraham**	CZE	Pull&Bear Aspar Team	DUCATI	Q2	1'34.374	1.935	0.883
13	Hector Barbera	SPA	Reale Avintia Racing	DUCATI	Q1	1'33.920	*0.357	0.134
14	Jack Miller	AUS	EG 0,0 Marc VDS	HONDA	Q1	1'33.933	*0.370	0.013
15	Loris Baz	FRA	Reale Avintia Racing	DUCATI	Q1	1'33.946	*0.383	0.013
16	Jonas Folger	GER	Monster Yamaha Tech 3	YAMAHA	Q1	1'33.987	*0.424	0.041
17	Pol Espargaro	SPA	Red Bull KTM Factory Racing	KTM	Q1	1'34.080	*0.517	0.093
18	Tito Rabat	SPA	EG 0,0 Marc VDS	HONDA	Q1	1'34.095	*0.532	0.015
19	Scott Redding	GBR	OCTO Pramac Racing	DUCATI	Q1	1'34.132	*0.569	0.037
20	Alex Rins	SPA	Team SUZUKI ECSTAR	SUZUKI	Q1	1'34.138	*0.575	0.006
21	Andrea Iannone	ITA	Team SUZUKI ECSTAR	SUZUKI	Q1	1'34.148	*0.585	0.010
22	Bradley Smith	GBR	Red Bull KTM Factory Racing	KTM	Q1	1'34.507	*0.944	0.359
23	Sam Lowes	GBR	Aprilia Racing Team Gresini	APRILIA	Q1	1'35.659	*2.096	1.152

*Gap with the fastest rider in the Q1 session
**Went forward from Q1 to Q2*

---

1 | MARC MARQUEZ
Thought about the championship for the whole race and only attacked on the last lap. Still took a lot of risks but calculated they were worth it for the extra five points. Went back to the top of the championship.

2 | DANILO PETRUCCI
Fought his way to second on Lap 6 then inherited the lead next time round when Lorenzo crashed. Led until the start of the final lap when Marquez pounced. Danilo's third podium of the year and his second in Italy.

3 | ANDREA DOVIZIOSO
His first podium at Misano kept Dovi level on points with Marquez. Never had any advantage over the opposition in any department and eased off towards the flag. Another intelligent race.

4 | MAVERICK VIÑALES
Happy with fourth on the new chassis' first wet-weather mileage. In trouble with the left side of the rear tyre all race but rode at his pace despite being pushed back to seventh from pole position early in the race.

5 | MICHELE PIRRO
Ducati's test rider had a wild-card for the second time this year. Despite two crashes on Saturday that compromised his qualifying, Michele again rode superbly. A fight with Miller prevented him challenging Viñales.

6 | JACK MILLER
Another great wet-weather ride. Felt he had the beating of Crutchlow and Viñales early on but probably delayed too long in switching maps and ran out of traction so couldn't hold Pirro off.

7 | SCOTT REDDING
Looked like he was reverting to his pre-Silverstone form when he struggled in practice and qualifying, but rode another solid race with no mistakes.

8 | ALEX RINS
A mature and effective ride from last place at the first corner to give Alex his best result of the year so far, in any conditions. Out-raced and out-qualified his team mate.

9 | JONAS FOLGER
Not his usual wet-weather form due to a change after warm-up that proved to be a step in the wrong direction. Not his usual self in dry practice either, appeared to still be suffering from his big Silverstone crash.

10 | BRADLEY SMITH
His best result so far on the KTM. Rode in a very controlled way until the final three laps then dropped into the 1min 48sec bracket and gapped his team mate significantly. Just the sort of result he needed.

11 | POL ESPARGARO
Not completely happy with his wet-weather set up, could follow when his team mate came past at half-distance but had no answer when Smith pressed in final laps.

12 | ALVARO BAUTISTA
Grateful to get to the flag and score points. Had no feeling from his tyres at any point in the race.

RACE LAP CHART

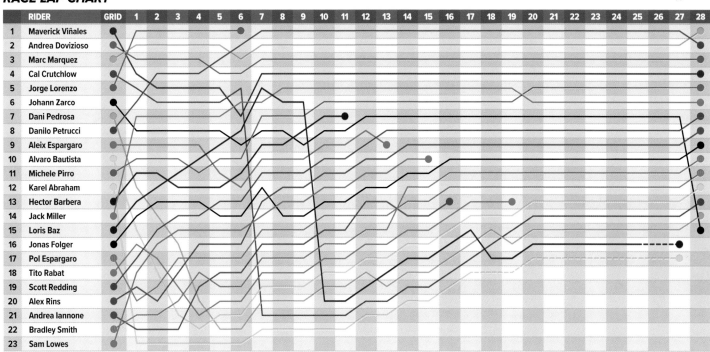

	RIDER	GRID	1	2	3	4	5	6	7	8	9	10	11	12	13	14	15	16	17	18	19	20	21	22	23	24	25	26	27	28
1	Maverick Viñales																													
2	Andrea Dovizioso																													
3	Marc Marquez																													
4	Cal Crutchlow																													
5	Jorge Lorenzo																													
6	Johann Zarco																													
7	Dani Pedrosa																													
8	Danilo Petrucci																													
9	Aleix Espargaro																													
10	Alvaro Bautista																													
11	Michele Pirro																													
12	Karel Abraham																													
13	Hector Barbera																													
14	Jack Miller																													
15	Loris Baz																													
16	Jonas Folger																													
17	Pol Espargaro																													
18	Tito Rabat																													
19	Scott Redding																													
20	Alex Rins																													
21	Andrea Iannone																													
22	Bradley Smith																													
23	Sam Lowes																													

RACE CLASSIFICATION AFTER 28 LAPS = 118.328 KM

	RIDER	NAT	TEAM	MACHINE	TIME	+ GAP	TYRES
1	Marc Marquez	SPA	Repsol Honda Team	HONDA	50'41.565		RS/RS
2	Danilo Petrucci	ITA	OCTO Pramac Racing	DUCATI	50'42.757	1.192	RS/RS
3	Andrea Dovizioso	ITA	Ducati Team	DUCATI	50'53.271	11.706	RS/RS
4	Maverick Viñales	SPA	Movistar Yamaha MotoGP	YAMAHA	50'58.124	16.559	RS/RS
5	Michele Pirro	ITA	Ducati Team	DUCATI	51'01.064	19.499	RS/RS
6	Jack Miller	AUS	EG 0,0 Marc VDS	HONDA	51'06.447	24.882	RS/RS
7	Scott Redding	GBR	OCTO Pramac Racing	DUCATI	51'15.437	33.872	RS/RS
8	Alex Rins	SPA	Team SUZUKI ECSTAR	SUZUKI	51'16.227	34.662	RS/RS
9	Jonas Folger	GER	Monster Yamaha Tech 3	YAMAHA	51'35.647	54.082	RS/RS
10	Bradley Smith	GBR	Red Bull KTM Factory Racing	KTM	51'39.529	57.964	RS/RS
11	Pol Espargaro	SPA	Red Bull KTM Factory Racing	KTM	51'42.005	60.440	RS/RS
12	Alvaro Bautista	SPA	Pull&Bear Aspar Team	DUCATI	51'58.921	77.356	RS/RS
13	Cal Crutchlow	GBR	LCR Honda	HONDA	52'17.153	95.588	RS/RS
14	Dani Pedrosa	SPA	Repsol Honda Team	HONDA	52'20.422	98.857	RS/RS
15	Johann Zarco	FRA	Monster Yamaha Tech 3	YAMAHA	52'43.777	122.212	RS/RS
16	Loris Baz	FRA	Reale Avintia Racing	DUCATI	50'56.522	1 lap	RS/RS
17	Karel Abraham	CZE	Pull&Bear Aspar Team	DUCATI	51'23.991	1 lap	RS/RS
NC	Tito Rabat	SPA	EG 0,0 Marc VDS	HONDA	35'17.899	9 laps	RS/RS
NC	Andrea Iannone	ITA	Team SUZUKI ECSTAR	SUZUKI	29'48.066	12 laps	RS/RS
NC	Sam Lowes	GBR	Aprilia Racing Team Gresini	APRILIA	27'43.503	13 laps	RS/RS
NC	Aleix Espargaro	SPA	Aprilia Racing Team Gresini	APRILIA	23'59.157	15 laps	RS/RS
NC	Hector Barbera	SPA	Reale Avintia Racing	DUCATI	20'17.102	17 laps	RS/RS
NC	Jorge Lorenzo	SPA	Ducati Team	DUCATI	10'59.028	22 laps	RS/RS

*Michelin wet tyre options
FRONT : Rain Soft / Rain Medium   **REAR** : Rain Soft / Rain Medium

CHAMPIONSHIP STANDINGS

	RIDER	NAT	TEAM	POINTS
1	Marc Marquez	SPA	Repsol Honda Team	199
2	Andrea Dovizioso	ITA	Ducati Team	199
3	Maverick Viñales	SPA	Movistar Yamaha MotoGP	183
4	Valentino Rossi	ITA	Movistar Yamaha MotoGP	157
5	Dani Pedrosa	SPA	Repsol Honda Team	150
6	Johann Zarco	FRA	Monster Yamaha Tech 3	110
7	Danilo Petrucci	ITA	OCTO Pramac Racing	95
8	Cal Crutchlow	GBR	LCR Honda	92
9	Jorge Lorenzo	SPA	Ducati Team	90
10	Jonas Folger	GER	Monster Yamaha Tech 3	84
11	Alvaro Bautista	SPA	Pull&Bear Aspar Team	62
12	Scott Redding	GBR	OCTO Pramac Racing	54
13	Jack Miller	AUS	EG 0,0 Marc VDS	53
14	Aleix Espargaro	SPA	Aprilia Racing Team Gresini	43
15	Loris Baz	FRA	Reale Avintia Racing	39
16	Andrea Iannone	ITA	Team SUZUKI ECSTAR	33
17	Pol Espargaro	SPA	Red Bull KTM Factory Racing	31
18	Karel Abraham	CZE	Pull&Bear Aspar Team	28
19	Alex Rins	SPA	Team SUZUKI ECSTAR	27
20	Tito Rabat	SPA	EG 0,0 Marc VDS	27
21	Hector Barbera	SPA	Reale Avintia Racing	23
22	Michele Pirro	ITA	Ducati Team	18
23	Bradley Smith	GBR	Red Bull KTM Factory Racing	14
24	Mika Kallio	FIN	Red Bull KTM Factory Racing	6
25	Sam Lowes	GBR	Aprilia Racing Team Gresini	2
26	Sylvain Guintoli	FRA	Team SUZUKI ECSTAR	1

---

13 | CAL CRUTCHLOW
Cautious early on but confident he could get on the podium. Unfortunately made a mistake and crashed after passing Miller. Got back on track with bent handlebars and no footrest to race for 22 laps and get in the points.

14 | DANI PEDROSA
Crashed in morning warm up and couldn't get any heat in his tyres in the race. Knocked four seconds off his time when the track started to dry out at the end of proceedings.

15 | JOHANN ZARCO
Started the last lap in seventh with a comfortable gap over Redding but ran out of fuel. Pushed over the line for the last point.

16 | LORIS BAZ
Very fast all weekend and decided to take a few risks despite the rear feeling very different in the wet. Shadowing Miller when he lost the front, remounted and crashed again chasing Bautista.

17 | KAREL ABRAHAM
A crash in warm up and another on the first lap, both at Turn 3. Picked the bike up but didn't get points. Karel described it as his worst race of the season.

DID NOT FINISH

TITO RABAT
Had no feel early on but then found some pace and crashed after half-distance while in the points.

ANDREA IANNONE
Pulled in because of arm pump caused by a tight wet suit, something that he has experienced before. Outshone by his team mate all weekend.

SAM LOWES
Running in the top ten having started on the back of the grid when the track started to dry just after half distance. His feeling with the front dropped too, and he crashed.

ALEIX ESPARGARO
Like his team mate, lost the front when the track went from soaking to merely wet. Not the way Aprilia wanted to celebrate 30 years in Grand Prix racing.

HECTOR BARBERA
Like his team mate took one risk too many when closing on Miller. Lucky to escape uninjured from a big highside.

JORGE LORENZO
Again led the early laps and had opened up a four-and-a-half second lead in just six laps when he lost concentration changing the map, used the back brake differently and highsided.

DID NOT RACE

VALENTINO ROSSI
At home recovering from breaking his right tibia and fibula in an enduro training accident.

A DAY OF CHAMPIONS

Marc Marquez strikes at his home circuit to open up what feels like a decisive lead. Best race of the year for Lorenzo, KTM and Aprilia.

It felt like we'd seen all three champions. Three epic races were won by Marc Marquez, Franco Morbidelli and Joan Mir, who all overcame strong challenges and rode like the champions they are or will surely become. In Marquez's case he also had to overcome an unruly Honda and by his own admission came closer to crashing than even he usually does. Inspired by what he truly regards as his home crowd, he was even more demonic than usual on left handers but struggled on the rights. Like every other rider, his set-up was compromised by the weather — again. Friday was completely wet, and FP3 was too cold to be relevant, so the only useful practice was a chunk of FP4. Not surprisingly, that meant that most of the rookies were in trouble on Sunday but, and this was definitely a surprise, so were most of the Ducatis.

The exception to that rule was Jorge Lorenzo, who led the race from the middle of the front row for longer than ever on a Ducati. Andrea Dovizioso was most definitely not an exception, he started the day level on points with Marquez at the top of the table and ended it with a deficit of 16 points.

But no matter what anyone else did, the story of the weekend was Valentino Rossi's return to the paddock just three weeks after breaking his right tibia and fibula. We have become

ABOVE, LEFT-RIGHT | Dani Pedrosa wasn't delighted with second place; Maverick Vinales also underachieved despite the aggressive helmet design; Scott Redding didn't enjoy Aragón

MAIN | Jorge Lorenzo led again, this time for more laps than ever before, but couldn't quite make the soft tyre last all race

FAR RIGHT | Aleix Espargaro gave Aprilia their best race yet and finished his closest to the winner despite a terrible start

accustomed to his miracles, but even by his standards putting the Yamaha on the front row, looking like a contender for the win, and finally finishing fifth was jaw-dropping. And jaws were positively subterranean after the race when Valentino informed us of the reason he couldn't hold off Viñales. It wasn't the leg, it was the now familiar sudden drop-off of the rear tyre's performance.

Variations on that theme dominated the way the race unfolded, with the exception of Marc Marquez who, as usual, did it his way seemingly unaffected by such mundane considerations. Maverick Viñales couldn't use his preferred soft tyres and had to wait for the medium to come to him. The same went for Pedrosa only he had to wait longer, mainly because he couldn't get past Maverick. The usually imperturbable Pedrosa couldn't hide his disappointment. Better qualifying and/or better early pace would have given him a shot at the win. It's tempting to say he would have won, but as Marc explained afterwards he was willing to risk everything for the victory in front of his fans. There was also the incentive of the extra five points with which to open the gap on Dovizioso.

If the front of the race felt like a return to order after the chaos that has characterised most of the season, the midfield looked revolutionary. Both Aprilia and KTM showed just how much progress they have made in the first year of their bikes' development. Aragón is a track which tests every aspect of a motorcycle and Aleix Espargaro was never out of the top ten in any session, qualified eighth, was second in warm-up and finished sixth just under seven seconds behind the winner. The new version of the aero fairing got a lot of praise and the only improvement that the rider had on his wish list was a bit more power. If Aleix couldn't think of anything else to ask for, that motorcycle has very little wrong with it. Over at KTM things were just as rosy. A new chassis with redesigned rear suspension proved another step forward and gave the factory their fourth top ten finish of the season but, much more significantly, only 14 seconds behind Marquez, a new best for KTM. The rider was Pol Espargaro who had to work hard to beat the factory test rider Mika Kallio, having his third wild-card ride of the season. The Finn

'I PUSHED HARD AND IN SOME CORNERS I JUST CLICKED THE OFF-BUTTON IN MY HEAD, EVEN IF I CRASHED TWICE YESTERDAY'
MARC MARQUEZ

MAIN   Marc Marquez forced the Honda do do his will, it wasn't easy

RIGHT, TOP-BOTTOM   KTM test rider impressed again, as did Pol Espargaro;
Jack Miller tried the hard rear tyre, probably a bad idea; It's fair to say that
Marc Marquez really wanted this one, his real home race

FAR RIGHT   Suzuki couldn't use their new chassis after a rained-off test and
Iannone suffered accordingly

MIRACLE MAN

Valentino Rossi's arrival at the circuit was closely studied. As Valentino got out of the car, an ex-racer gasped "It's the right shape!" By which he meant that the leg had no swelling and therefore no infection, fluid build-up or other issues. Clearly, this had been a considerably less serious injury than his Mugello injury of 2010 and surgery had gone as well as it possibly could. Predictably, he passed the medical test on Thursday but could he really race? Could he even ride?

out-qualified Espargaro and led him until three-quarters distance, finishing just three seconds behind in 11th. All of which looked bad for Bradley Smith, who was hoping to build on his great result in San Marino but yet again suffered from his problems with the Michelins. His future prospects may also suffer from Mika Kallio.

Suzuki did not enjoy the same encouragement. Their plan to use a new chassis was thwarted by wet weather at their post-Misano test and they rescheduled to join KTM at a test on Monday to finalise plans for the three flyaway races.

Leaving Aragón, no-one expected any factory to pull any miracles out of their corporate sleeves. The sight and sound of Marc Marquez, with his favoured hard tyres front and rear, fighting his way to the lead despite the Honda's recalcitrance showed just what the rest have to deal with. Yes, it was a difficult weekend on which to get things right and while Marc had worked it out by race day his two closest rivals couldn't get on the podium. That other habitual defier of expectations Valentino Rossi also continued to amaze and astound, which doesn't alter the fact that elusive tenth title continues to be out of reach. It now feels like a three-man race at best, but if we're honest, and with the usual disclaimers about acts of god, Aragón showed us where all of the 2017 titles are going.

When Valentino came out of the Yamaha truck's office on Friday morning he had to descend an aluminium staircase with about a dozen steps. He made it down three walking normally then the leg buckled. He did eight laps and was 18th, 2.8sec off the pace. In FP2 he did 13 laps and closed the gap by 0.7sec. It didn't look promising. On Saturday morning he walked down the steps almost normally and did 19 laps in FP3 to finish tenth and go direct to Q2 where he was just 0.18sec slower than pole man Viñales to be third fastest for a front-row start. If you're looking for a miracle, there it is. On race day he skipped down the steps to his bike.

14 | ARAGÓN

RACE RESULTS

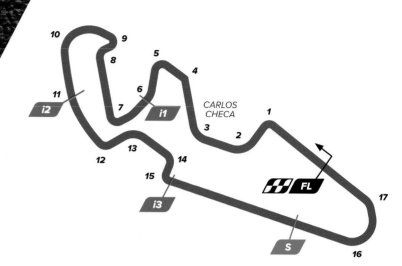

Sectors
Speed Trap
Finish Line

WINNER | MARC MARQUEZ

CIRCUIT LENGTH 5.1 KM | 3.15 MILES

NO. OF LAPS 23

RACE DISTANCE 116.8 KM | 72.5 MILES

CIRCUIT RECORD LAP 1'48.120 | 169.0 KM/H
JORGE LORENZO (2015)

CIRCUIT BEST LAP 1'46.635 | 171.4 KM/H
MARC MARQUEZ (2015)

RACE CONDITION DRY

AIR 27°C

HUMIDITY 44%

GROUND 40°C

TISSOT SWISS WATCHES SINCE 1853 | MotoGP
OFFICIAL TIMEKEEPER

MICHELIN | MotoGP
OFFICIAL MotoGP™ CLASS TYRE

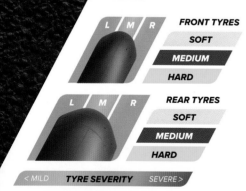

FRONT TYRES
SOFT
MEDIUM
HARD

REAR TYRES
SOFT
MEDIUM
HARD

< MILD **TYRE SEVERITY** SEVERE >

QUALIFYING RESULTS

	RIDER	NAT	TEAM	MACHINE	QP/TIME	GAP 1ST/PREV	
1	Maverick Viñales	SPA	Movistar Yamaha MotoGP	YAMAHA	Q2 1'47.635		
2	Jorge Lorenzo**	SPA	Ducati Team	DUCATI	Q2 1'47.735	0.100	0.100
3	Valentino Rossi	ITA	Movistar Yamaha MotoGP	YAMAHA	Q2 1'47.815	0.180	0.080
4	Cal Crutchlow	GBR	LCR Honda	HONDA	Q2 1'47.830	0.195	0.015
5	Marc Marquez	SPA	Repsol Honda Team	HONDA	Q2 1'47.963	0.328	0.133
6	Dani Pedrosa	SPA	Repsol Honda Team	HONDA	Q2 1'48.107	0.472	0.144
7	Andrea Dovizioso	ITA	Ducati Team	DUCATI	Q2 1'48.137	0.502	0.030
8	Aleix Espargaro	SPA	Aprilia Racing Team Gresini	APRILIA	Q2 1'48.159	0.524	0.022
9	Alvaro Bautista	SPA	Pull&Bear Aspar Team	DUCATI	Q2 1'48.187	0.552	0.028
10	Andrea Iannone	ITA	Team SUZUKI ECSTAR	SUZUKI	Q2 1'48.289	0.654	0.102
11	Johann Zarco**	FRA	Monster Yamaha Tech 3	YAMAHA	Q2 1'48.402	0.767	0.113
12	Mika Kallio	FIN	Red Bull KTM Factory Racing	KTM	Q2 1'48.471	0.836	0.069
13	Jack Miller	AUS	EG 0,0 Marc VDS	HONDA	Q1 1'48.307	*0.128	0.009
14	Pol Espargaro	SPA	Red Bull KTM Factory Racing	KTM	Q1 1'48.387	*0.208	0.080
15	Karel Abraham	CZE	Pull&Bear Aspar Team	DUCATI	Q1 1'48.467	*0.288	0.080
16	Danilo Petrucci	ITA	OCTO Pramac Racing	DUCATI	Q1 1'48.908	*0.729	0.441
17	Loris Baz	FRA	Reale Avintia Racing	DUCATI	Q1 1'48.911	*0.732	0.003
18	Jonas Folger	GER	Monster Yamaha Tech 3	YAMAHA	Q1 1'49.034	*0.855	0.123
19	Hector Barbera	SPA	Reale Avintia Racing	DUCATI	Q1 1'49.052	*0.873	0.018
20	Alex Rins	SPA	Team SUZUKI ECSTAR	SUZUKI	Q1 1'49.233	*1.054	0.181
21	Tito Rabat	SPA	EG 0,0 Marc VDS	HONDA	Q1 1'49.258	*1.079	0.025
22	Scott Redding	GBR	OCTO Pramac Racing	DUCATI	Q1 1'49.288	*1.109	0.030
23	Bradley Smith	GBR	Red Bull KTM Factory Racing	KTM	Q1 1'49.578	*1.399	0.290
24	Sam Lowes	GBR	Aprilia Racing Team Gresini	APRILIA	Q1 1'50.769	*2.590	1.191

Gap with the fastest rider in the Q1 session
** Went forward from Q1 to Q2*

1 | MARC MARQUEZ
The bike wasn't up to winning but Marc was. He had to fight his way past Dovizioso, Rossi and Lorenzo, none of whom were easy meat, then hold off a late attack from Pedrosa. This was a win at his real home track and it felt like a crucial one.

2 | DANI PEDROSA
Stuck behind Viñales for too long so couldn't quite get to his teammate with a very fast late charge that included the fastest lap of the race. Average qualifying didn't help either.

3 | JORGE LORENZO
Led the race for more laps than he's done before on the Ducati and finished closer to the winner than he's done before. Unlike most of the opposition, used the soft tyre.

4 | MAVERICK VIÑALES
Couldn't use his preferred soft tyre and suffered accordingly early on. By the time he got the medium working the leaders were gone and Mack could only fight his teammate.

5 | VALENTINO ROSSI
Astoundingly competitive just three weeks after his broken leg. Said the now expected rear-tyre drop was what affected him at the end of the race, not his injury. Just another miracle to add to the collection.

6 | ALEIX ESPARGARO
A suberb ride, the closest the Aprilia has been to the winner by a good margin. As low as 12th on the first lap before a great fightback.

7 | ANDREA DOVIZIOSO
Badly affected by the lack of proper testing time caused by the mixed weather conditions. Like his teammate used the soft rear tyre but could only run with the leaders to just over half-distance.

8 | ALVARO BAUTISTA
Top independent Ducati only eight seconds behind Marquez. Went with the soft rear tyre without knowing what would happen after the seventh lap. Used all his experience to produce another good result.

9 | JOHANN ZARCO
Like the other rookies, didn't have the time to get the set-up he needed to get the best out of his bike. Consequently wasn't able to push as he is used to doing.

10 | POL ESPARGARO
A fourth top-ten finish for the KTM but the really impressive thing was the gap to the winner, just 14 seconds.

11 | MIKA KALLIO
KTM's test rider said they had a great test here and he backed his words up by going direct to Q2 and then finishing only three seconds behind Espargaro in his third wild-card ride of the year. Solid proof of the Austrian factory's progress.

12 | ANDREA IANNONE
The result doesn't look good but Andrea was more competitive than recently, especially in qualifying. Like others, couldn't get the tyres working in the race.

RACE LAP CHART

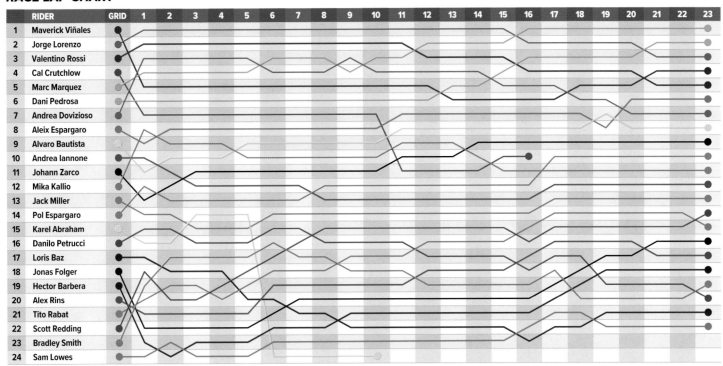

RIDER	GRID	1	2	3	4	5	6	7	8	9	10	11	12	13	14	15	16	17	18	19	20	21	22	23
1 Maverick Viñales																								
2 Jorge Lorenzo																								
3 Valentino Rossi																								
4 Cal Crutchlow																								
5 Marc Marquez																								
6 Dani Pedrosa																								
7 Andrea Dovizioso																								
8 Aleix Espargaro																								
9 Alvaro Bautista																								
10 Andrea Iannone																								
11 Johann Zarco																								
12 Mika Kallio																								
13 Jack Miller																								
14 Pol Espargaro																								
15 Karel Abraham																								
16 Danilo Petrucci																								
17 Loris Baz																								
18 Jonas Folger																								
19 Hector Barbera																								
20 Alex Rins																								
21 Tito Rabat																								
22 Scott Redding																								
23 Bradley Smith																								
24 Sam Lowes																								

RACE CLASSIFICATION AFTER 23 LAPS = 116.771 KM

	RIDER	NAT	TEAM	MACHINE	TIME	+ GAP	TYRES
1	Marc Marquez	SPA	Repsol Honda Team	HONDA	42'06.816		H/H
2	Dani Pedrosa	SPA	Repsol Honda Team	HONDA	42'07.695	0.879	M/M
3	Jorge Lorenzo	SPA	Ducati Team	DUCATI	42'08.844	2.028	M/S
4	Maverick Viñales	SPA	Movistar Yamaha MotoGP	YAMAHA	42'12.072	5.256	M/H
5	Valentino Rossi	ITA	Movistar Yamaha MotoGP	YAMAHA	42'12.698	5.882	M/H
6	Aleix Espargaro	SPA	Aprilia Racing Team Gresini	APRILIA	42'13.778	6.962	M/M
7	Andrea Dovizioso	ITA	Ducati Team	DUCATI	42'14.271	7.455	M/S
8	Alvaro Bautista	SPA	Pull&Bear Aspar Team	DUCATI	42'14.726	7.910	M/S
9	Johann Zarco	FRA	Monster Yamaha Tech 3	YAMAHA	42'19.818	13.002	S/S
10	Pol Espargaro	SPA	Red Bull KTM Factory Racing	KTM	42'20.891	14.075	M/M
11	Mika Kallio	FIN	Red Bull KTM Factory Racing	KTM	42'24.008	17.192	M/M
12	Andrea Iannone	ITA	Team SUZUKI ECSTAR	SUZUKI	42'27.448	20.632	M/M
13	Jack Miller	AUS	EG 0,0 Marc VDS	HONDA	42'30.702	23.886	M/H
14	Scott Redding	GBR	OCTO Pramac Racing	DUCATI	42'32.339	25.523	M/S
15	Tito Rabat	SPA	EG 0,0 Marc VDS	HONDA	42'32.898	26.082	M/S
16	Jonas Folger	GER	Monster Yamaha Tech 3	YAMAHA	42'37.118	30.302	M/M
17	Alex Rins	SPA	Team SUZUKI ECSTAR	SUZUKI	42'38.690	31.874	M/H
18	Hector Barbera	SPA	Reale Avintia Racing	DUCATI	42'38.764	31.948	M/S
19	Bradley Smith	GBR	Red Bull KTM Factory Racing	KTM	42'43.112	36.296	M/S
20	Danilo Petrucci	ITA	OCTO Pramac Racing	DUCATI	42'44.658	37.842	M/M
21	Loris Baz	FRA	Reale Avintia Racing	DUCATI	42'54.415	47.599	M/M
22	Sam Lowes	GBR	Aprilia Racing Team Gresini	APRILIA	42'54.463	47.647	M/M
NC	Cal Crutchlow	GBR	LCR Honda	HONDA	29'26.285	7 laps	H/H
NC	Karel Abraham	CZE	Pull&Bear Aspar Team	DUCATI	19'25.442	13 laps	S/S

CHAMPIONSHIP STANDINGS

	RIDER	NAT	TEAM	POINTS
1	Marc Marquez	SPA	Repsol Honda Team	224
2	Andrea Dovizioso	ITA	Ducati Team	208
3	Maverick Viñales	SPA	Movistar Yamaha MotoGP	196
4	Dani Pedrosa	SPA	Repsol Honda Team	170
5	Valentino Rossi	ITA	Movistar Yamaha MotoGP	168
6	Johann Zarco	FRA	Monster Yamaha Tech 3	117
7	Jorge Lorenzo	SPA	Ducati Team	106
8	Danilo Petrucci	ITA	OCTO Pramac Racing	95
9	Cal Crutchlow	GBR	LCR Honda	92
10	Jonas Folger	GER	Monster Yamaha Tech 3	84
11	Alvaro Bautista	SPA	Pull&Bear Aspar Team	70
12	Jack Miller	AUS	EG 0,0 Marc VDS	56
13	Scott Redding	GBR	OCTO Pramac Racing	56
14	Aleix Espargaro	SPA	Aprilia Racing Team Gresini	53
15	Loris Baz	FRA	Reale Avintia Racing	39
16	Andrea Iannone	ITA	Team SUZUKI ECSTAR	37
17	Pol Espargaro	SPA	Red Bull KTM Factory Racing	37
18	Karel Abraham	CZE	Pull&Bear Aspar Team	28
19	Tito Rabat	SPA	EG 0,0 Marc VDS	28
20	Alex Rins	SPA	Team SUZUKI ECSTAR	27
21	Hector Barbera	SPA	Reale Avintia Racing	23
22	Michele Pirro	ITA	Ducati Team	18
23	Bradley Smith	GBR	Red Bull KTM Factory Racing	14
24	Mika Kallio	FIN	Red Bull KTM Factory Racing	11
25	Sam Lowes	GBR	Aprilia Racing Team Gresini	2
26	Sylvain Guintoli	FRA	Team SUZUKI ECSTAR	1

13 | JACK MILLER
Used the hard rear tyre but couldn't get it working early enough to finish above his qualifying position.

14 | SCOTT REDDING
This doesn't look like a good result until you remember that Scott qualified 22nd and most Ducati riders, especially from the satellite and customer teams, suffered. Satisfied with his race pace not the result.

15 | TITO RABAT
Started a long way back in 21st but was pleased to make enough progress to take the final point.

16 | JONAS FOLGER
A strange crash in FP3 in which he hurt his neck on the edge of the screen set Jonas back, and he never got to grips with the track. The first race he has finished out of the points in MotoGP.

17 | ALEX RINS
Not a good weekend. Used the hard tyre but was never as competitive as we've come to expect. Another rookie with a tale of woe.

18 | HECTOR BARBERA
Like most Ducati riders, never found a setting he was remotely comfortable with. Thought everyone's pace would drop as it did in Catalunya, but was disappointed.

19 | BRADLEY SMITH
Rode a decent race on the soft tyre but compromised by dreadful qualifying. More importantly, didn't lay a glove on Kallio in their internecine struggle for a place in the race team next season.

20 | DANILO PETRUCCI
Never troubled the leaders. Like many Ducati riders the wet Friday sessions and cold Saturday morning ruined his weekend.

21 | LORIS BAZ
Had no grip anywhere, anytime. His only victory was in the last-lap fight with Lowes.

22 | SAM LOWES
Like a lot of the rookies, struggled but at least was able to get to the flag.

DID NOT FINISH

CAL CRUTCHLOW
Chose the hard front tyre, which was a risk. Ran off-track then crashed mainly due to problems with his brake lever, which he could not adjust as he still had his left index finger in a cast to protect the recently repaired ligament.

KAREL ABRAHAM
Crashed at the Corkscrew when he lost the front early on.

HURRICANE DOVI

Andrea Dovizioso wins a thrilling last lap battle to reduce Marc Marquez's championship lead. Petrucci third, the Yamahas nowhere.

It is so rare to get a head-to-head race between the best two men, currently, in the world with no interference from outside factors like injuries, machinery or tyres. It is rarer still when this encounter happens at a crucial stage of the championship, and even rarer when it is decided by a last lap of such epic proportions that even old hands struggle to recall its equal.

The Japanese Grand Prix of 2017 was such an event, won by Andrea Dovizioso with an impossibly precise manoeuvre down into one of the most difficult corners of the year in the worst weather you can run a motorcycle race in. The man he beat was Marc Marquez, who's started the final lap with a small but significant lead. Everything changed at Turn 8 when Marc got on the gas too hard, too early and the rear stepped out. By his standards it was a minor indiscretion but it was enough to give Dovi a chance; a perfect entry onto the back straight put him in position to outbrake Marc at Turn 11. This is a downhill, off-camber, 90-degree right at the end of the fastest straight that demands total precision or your exit speed is destroyed. Under that pressure, in those conditions, Dovi made the move stick, which should have been it, but Marc found a way to attack around the outside in the next left. This was the tactic that won Toni Elias the 250cc race in 2002 when he mugged Marco Melandri and a much less dangerous move than

'I KNEW THAT HE WAS GOING TO ATTACK ME IN THE FINAL TWO CORNERS BUT I WAS PREPARED. IT WAS ABSOLUTELY VITAL TO WIN HERE'

ANDREA DOVIZIOSO

the one Marc tried in Austria. Andrea was calm enough to let Marc make his move round the outside on the left hander that is the first part of the esses that end the lap and then use the right line to get to the line first by a quarter of a second. Thus Marc's championship lead was reduced to 11 points with three races left.

All of this took place in the heavy rain that affected every session of the meeting. It would have been one of the great races in any conditions, at the very least it was one of the greatest wet-weather races and deserves to be ranked with the very best we've seen in the MotoGP era. It was that good. It also confirmed Danilo Petrucci's reputation as a threat any time it rains. He was one of the few to go with the extra-soft rear tyre and he did have to restrain his natural instincts at times. However, the tyre was not to blame for his position. That, said Danilo, was down to the two usual problems. "Dovi and Marc."

The pleasant surprise of the weekend was the form of the Suzukis in fourth and fifth places, particularly the combativeness of Andrea Iannone. Andrea and Alex Rins both used a new aero fairing, dubbed "the moustache" by the team and for the first time both went straight to the final qualifying session. In the race they had to deal with Zarco's Yamaha before Iannone asserted his authority. Johann Zarco was Yamaha's only success of the weekend, and that was mainly because he started from pole. Tyre wear, Yamaha's perpetual bugbear, hit him hard in the final laps and he was passed by not just the Suzukis but Lorenzo's Ducati and Espargaro's Aprilia. Zarco still beat the factory bike of Viñales, who seemed happy to finish in the top ten. As for Valentino Rossi, he was an early crasher, making it two big get-offs in the weekend. Valentino pointedly observed that he was trying to keep up with the Aprilia when he crashed. Any chance of Yamaha winning the title disappeared.

Jorge Lorenzo had one of those curious races where he leads then drops back rapidly only to charge again in the final laps. His drop was precipitated by Zarco pushing him off track, it was a move not too far removed from the one Zarco put on Rossi in Texas and Jorge was as unamused as Valentino. This time Jorge's

MAIN One of the finest head-to-head races between the championship contenders you are likely to see

BELOW, LEFT-RIGHT Johann Zarco started from pole but lost a lot of places when his tyre went off; Jorge Lorenzo led as usual but got lost in the middle of the race after a sideswipe from Zarco; Andrea Iannone with new fairing and very cool retro helmet design had his best race for Suzuki

RIGHT Danilo Petrucci heading for third, with no complaints

MAIN | *Aleix Espargaro and Aprilia's new fairing had a slightly disappointing race*

RIGHT, TOP-BOTTOM | *As usual test rider Katsuyuki Nakasuga was a Yamaha wild card; Loris Baz is always fast in the wet, Motegi was no exception; KTM had no data for the circuit and precious little for wet conditions so Pol's 11th place wasn't a disaster*

FAR RIGHT | *Sam Lowes had a solid weekend and scored points for the second time*

WET, WET, WET

The Japanese Grand Prix of 2017 was the wettest anyone could remember. It rained in every session from the first free practice for Moto3 on Friday morning right through to the MotoGP race on Sunday afternoon. The only significant period of dry tarmac came at the end of Moto2 qualifying when the whole field was able to use slicks for at least half-a-dozen laps at the end of the session.

Only two sets of slicks were used in MotoGP, one by Valentino Rossi and one by Marc Marquez. Rossi decided to gamble hugely

in Q2 after crashing his preferred bike in FP4 but found himself 15 seconds off the pace. Marquez set a stunning mark then decided to also try slicks on his second run, with equally dire results plus the loss of pole position. He said he did it because Rossi did then later claimed he had learnt a lot about slicks on a drying track and said the front row had been his objective anyway. It is unlikely Honda's top management, present in force as usual at their track, agreed.

Michelin withdrew the soft front tyre because of fears about its longevity on drying tarmac. They needn't have worried, the rain never stopped and they had to supply an extra set of wet

charge took him three places back up the order in six laps while equalling or bettering the leading pair's lap times. Aprilia and KTM had encouraging races, or rather they had great qualifying then races hindered by lack of data. The KTMs had never turned a wheel on the Twin Ring circuit before and also had precious little wet-weather track time anywhere. There was also the matter of Michelin withdrawing the soft front-tyre option before the race on safety grounds, which particularly affected the Aspar Ducati riders.

Before the first practice session Andrea Dovizioso and Marc Marquez agreed that the Ducati had an advantage at Motegi, they felt the same way afterwards as well. Dovi was noticeably upbeat beforehand; however, saying that you have to beat Marquez and doing it are two very different things. Andrea's celebrations after the race were much less muted than usual; he knew what he had just done, something very few can claim, he had beaten Marc Marquez in a straight fight. Twice. He did admit that he didn't think he had the speed but still found the steel to take Turn 10 perfectly which gave him the speed onto the straight to execute that impossibly accurate pass and then calmly ignore the sort of last-corner attack that only Marc Marquez can conjure up. And it demonstrated Andrea Dovizioso's newly-found total faith in his own abilities. In short, it was as good a race as you could hope to see.

tyres as per regulations for events where treaded tyres are used every session.

So was this the wettest race ever? There certainly hasn't been a race in the MotoGP era where every session was wet. Even the thoroughly soaking Pacific GP of 2009 at Motegi was dry for the first free-practice session. Isle of Man TTs lasted too long to be permanently wet, records for various GPs at such notoriously precipitation-prone places as Ulster, Nürburgring and Spa do not prove they suffered like Motegi this year. So unless anyone can prove otherwise this was the only totally wet Grand Prix in history.

ROUND 15 | JAPAN

RACE RESULTS

WINNER | *ANDREA DOVIZIOSO*

CIRCUIT LENGTH | *4.8 KM* | *2.98 MILES*

NO. OF LAPS | *24*

RACE DISTANCE | *115.2 KM* | *71.5 MILES*

CIRCUIT RECORD LAP | *1'45.350* | *164.0 KM/H*
JORGE LORENZO (2014)

CIRCUIT BEST LAP | *1'43.790* | *166.5 KM/H*
JORGE LORENZO (2015)

RACE CONDITION | *WET*

AIR | *14°C*

HUMIDITY | *97%*

GROUND | *15°C*

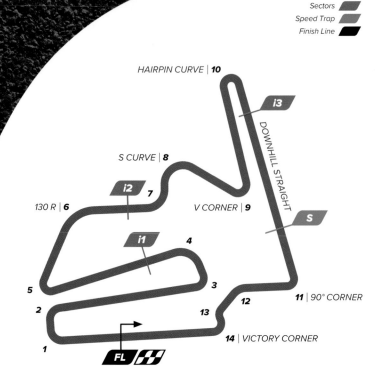

Sectors
Speed Trap
Finish Line

HAIRPIN CURVE | 10
i3
DOWNHILL STRAIGHT
S CURVE | 8
i2 7
130 R | 6
V CORNER | 9
S
i1
4
5
3
2
12
11 | 90° CORNER
13
1
14 | VICTORY CORNER
FL

TISSOT | *motoGP*
SWISS WATCHES SINCE 1853

OFFICIAL TIMEKEEPER

MICHELIN | *motoGP*

OFFICIAL MotoGP™ CLASS TYRE

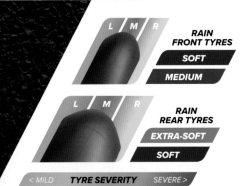

L M R
RAIN FRONT TYRES
SOFT
MEDIUM

L M R
RAIN REAR TYRES
EXTRA-SOFT
SOFT

< MILD   **TYRE SEVERITY**   SEVERE >

QUALIFYING RESULTS

	RIDER	NAT	TEAM	MACHINE	QP/TIME		GAP 1ST/PREV	
1	Johann Zarco	FRA	Monster Yamaha Tech 3	YAMAHA	Q2	1'53.469	297.7	
2	Danilo Petrucci	ITA	OCTO Pramac Racing	DUCATI	Q2	1'53.787	0.318	0.318
3	Marc Marquez	SPA	Repsol Honda Team	HONDA	Q2	1'53.903	0.434	0.116
4	Aleix Espargaro	SPA	Aprilia Racing Team Gresini	APRILIA	Q2	1'53.947	0.478	0.044
5	Jorge Lorenzo	SPA	Ducati Team	DUCATI	Q2	1'54.235	0.766	0.288
6	Dani Pedrosa	SPA	Repsol Honda Team	HONDA	Q2	1'54.342	0.873	0.107
7	Bradley Smith**	GBR	Red Bull KTM Factory Racing	KTM	Q2	1'54.872	1.403	0.530
8	Pol Espargaro**	SPA	Red Bull KTM Factory Racing	KTM	Q2	1'54.906	1.437	0.034
9	Andrea Dovizioso	ITA	Ducati Team	DUCATI	Q2	1'55.064	1.595	0.158
10	Alex Rins	SPA	Team SUZUKI ECSTAR	SUZUKI	Q2	1'55.483	2.014	0.419
11	Andrea Iannone	ITA	Team SUZUKI ECSTAR	SUZUKI	Q2	1'55.617	2.148	0.134
12	Valentino Rossi	ITA	Movistar Yamaha MotoGP	YAMAHA	Q2	1'57.786	4.317	2.169
13	Loris Baz	FRA	Reale Avintia Racing	DUCATI	Q1	1'55.862	*0.604	0.018
14	Maverick Viñales	SPA	Movistar Yamaha MotoGP	YAMAHA	Q1	1'55.916	*0.658	0.054
15	Cal Crutchlow	GBR	LCR Honda	HONDA	Q1	1'55.952	*0.694	0.036
16	Alvaro Bautista	SPA	Pull&Bear Aspar Team	DUCATI	Q1	1'56.292	1.034	0.340
17	Hector Barbera	SPA	Reale Avintia Racing	DUCATI	Q1	1'56.668	*1.410	0.376
18	Sam Lowes	GBR	Aprilia Racing Team Gresini	APRILIA	Q1	1'56.771	*1.513	0.103
19	Tito Rabat	SPA	EG 0,0 Marc VDS	HONDA	Q1	1'56.903	*1.645	0.132
20	Karel Abraham	CZE	Pull&Bear Aspar Team	DUCATI	Q1	1'57.144	*1.886	0.241
21	Hiroshi Aoyama	JPN	EG 0,0 Marc VDS	HONDA	Q1	1'57.157	*1.899	0.013
22	Scott Redding	GBR	OCTO Pramac Racing	DUCATI	Q1	1'57.787	*2.529	0.630
23	Katsuyuki Nakasuga	JPN	Yamalube Yamaha Factory Racing	YAMAHA	Q1	1'57.861	*2.603	0.074
24	Kohta Nozane	JPN	Monster Yamaha Tech 3	YAMAHA	Q1	2'01.730	*6.472	3.869

* Gap to the fastest rider in the Q1 session
** Went forward from Q1 to Q2

1 ANDREA DOVIZIOSO
Utterly brilliant. Had to beat Marquez at this track where the Ducati has an advantage and won another last-lap showdown with wonderfully precise riding and the coolest of cool heads in the worst possible conditions. Reduced Marquez's lead to 11 points.

2 MARC MARQUEZ
Looked like he had it won until a small mistake half way round the last lap put Dovi in range for his last-gasp attack. Conceded that the Italian always had the advantage at Motegi and happy to limit the damage to his championship lead. It was his 100th podium; Marc is the youngest rider to reach that mark.

3 DANILO PETRUCCI
Gambled on the extra-soft rear tyre and scored his fourth podium of the year. For once there were no what-ifs, this was the best Danilo could have done.

4 ANDREA IANNONE
His best result for Suzuki. Used the new 'moustache' aero fairing to good effect. Involved in a great dice with Zarco and his teammate Rins. Looked to have lost out but asserted his authority with forceful final laps.

5 ALEX RINS
Contributed to Suzuki's great weekend with his best result in MotoGP despite being pushed back to 15th at the first corner. Had to give best to his teammate, but a deeply impressive performance.

6 JORGE LORENZO
Led the first lap but dropped back after contact with Zarco. Lost feel with the rear and dropped to ninth then charged over the last six laps, making three passes.

7 ALEIX ESPARGARO
It's a measure of Aprilia's progress that seventh was a disappointment to rider and team. Suffered spin that hadn't shown itself even in warm up.

8 JOHANN ZARCO
Started from pole and settled into fourth place trying to conserve his tyre but ran out of grip six laps from the flag and lost four places.

9 MAVERICK VIÑALES
How bad were things at Yamaha? Maverick didn't expect to finish this high. Yamaha's usual bugbear of rear grip was the problem, Mack could neither catch Aleix Espargaro early on or hold off Lorenzo in the closing stages.

10 LORIS BAZ
Couldn't see through the spray early on but when he could attack he made good progress. Improved massively on his Friday times.

11 POL ESPARGARO
Couldn't quite live up to the promise of qualifying when both KTMs went through to Q2, but considering the bike had never set a wheel on Motegi before and how little data the team have for wet conditions this was another good result.

12 KATSUYUKI NAKASUGA
Yamaha's veteran test rider entered, as usual, as a wild card and as usual did a professional job. And as usual he most likely was testing parts for 2018.

RACE LAP CHART

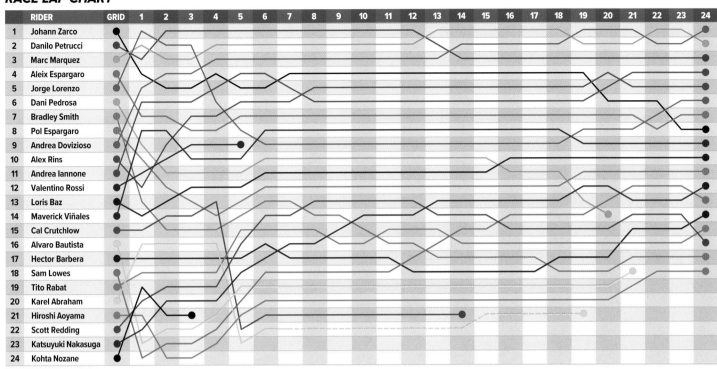

----- Dashed line: Lapped rider

	RIDER	GRID	1	2	3	4	5	6	7	8	9	10	11	12	13	14	15	16	17	18	19	20	21	22	23	24
1	Johann Zarco																										
2	Danilo Petrucci																										
3	Marc Marquez																										
4	Aleix Espargaro																										
5	Jorge Lorenzo																										
6	Dani Pedrosa																										
7	Bradley Smith																										
8	Pol Espargaro																										
9	Andrea Dovizioso																										
10	Alex Rins																										
11	Andrea Iannone																										
12	Valentino Rossi																										
13	Loris Baz																										
14	Maverick Viñales																										
15	Cal Crutchlow																										
16	Alvaro Bautista																										
17	Hector Barbera																										
18	Sam Lowes																										
19	Tito Rabat																										
20	Karel Abraham																										
21	Hiroshi Aoyama																										
22	Scott Redding																										
23	Katsuyuki Nakasuga																										
24	Kohta Nozane																										

RACE CLASSIFICATION AFTER 24 LAPS = 115.224 KM

	RIDER	NAT	TEAM	MACHINE	TIME	+ GAP	TYRES
1	Andrea Dovizioso	ITA	Ducati Team	DUCATI	47'14.236		RM/RS
2	Marc Marquez	SPA	Repsol Honda Team	HONDA	47'14.485	0.249	RM/RS
3	Danilo Petrucci	ITA	OCTO Pramac Racing	DUCATI	47'24.793	10.557	RE-S/RS
4	Andrea Iannone	ITA	Team SUZUKI ECSTAR	SUZUKI	47'33.081	18.845	RM/RS
5	Alex Rins	SPA	Team SUZUKI ECSTAR	SUZUKI	47'37.218	22.982	RM/RS
6	Jorge Lorenzo	SPA	Ducati Team	DUCATI	47'38.700	24.464	RM/RS
7	Aleix Espargaro	SPA	Aprilia Racing Team Gresini	APRILIA	47'42.246	28.010	RM/RS
8	Johann Zarco	FRA	Monster Yamaha Tech 3	YAMAHA	47'43.711	29.475	RM/RS
9	Maverick Viñales	SPA	Movistar Yamaha MotoGP	YAMAHA	47'50.811	36.575	RM/RS
10	Loris Baz	FRA	Reale Avintia Racing	UCATI	48'02.742	48.506	RM/RS
11	Pol Espargaro	SPA	Red Bull KTM Factory Racing	KTM	48'10.593	56.357	RE-S/RS
12	Katsuyuki Nakasuga	JPN	Yamalube Yamaha Factory Racing	YAMAHA	48'14.417	60.181	RM/RS
13	Sam Lowes	GBR	Aprilia Racing Team Gresini	APRILIA	48'15.216	60.980	RM/RS
14	Hector Barbera	SPA	Reale Avintia Racing	DUCATI	48'17.354	63.118	RM/RS
15	Tito Rabat	SPA	EG 0,0 Marc VDS	HONDA	48'17.750	63.514	RM/RS
16	Scott Redding	GBR	OCTO Pramac Racing	DUCATI	48'18.398	64.162	RM/RS
17	Bradley Smith	GBR	Red Bull KTM Factory Racing	KTM	48'20.507	66.271	RE-S/RS
18	Hiroshi Aoyama	JPN	EG 0,0 Marc VDS	HONDA	48'27.486	73.250	RM/RS
NC	Alvaro Bautista	SPA	Pull&Bear Aspar Team	DUCATI	42'23.775	3 laps	RE-S/RS
NC	Dani Pedrosa	SPA	Repsol Honda Team	HONDA	40'17.272	4 laps	RE-S/RS
NC	Karel Abraham	CZE	Pull&Bear Aspar Team	DUCATI	40'52.411	5 laps	RE-S/RS
NC	Cal Crutchlow	GBR	LCR Honda	HONDA	29'18.059	10 laps	RM/RS
NC	Valentino Rossi	ITA	Movistar Yamaha MotoGP	YAMAHA	10'08.415	19 laps	RM/RS
NC	Kohta Nozane	JPN	Monster Yamaha Tech 3	YAMAHA	6'16.600	21 laps	RM/RS

*Michelin wet tyre options
FRONT : Rain Soft / Rain Medium   **REAR** : Rain Extra-Soft / Rain Soft

CHAMPIONSHIP STANDINGS

	RIDER	NAT	TEAM	POINTS
1	Marc Marquez	SPA	Repsol Honda Team	244
2	Andrea Dovizioso	ITA	Ducati Team	233
3	Maverick Viñales	SPA	Movistar Yamaha MotoGP	203
4	Dani Pedrosa	SPA	Repsol Honda Team	170
5	Valentino Rossi	ITA	Movistar Yamaha MotoGP	168
6	Johann Zarco	FRA	Monster Yamaha Tech 3	125
7	Jorge Lorenzo	SPA	Ducati Team	116
8	Danilo Petrucci	ITA	OCTO Pramac Racing	111
9	Cal Crutchlow	GBR	LCR Honda	92
10	Jonas Folger	GER	Monster Yamaha Tech 3	84
11	Alvaro Bautista	SPA	Pull&Bear Aspar Team	70
12	Aleix Espargaro	SPA	Aprilia Racing Team Gresini	62
13	Jack Miller	AUS	EG 0,0 Marc VDS	56
14	Scott Redding	GBR	OCTO Pramac Racing	56
15	Andrea Iannone	ITA	Team SUZUKI ECSTAR	50
16	Loris Baz	FRA	Reale Avintia Racing	45
17	Pol Espargaro	SPA	Red Bull KTM Factory Racing	42
18	Alex Rins	SPA	Team SUZUKI ECSTAR	38
19	Tito Rabat	SPA	EG 0,0 Marc VDS	29
20	Karel Abraham	CZE	Pull&Bear Aspar Team	28
21	Hector Barbera	SPA	Reale Avintia Racing	25
22	Michele Pirro	ITA	Ducati Team	18
23	Bradley Smith	GBR	Red Bull KTM Factory Racing	14
24	Mika Kallio	FIN	Red Bull KTM Factory Racing	11
25	Sam Lowes	GBR	Aprilia Racing Team Gresini	5
26	Katsuyuki Nakasuga	JPN	Yamalube Yamaha Factory Racing	4
27	Sylvain Guintoli	FRA	Team SUZUKI ECSTAR	1

13 | SAM LOWES
Competitive all weekend. A solid race for his second points-scoring finish of the year.

14 | HECTOR BARBERA
Puzzled that he couldn't find grip on a track which is usually very grippy in the wet. Although he expected better, relieved to get a couple of points.

15 | TITO RABAT
Marooned in the spray early on then diced with Nakasuga and Redding, taking the final point on the last lap.

16 | SCOTT REDDING
Another awful weekend in conditions that should have favoured Scott. Never improved on FP1.

17 | BRADLEY SMITH
The highlight of the weekend was qualifying seventh after both KTMs went from Q1 to Q2. A small crash in warm-up set him on edge for the start and Bradley did not have the race he was hoping for. Like his teammate, lack of data was a problem.

18 | HIROSHI AOYAMA
Thought he had a chance in the conditions but lack of grip and an early coming together ruined his race.

DID NOT FINISH

ALVARO BAUTISTA
Unhappy to be prevented from using the soft front. Lost all his reference from Friday and Saturday. Crashed four laps from the flag.

DANI PEDROSA
His extra-soft rear tyre span so much he couldn't stay in a points-scoring position, so Dani pulled in.

KAREL ABRAHAM
Had an off-throttle highside in the final left hander on Lap 5. Changed bikes but then retired.

CAL CRUTCHLOW
A thoroughly miserable weekend. Qualified 15th, crashed on Lap 5 but managed to get back to the pits and go out on his spare bike only to crash that too.

VALENTINO ROSSI
Apart from a flash of brilliance in FP3 with the extra-soft rear this was a weekend in search of rear grip. Crashed while trying to keep pace with Aleix Espargaro, his second big crash of the weekend. No longer mathematically able to win title.

KOHTA NOZANE
Yamaha's young test rider impressed. Raced despite breaking a bone in his right hand in FP4 and slid off early on.

DID NOT RACE

JONAS FOLGER
Suffering from Epstein-Barr virus and liable to be out for several races. Replaced by Nozane.

JACK MILLER
Broke his leg in a trials bike accident, recovering at home. Replaced by Aoyama.

MotoGP SEASON REVIEW | 165

TAKE NO PRISONERS

Marc Marquez wins after a magnificent no-holds-barred mass brawl. Rossi pips Viñales and Zarco for second, Dovizioso in purgatory.

This was the race that had everything. Factory bikes and satellite bikes in a group fight, a local hero, more overtaking moves than you could count, some serious contact, and no crashes from the eight-man leading group. They were Marquez, Rossi, Viñales, Zarco, Iannone, Crutchlow, Miller and Rins, and they overtook each other at least 70 times on probably the best circuit in the world for motorcycle racing. It was even better than the 2015 race and right up there with the two-stroke epic of 2000, all of which featured Valentino Rossi.

This time he reminded us what he can do on the great old circuits he loves but even Valentino's ability to turn back the years couldn't deny Marc Marquez. Somehow, when it seemed no-one could lead for more than a couple of corners he fashioned a breakaway that left the others squabbling over second place. There is always an element of luck in a group fight, but Marc seems to make his own.

He was also helped by disarray at Ducati and extended his championship lead to what looked like a decisive 33 points. Andrea Dovizioso, the only man with a realistic chance of stopping Marquez, had a nightmare. A crash in FP4 meant his qualifying was disrupted so he started 11th, and on the second lap of the

ABOVE, LEFT-RIGHT Alex Rins had his best dry race in MotoGP; Aussie veteran Broc Parkes stood in for Jonas Folger; What the crowd wanted - Jack Miller leads the early laps

MAIN The most thrilling sight in racing, the leaders fly into Doohan's in close formation

RIGHT Valentino Rossi reminded everyone what he can do on the great tracks he loves so much

race he ran wide at Doohan's trying to get to the leading group. That was effectively the end of Dovi's race and more than likely his championship chances. He ended up fighting over 11th place with Scott Redding and Dani Pedrosa, losing out to both of them, a victim of Ducati's perennial mid-corner turning problems which are massively amplified by Phillip Island's sweeping curves.

Marc Marquez wanted a quiet race to concentrate on the championship. That hope evaporated when Zarco smacked into him on the third lap after which Marc smacked into Rossi, Zarco smacked into most people and Iannone had a good go too in search of his first Suzuki podium. Before they could fight for the lead the gang had to dispense with Jack Miller who delighted the hard-core Aussie crowd by returning to action one day sooner than Rossi had done after breaking his tibia and fibula in a training accident. He led the first four laps but gave his tyres too much of a hard time. They never quite got rid of him though. Nor Andrea Iannone who proved that his and Suzuki's Motegi form was not a flash in a very wet pan. The ever more impressive Alex Rins again backed his teammate up although the best he could do was stay on the back of the group.

Valentino Rossi matched his young rivals blow for blow and gave every impression of having enjoyed the experience: "If this. Is the game, I am ready." And as for the fairing bashing: "You need to be a little more stupid, more aggressive than they are." A little later, in his press debrief he wasn't quite so phlegmatic, particularly about Zarco and Iannone who, as in 2015, was the one to dash Valentino's hopes. This time with an outbraking move that let Marquez escape and ended Valentino's chance of winning.

After that the race was Marc's to loose. The three Yamahas pulled away to fight for the remaining podium positions with Valentino using all his cunning and experience to beat Viñales to the line by a few thousandths of a second with Zarco the same distance further back. The French rookie, it is difficult to remember that this is his first year in MotoGP, was positively mystical about the race. "I lived things today I never thought I would live in my life." That and other remarks about having to

> ## 'I WAS THINKING I HAD TO STAY CALM AND MANAGE THE TYRES, BUT THEN ZARCO HIT ME AND I REALISED IT WAS GOING TO BE A BATTLE'
> *MARC MARQUEZ*

FROM TOP LEFT, CLOCKWISE | *The KTMs were this far apart for the whole race; The Yamahas sandwich Marquez coming out of Siberia; Marc Marquez had more than one reason to smile; The battle for tenth - more significant than it seemed*

MAIN | *Marc Marquez's late-race push opened up this small but vital lead*

FIVE MORE YEARS

Michelin and Dorna announced at Phillip Island that the French tyre manufacturer will continue as the spec-tyre supplier to MotoGP for at least another five years. That will take the agreement through to the end of the 2023 and give the teams the stability they crave. Dorna CEO Carmelo Ezpeleta duly said nice things about Michelin's willingness to respond in a flexible manner to such things as the need for three different rear tyre compounds, which he cited as one of the major reasons

be there at 300kph to understand and a slightly more cutting comment about obviously not being the only aggressive one out there were delivered in a quiet monotone with a faraway look. He really is bike racing's warrior monk; fast like Viñales, feared like Iannone. He didn't make the podium but he did wrap up the Rookie of the Year title.

Behind the enthralling fight that eventually spat out Crutchlow, Miller and the Suzukis, the KTMs fought each other well clear of the remaining factory and satellite bikes for their first double top-ten finish. Another milestone for the Austrian factory.

Despite many attempts to crash, the leaders all stayed on, the only casualty of the race was Aleix Espargaro who was with the leaders when he slid off at the first corner and broke his hand. It was enough to put him out of the next race. The only other low point was the booing of Marquez by some of the fans gathered under the podium after the usual, and much appreciated, controlled track invasion. I believe the local term for such people is 'bogans.'

In the euphoria following if not the best then certainly the most entertaining race in years it was easy to ignore the ramifications of the result. Yet again Marc Marquez proved that he can win any type of race and even control such an unruly gang fight. More than once, he could be seen taking a long look behind him to check on the whereabouts of Dovizioso. The answer was just where he wanted him, well behind and out of the top-ten. So Marc pushed really hard, he said, for three or four laps. Just like that he broke clear of the fight, a feat that had looked impossible for the previous 20 laps, and secured all the points. Andrea Dovizioso then got mugged on the line by Marc's teammate Dani Pedrosa as well as fellow Ducati rider Scott Redding, who declined to follow his team's instruction to let Dovi back past. A bad weekend can always get worse.

FROM TOP LEFT, CLOCKWISE | *The KTMs were this far apart for the whole race; The Yamahas sandwich Marquez coming out of Siberia; Marc Marquez had more than one reason to smile; The battle for tenth - more significant than it seemed*

MAIN | *Marc Marquez's late-race push opened up this small but vital lead*

the championship was now so competitive and had so many different race winners.

Michelin's director of motorsport, Pascal Couasnon, identified two main reason the company goes racing. There is of course the desire to associate the brand with racing, but there is also technology transfer. Some tread-compounds developed at MotoGP will be in commercially available racing tyres from next year and were used at the Bol d'Or this year. Lessons learnt on track are already being applied to road tyres and the technology

will trickle down over the next two years. As qualifying tyres have no relevance to these areas, Michelin have no interest in bringing them back.

Interestingly, both Ezpeleta and Couasnon mentioned that quality control is the area they are looking for improvements in - but that doesn't mean that every time a rider complains about a tyre he's right.

Michelin image courtesy of www.michelinmotorsport.com

ROUND 16 | AUSTRALIA

Sectors
Speed Trap
Finish Line

RACE RESULTS

WINNER | MARC MARQUEZ

CIRCUIT LENGTH | ?? KM ?? MILES

NO. OF LAPS | 27

RACE DISTANCE | 120.1 KM 74.5 MILES

CIRCUIT RECORD LAP | 1'28.108 181.7 KM/H
MARC MARQUEZ (2013)

CIRCUIT BEST LAP | 1'27.899 182.1 KM/H
JORGE LORENZO (2013)

RACE CONDITION | DRY

AIR | 16°C

HUMIDITY | 79%

GROUND | 29°C

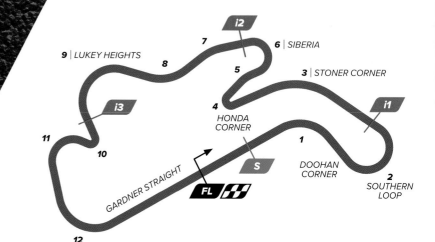

9 | LUKEY HEIGHTS
i2
7
6 | SIBERIA
8
5
3 | STONER CORNER
i3
4
HONDA CORNER
i1
11
10
1
DOOHAN CORNER
2 SOUTHERN LOOP
S
GARDNER STRAIGHT
FL
12

TISSOT
SWISS WATCHES SINCE 1853 | motoGP™
OFFICIAL TIMEKEEPER

MICHELIN | motoGP™
OFFICIAL MotoGP™ CLASS TYRE

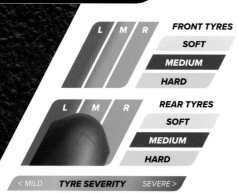

L M R
FRONT TYRES
SOFT
MEDIUM
HARD

L M R
REAR TYRES
SOFT
MEDIUM
HARD

< MILD **TYRE SEVERITY** SEVERE >

QUALIFYING RESULTS

	RIDER	NAT	TEAM	MACHINE	QP/TIME	GAP 1ST/PREV	
1	Marc Marquez	SPA	Repsol Honda Team	HONDA	Q2 1'28.386		
2	Maverick Viñales	SPA	Movistar Yamaha MotoGP	YAMAHA	Q2 1'28.719	0.333	0.333
3	Johann Zarco	FRA	Monster Yamaha Tech 3	YAMAHA	Q2 1'28.744	0.358	0.025
4	Andrea Iannone	ITA	Team SUZUKI ECSTAR	SUZUKI	Q2 1'28.937	0.551	0.193
5	Jack Miller	AUS	EG 0,0 Marc VDS	HONDA	Q2 1'28.964	0.578	0.027
6	Pol Espargaro	SPA	Red Bull KTM Factory Racing	KTM	Q2 1'29.030	0.644	0.066
7	Valentino Rossi**	ITA	Movistar Yamaha MotoGP	YAMAHA	Q2 1'29.203	0.817	0.173
8	Aleix Espargaro	SPA	Aprilia Racing Team Gresini	APRILIA	Q2 1'29.271	0.885	0.068
9	Bradley Smith**	GBR	Red Bull KTM Factory Racing	KTM	Q2 1'29.321	0.935	0.050
10	Cal Crutchlow	GBR	LCR Honda	HONDA	Q2 1'29.429	1.043	0.108
11	Andrea Dovizioso	ITA	Ducati Team	DUCATI	Q2 1'29.496	1.110	0.067
12	Dani Pedrosa	SPA	Repsol Honda Team	HONDA	Q2 1'29.546	1.160	0.050
13	Alex Rins	SPA	Team SUZUKI ECSTAR	SUZUKI	Q1 1'29.824	*0.478	0.119
14	Tito Rabat	SPA	EG 0,0 Marc VDS	HONDA	Q1 1'29.847	*0.501	0.023
15	Karel Abraham	CZE	Pull&Bear Aspar Team	DUCATI	Q1 1'29.961	*0.615	0.114
16	Jorge Lorenzo	SPA	Ducati Team	DUCATI	Q1 1'30.085	*0.739	0.124
17	Loris Baz	FRA	Reale Avintia Racing	DUCATI	Q1 1'30.224	*0.878	0.139
18	Danilo Petrucci	ITA	OCTO Pramac Racing	DUCATI	Q1 1'30.471	*1.125	0.247
19	Hector Barbera	SPA	Reale Avintia Racing	DUCATI	Q1 1'30.543	*1.197	0.072
20	Scott Redding	GBR	OCTO Pramac Racing	DUCATI	Q1 1'30.806	*1.460	0.263
21	Broc Parkes	AUS	Monster Yamaha Tech 3	YAMAHA	Q1 1'30.889	*1.543	0.083
22	Alvaro Bautista	SPA	Pull&Bear Aspar Team	DUCATI	Q1 1'30.900	*1.554	0.011
23	Sam Lowes	GBR	Aprilia Racing Team Gresini	APRILIA	Q1 1'31.158	*1.812	0.258

Gap to the fastest rider in the Q1 session
**Went forward from Q1 to Q2*

1 | MARC MARQUEZ
Banged fairings with everyone before making a break with five laps to go for his sixth win of the year and his ninth podium in the last ten races. More importantly, he took advantage of Doivizioso's troubles to open up a lead of 33 points with only 50 left on the table.

2 | VALENTINO ROSSI
Finished with rubber marks on his leathers and his bike after being at the centre of the action for the entire race, culminating in outfoxing Zarco and Vinales on the last lap. Couldn't

match Marquez but regained fourth in the points table.

3 | MAVERICK VIÑALES
With he leaders all race. Had the same plan as Marquez, to push over the last five laps, but was thwarted by running wide at Turn 1 and bouncing off Zarco and Iannone. After that is was an all-Yamaha fight for the lower two steps of the podium. Used the soft rear tyre, unlike his teammate.

4 | JOHANN ZARCO
Said he experienced things he never thought he would during the race. His soft tyres lasted the race despite the level of aggression he showed - which as usual was extremely high, and only missed out on a podium by one-hundredth of a second.

5 | CAL CRUTCHLOW
Nearly didn't race after a massive crash in warm up. With the lead group after half-a-dozen laps, then stayed with them, picking off Miller as he tired and Iannone on the last lap. A gutsy race to a better result than seemed possible.

6 | ANDREA IANNONE
Involved with the leaders all race and a big part of the gloves-off fight. Looked on for a podium finish until the final few las when he lost some feel. Delighted with the race, disappointed with the finishing position.

7 | JACK MILLER
Just 23 days after breaking his leg, Jack led the opening laps of his home GP to the delight of the fans. That early effort affected his rear grip in the second half of the race he couldn't push as hard, but still a magnificent effort.

8 | ALEX RINS
A great first corner put him on the back of the leading group, where he stayed all race. Couldn't get involved in the fight but ran the leaders' pace. Lost rear grip over the final laps and dropped back without losing a place.

9 | POL ESPARGARO
Went straight to Q2, had a superb start but got dropped by the lead group quite rapidly and settled into a race with his teammate. Another impressive result.

10 | BRADLEY SMITH
Looked much more like his old self and only beaten by a fraction of a second by his teammate. Got to Q2 via Q1 for the second race running.

11 | SCOTT REDDING
Top Ducati after qualifying 20th and not starting well. But he had good pace front he start and made steady progress through the field before becoming involve in a great fight with Pedrosa and Dovizioso. If there were any team orders, Scott took no notice and won that fight.

RACE LAP CHART

	RIDER	GRID	1	2	3	4	5	6	7	8	9	10	11	12	13	14	15	16	17	18	19	20	21	22	23	24	25	26	27
1	Marc Marquez																												
2	Maverick Viñales																												
3	Johann Zarco																												
4	Andrea Iannone																												
5	Jack Miller																												
6	Pol Espargaro																												
7	Valentino Rossi																												
8	Aleix Espargaro																												
9	Bradley Smith																												
10	Cal Crutchlow																												
11	Andrea Dovizioso																												
12	Dani Pedrosa																												
13	Alex Rins																												
14	Tito Rabat																												
15	Karel Abraham																												
16	Jorge Lorenzo																												
17	Loris Baz																												
18	Danilo Petrucci																												
19	Hector Barbera																												
20	Scott Redding																												
21	Broc Parkes																												
22	Alvaro Bautista																												
23	Sam Lowes																												

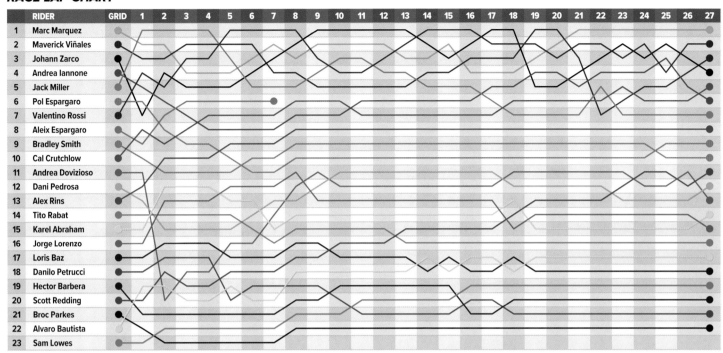

RACE CLASSIFICATION AFTER 27 LAPS = 120.096 KM

	RIDER	NAT	TEAM	MACHINE	TIME	+ GAP	TYRES
1	Marc Marquez	SPA	Repsol Honda Team	HONDA	40'49.772		M/S
2	Valentino Rossi	ITA	Movistar Yamaha MotoGP	YAMAHA	40'51.571	1.799	M/S
3	Maverick Viñales	SPA	Movistar Yamaha MotoGP	YAMAHA	40'51.598	1.826	M/M
4	Johann Zarco	FRA	Monster Yamaha Tech 3	YAMAHA	40'51.614	1.842	S/S
5	Cal Crutchlow	GBR	LCR Honda	HONDA	40'53.617	3.845	M/S
6	Andrea Iannone	ITA	Team SUZUKI ECSTAR	SUZUKI	40'53.643	3.871	M/S
7	Jack Miller	AUS	EG 0,0 Marc VDS	HONDA	40'55.391	5.619	M/S
8	Alex Rins	SPA	Team SUZUKI ECSTAR	SUZUKI	41'01.980	12.208	M/S
9	Pol Espargaro	SPA	Red Bull KTM Factory Racing	KTM	41'06.023	16.251	M/S
10	Bradley Smith	GBR	Red Bull KTM Factory Racing	KTM	41'06.034	16.262	M/S
11	Scott Redding	GBR	OCTO Pramac Racing	DUCATI	41'11.424	21.652	M/S
12	Dani Pedrosa	SPA	Repsol Honda Team	HONDA	41'11.440	21.668	M/S
13	Andrea Dovizioso	ITA	Ducati Team	DUCATI	41'11.464	21.692	M/S
14	Karel Abraham	CZE	Pull&Bear Aspar Team	DUCATI	41'15.882	26.110	M/S
15	Jorge Lorenzo	SPA	Ducati Team	DUCATI	41'15.940	26.168	M/S
16	Tito Rabat	SPA	EG 0,0 Marc VDS	HONDA	41'16.024	26.252	M/S
17	Alvaro Bautista	SPA	Pull&Bear Aspar Team	DUCATI	41'26.149	36.377	S/S
18	Loris Baz	FRA	Reale Avintia Racing	DUCATI	41'29.426	39.654	M/S
19	Sam Lowes	GBR	Aprilia Racing Team Gresini	APRILIA	41'30.172	40.400	M/S
20	Hector Barbera	SPA	Reale Avintia Racing	DUCATI	41'35.673	45.901	M/S
21	Danilo Petrucci	ITA	OCTO Pramac Racing	DUCATI	41'38.540	48.768	M/M
22	Broc Parkes	AUS	Monster Yamaha Tech 3	YAMAHA	41'47.483	57.711	M/M
NC	Aleix Espargaro	SPA	Aprilia Racing Team Gresini	APRILIA	10'40.746	20 laps	M/S

CHAMPIONSHIP STANDINGS

	RIDER	NAT	TEAM	POINTS
1	Marc Marquez	SPA	Repsol Honda Team	269
2	Andrea Dovizioso	ITA	Ducati Team	236
3	Maverick Viñales	SPA	Movistar Yamaha MotoGP	219
4	Valentino Rossi	ITA	Movistar Yamaha MotoGP	188
5	Dani Pedrosa	SPA	Repsol Honda Team	174
6	Johann Zarco	FRA	Monster Yamaha Tech 3	138
7	Jorge Lorenzo	SPA	Ducati Team	117
8	Danilo Petrucci	ITA	OCTO Pramac Racing	111
9	Cal Crutchlow	GBR	LCR Honda	103
10	Jonas Folger	GER	Monster Yamaha Tech 3	84
11	Alvaro Bautista	SPA	Pull&Bear Aspar Team	70
12	Jack Miller	AUS	EG 0,0 Marc VDS	65
13	Aleix Espargaro	SPA	Aprilia Racing Team Gresini	62
14	Scott Redding	GBR	OCTO Pramac Racing	61
15	Andrea Iannone	ITA	Team SUZUKI ECSTAR	60
16	Pol Espargaro	SPA	Red Bull KTM Factory Racing	49
17	Alex Rins	SPA	Team SUZUKI ECSTAR	46
18	Loris Baz	FRA	Reale Avintia Racing	45
19	Karel Abraham	CZE	Pull&Bear Aspar Team	30
20	Tito Rabat	SPA	EG 0,0 Marc VDS	29
21	Hector Barbera	SPA	Reale Avintia Racing	25
22	Bradley Smith	GBR	Red Bull KTM Factory Racing	20
23	Michele Pirro	ITA	Ducati Team	18
24	Mika Kallio	FIN	Red Bull KTM Factory Racing	11
25	Sam Lowes	GBR	Aprilia Racing Team Gresini	5
26	Katsuyuki Nakasuga	JPN	Yamalube Yamaha Factory Racing	4
27	Sylvain Guintoli	FRA	Team SUZUKI ECSTAR	1

12 | DANI PEDROSA
Never fast except in the wet Sunday warm up, which also meant he couldn't test the set-up he used for the race. Did manage to help his teammate by keeping Dovizioso behind him.

13 | ANDREA DOVIZIOSO
His championship hopes took a terrible blow. Bad qualifying followed by running wide at Doohan's on the second lap gave Dovi a task the Ducati cannot manage at this track.

14 | KAREL ABRAHAM
Not a great result but one of his best races. Fought with the factory Ducatis and Pedrosa for most of the race and won a last-lap dice with Lorenzo despite, like most Ducatis, suffering a drop in rear tyre performance.

15 | JORGE LORENZO
An awful weekend. Not on the radar in qualifying or the race. Experienced all the same problems he had in preseason testing here.

16 | TITO RABAT
Disappointed to miss out on points but happy with his speed and distance to the winner.

17 | ALVARO BAUTISTA
Another Ducati rider who suffered all weekend. Crashed twice in free practice and never anywhere but well downfield.

18 | LORIS BAZ
In the midfield group after a good start and looking competitive until moved off line by Redding. Then

used up his rear tyre getting back to them and couldn't push in the second half of the race.

19 | SAM LOWES
Made up for disappointing qualifying with a good race, picking up three places.

20 | HECTOR BARBERA
No rear grip from the second lap. Changing to lower-power engine maps didn't help so Hector couldn't challenge for the points.

21 | DANILO PETRUCCI
A truly awful weekend in both qualifying and the race, for which Danilo had no explanation.

22 | BROC PARKES
Stood in for Folger and out-qualified a couple of the regulars. Started well but couldn't find rear grip from early in the race.

DID NOT FINISH

ALEIX ESPARGARO
Crashed at Doohan's trying to overtake Miller and make up for a bad start. Broke a bone in his left hand.

DID NOT RACE

JONAS FOLGER
Awaiting results after tests for Epstein-Barr virus. Replaced by Parkes.

DEFERRED GRATIFICATION

Andrea Dovizioso had to win and he did, Marc Marquez had to be off the podium and he was, so the fight goes to the last round

Another wet race, another perfect performance by Professor Dovizioso this time with Jorge Lorenzo in a strong supporting role. Two things had to happen for the championship to stay alive and go to a last-round showdown, and both did. Dovi had to win and Marquez had to have the sort of weekend we thought he and the Honda had grown out of. Marc qualified seventh, off the front two rows for only the second time in his 88 MotoGP starts, despite his teammate Dani Pedrosa being on pole, and there was an epic save in FP4 followed by a crash in qualifying. The bike looked nervous and snappy, Marc looked as close to the edge as ever but nowhere near as fast as usual. Dovi, on the other hand, calmly and clinically put his Ducati on the front row for only the fourth time this season.

The race followed the same pattern, only much wetter, but there was another potentially crucial twist before the start. Danilo Petrucci's Ducati stopped on the warm-up lap, so he started from the back of the grid on his second bike. That effectively robbed Dovizioso of one ally in his fight against Marquez, a fight which had to prevent Marc from getting on the podium. If Marquez did stand on the podium he would be World Champion no matter what Dovi did.

'IT WAS A TRULY PERFECT WEEKEND: WE WERE QUICK IN EVERY SESSION, BOTH IN THE DRY AND IN THE WET, AND TODAY IN THE RAIN WE DOMINATE'

ANDREA DOVIZIOSO

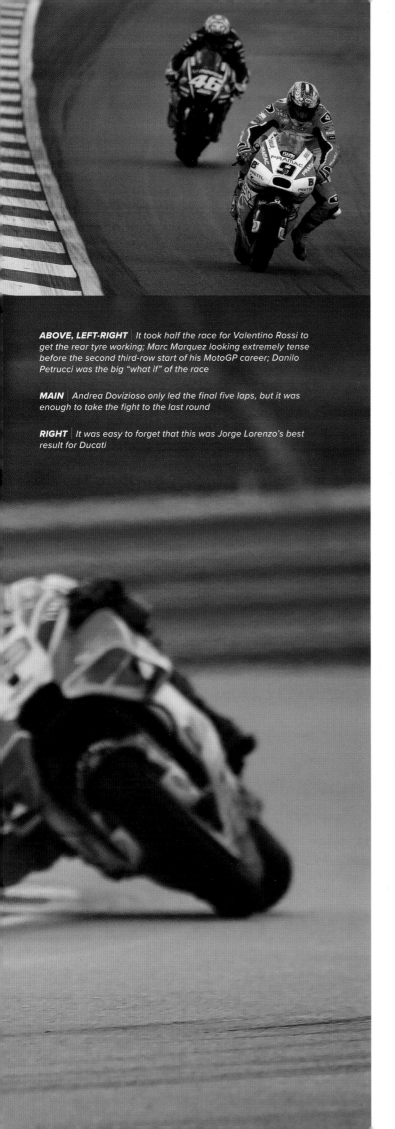

ABOVE, LEFT-RIGHT It took half the race for Valentino Rossi to get the rear tyre working; Marc Marquez looking extremely tense before the second third-row start of his MotoGP career; Danilo Petrucci was the big "what if" of the race

MAIN Andrea Dovizioso only led the final five laps, but it was enough to take the fight to the last round

RIGHT It was easy to forget that this was Jorge Lorenzo's best result for Ducati

All this might have been irrelevant if Johann Zarco could have made his soft rear tyre last. The Frenchman got the holeshot and took a second–and-a-half out of the field in the first lap, but only added a couple more tenths before being steadily reeled in by the Ducatis of not just Dovizioso but also Jorge Lorenzo. Marquez started like a demon but was quickly pushed back to fourth where he would stay after deciding an attack on Zarco would be a risk too far. Lorenzo was first past the Yamaha and applied his usual ferocious focus to the job of repeatedly lowering the fastest lap time on a very tricky surface. Dovi followed, trading fastest lap times with his teammate as the pair pulled well clear of any possible challenge. The question now was where and how Dovizioso would take the lead and the win that would keep the championship alive. Lorenzo had said back in Aragon that he understood what his job was and unequivocally said he would help Dovi but not until the last two races when the situation should be clear. Jorge certainly kept Andrea honest with his pace but five laps from home he went wide at the final corner and Dovi was through, never to be headed again. At first it looked like a deliberate move but TV replays showed that he had lost the front and he put enough force through his knee to hold the bike up to turn the kneeslider and the leg of his leathers through 90 degrees so the unprotected kangaroo hide left a long arc of red on the tarmac. It was a big moment.

Jorge later said that he decided it was too risky to mount a counterattack given the circumstances, but as he hasn't usually managed to bite back in races this year and is never quite as fast as he can be if the front tyre is sending him that sort of message, that may have been bluster. Whatever, it was still Jorge's best result for the factory. Ducati management did send a coded message to his dashboard but Jorge claimed he didn't see it, having learnt his lesson about getting distracted in the wet when he crashed out of the lead at Misano.

Further back down the field, there was enough action to keep the record crowd interested. The pack was shuffled mainly according to tyre choice. Those with the soft option started fast and spent

TEAM ORDERS

This is always a tricky subject as such things are technically illegal. However, no-one was in any doubt that the message Ducati team management flashed-up on Jorge Lorenzo's dashboard – SUGGEST MAPPING 8 – was anything other than a not-very-subtle hint to move over and let Andrea Dovizioso through for the win. Indeed, Gigi Dall'igna later confirmed it to Italian TV. However, Jorge said that he didn't see it and that he didn't need to see it to know what to do. In other words, Jorge was well aware of his responsibilities to his employers.

the second half of the race in conservation mode, those with the medium tyre had to suffer a tricky opening few laps but could take advantage when the tyre came in. A distinctly unhappy Valentino Rossi was among the later group, but he was still better off than his team mate Maverick Viñales who had to fight his way into the top ten from as low as 16th. Both men again had to watch the satellite Tech 3 bike of Johann Zarco not just beat them comprehensively but finish in a safe podium position.

The exception was Danilo Petrucci who ripped through the field from the back of the grid on medium tyres to reach sixth place at half-distance and stayed there, his rear Michelin shot. Where would Danilo have finished if he'd started from his qualifying position ten places further forward? He thought on the podium, certainly in front of Marquez thus depriving the championship leader of what could have been a vital point or two. As it was, all Andrea Dovizioso could do was reduce Marquez's lead from 33 to 19 points, still a very high hurdle to clear at the final round. However, this victory made it six wins each for the season, a true reflection of the way the season had panned out. Since the Summer break, no other rider had won a race or, frankly, looked likely to. Marc continued his work of compensating for the Honda's weaknesses while Dovi has added iron self-belief to his formidable technical skills. Of course Marquez left Sepang and headed for Valencia as a strong favourite for his fourth MotoGP title in five years, but as one ex-World champ remarked even Marc would be having a little trouble sleeping.

ABOVE, LEFT-RIGHT | *Loris Baz enlivened the early stages with a typically spirited ride; Michael van der Mark finally got to make his MotoGP debut; Maverick Viñales was unrecognisably invisible all weekend*

MAIN | *Yet again Johann Zarco amazed, he led the first half of the race then hung on for third on worn soft tyres.*

LEFT | *Joy is unrestrained as Ducati take the fight to Valencia*

In Jorge's defence it is worth noting that he crashed when distracted at Misano so it is no surprise that, like most racers, he didn't look at his dash or pitboard every lap. Also, when passed this year, he has never shown a tendency to fight back. When it happened, it happened after an interval of several laps. It is most likely that what we saw was an honest race.

In any case, nobody in the paddock thought this was anything other than the right thing to do. Even Marc Marquez expressed his admiration for Ducati's professionalism.

ROUND 17 | MALAYSIA

RACE RESULTS

WINNER ANDREA DOVIZIOSO

CIRCUIT LENGTH 5.5 KM | 3.44 MILES

NO. OF LAPS 20

RACE DISTANCE 110.9 KM | 68.8 MILES

CIRCUIT RECORD LAP 2'00.606 | 165.4 KM/H
JORGE LORENZO (2015)

CIRCUIT BEST LAP 1'59.053 | 167.6 KM/H
DANI PEDROSA (2015)

RACE CONDITION WET

AIR 25°C

HUMIDITY 89%

GROUND 33°C

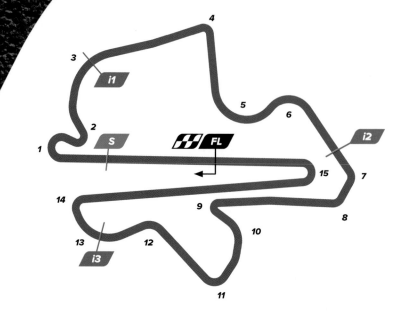

Sectors
Speed Trap
Finish Line

TISSOT | MotoGP
SWISS WATCHES SINCE 1853
OFFICIAL TIMEKEEPER

MICHELIN | MotoGP
OFFICIAL MotoGP™ CLASS TYRE

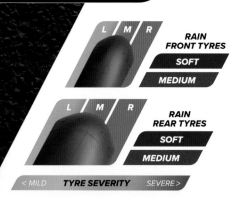

L M R — **RAIN FRONT TYRES**
SOFT
MEDIUM

L M R — **RAIN REAR TYRES**
SOFT
MEDIUM

< MILD **TYRE SEVERITY** SEVERE >

QUALIFYING RESULTS

	RIDER	NAT	TEAM	MACHINE	QP/TIME		GAP 1ST/PREV	
1	Dani Pedrosa	SPA	Repsol Honda Team	HONDA	Q2	1'59.212		
2	Johann Zarco	FRA	Monster Yamaha Tech 3	YAMAHA	Q2	1'59.229	0.017	0.017
3	Andrea Dovizioso	ITA	Ducati Team	DUCATI	Q2	1'59.236	0.024	0.007
4	Valentino Rossi	ITA	Movistar Yamaha MotoGP	YAMAHA	Q2	1'59.498	0.286	0.262
5	Maverick Viñales	SPA	Movistar Yamaha MotoGP	YAMAHA	Q2	1'59.538	0.326	0.040
6	Jorge Lorenzo	SPA	Ducati Team	DUCATI	Q2	1'59.622	0.410	0.084
7	Marc Marquez	SPA	Repsol Honda Team	HONDA	Q2	1'59.694	0.482	0.072
8	Alex Rins**	SPA	Team SUZUKI ECSTAR	SUZUKI	Q2	1'59.992	0.780	0.298
9	Andrea Iannone	ITA	Team SUZUKI ECSTAR	SUZUKI	Q2	2'00.119	0.907	0.127
10	Cal Crutchlow	GBR	LCR Honda	HONDA	Q2	2'00.181	0.969	0.062
11	Jack Miller	AUS	EG 0,0 Marc VDS	HONDA	Q2	2'00.326	1.114	0.145
12	Pol Espargaro**	SPA	Red Bull KTM Factory Racing	KTM	Q2	2'00.770	1.558	0.444
13	Danilo Petrucci	ITA	OCTO Pramac Racing	DUCATI	Q1	2'00.351	*0.213	0.164
14	Scott Redding	GBR	OCTO Pramac Racing	DUCATI	Q1	2'00.451	*0.313	0.100
15	Alvaro Bautista	SPA	Pull&Bear Aspar Team	DUCATI	Q1	2'00.469	*0.331	0.018
16	Bradley Smith	GBR	Red Bull KTM Factory Racing	KTM	Q1	2'00.718	*0.580	0.249
17	Loris Baz	FRA	Reale Avintia Racing	DUCATI	Q1	2'01.050	*0.912	0.332
18	Sam Lowes	GBR	Aprilia Racing Team Gresini	APRILIA	Q1	2'01.207	*1.069	0.157
19	Tito Rabat	SPA	EG 0,0 Marc VDS	HONDA	Q1	2'01.228	*1.090	0.021
20	Hector Barbera	SPA	Reale Avintia Racing	DUCATI	Q1	2'01.413	*1.275	0.185
21	Karel Abraham	CZE	Pull&Bear Aspar Team	DUCATI	Q1	2'01.570	*1.432	0.157
22	Michael van der Mark	NED	Monster Yamaha Tech 3	YAMAHA	Q1	2'02.376	*2.238	0.806

*Gap to the fastest rider in the Q1 session
** Went forward from Q1 to Q2

1 | ANDREA DOVIZIOSO
He had to win and he did. Another masterful exhibition by The Professor; had to work his way to the front after a less than perfect start then stay with his teammate as he pushed hard. Never put a wheel wrong all weekend.

2 | JORGE LORENZO
His best result for Ducati. No repeat of the mistake of Misano, led most of the race until a big moment five laps from home let his teammate through. That warning from the front tyre, among other things, meant he wasn't going to push for the win.

3 | JOHANN ZARCO
A second podium of the year for the rookie from his third consecutive front-row start. Led early on using the soft rear tyre, realised he couldn't fight with the Ducatis yet had enough left to respond when Marquez closed. Again embarrassed the factory bikes.

4 | MARC MARQUEZ
Took some comfort from Honda winning that. Constructors' Championship but realised this was not a race to win the rider's title but rather one to get closer to it. Even trying to chase down Zarco was a risk too far.

5 | DANI PEDROSA
Started from pole. Went with the soft rear tyre and a major, experimental set-up change with gave Dani the wet-weather feeling he'd not found all season. Pleased with the result and its implications.

6 | DANILO PETRUCCI
Had to start from back of grid after his bike stopped on sighting lap.

7 | VALENTINO ROSSI
The now-expected wet-weather problems with lack of traction meant Valentino didn't get going until halfway through the race. Got way from Baz and Espargaro but couldn't follow Petrucci when he came past.

8 | JACK MILLER
A second top-ten finish since. Breaking his leg. In trouble with the left side of the tyre in the first half then worked his way up from 13th as you'd expect. From a man with his feel for a wet track.

9 | MAVERICK VIÑALES
Another awful wet race. Like his teammate, much slower than he'd been in very similar conditions on Friday afternoon. Thought he'd made a breakthrough in warm up at. Phillip Island, but that also proved illusory.

10 | POL ESPARGARO
The factory's seventh top-ten finish of the year started with a dice with Rossi and ended with losing out to Vinales on the vey last lap. As Pol said, that shows just how far the team has come in s short time.

11 | ALVARO BAUTISTA
Gambled on the soft rear and, like others, paid the price in the second half of the race. Still a better race than he is used to under such conditions.

RACE LAP CHART

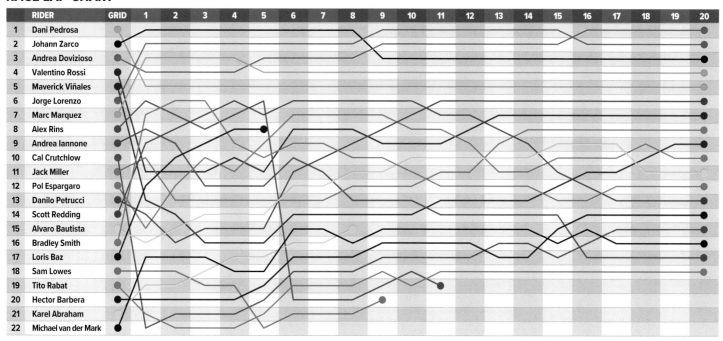

	RIDER	GRID	1	2	3	4	5	6	7	8	9	10	11	12	13	14	15	16	17	18	19	20
1	Dani Pedrosa																						
2	Johann Zarco																						
3	Andrea Dovizioso																						
4	Valentino Rossi																						
5	Maverick Viñales																						
6	Jorge Lorenzo																						
7	Marc Marquez																						
8	Alex Rins																						
9	Andrea Iannone																						
10	Cal Crutchlow																						
11	Jack Miller																						
12	Pol Espargaro																						
13	Danilo Petrucci																						
14	Scott Redding																						
15	Alvaro Bautista																						
16	Bradley Smith																						
17	Loris Baz																						
18	Sam Lowes																						
19	Tito Rabat																						
20	Hector Barbera																						
21	Karel Abraham																						
22	Michael van der Mark																						

RACE CLASSIFICATION AFTER 20 LAPS = 110.86 KM

	RIDER	NAT	TEAM	MACHINE	TIME	+ GAP	TYRES
1	Andrea Dovizioso	ITA	Ducati Team	DUCATI	44'51.497		RM/RM
2	Jorge Lorenzo	SPA	Ducati Team	DUCATI	44'52.240	0.743	RM/RM
3	Johann Zarco	FRA	Monster Yamaha Tech 3	YAMAHA	45'01.235	9.738	RM/RS
4	Marc Marquez	SPA	Repsol Honda Team	HONDA	45'09.260	17.763	RM/RM
5	Dani Pedrosa	SPA	Repsol Honda Team	HONDA	45'20.641	29.144	RM/RS
6	Danilo Petrucci	ITA	OCTO Pramac Racing	DUCATI	45'21.877	30.380	RM/RM
7	Valentino Rossi	ITA	Movistar Yamaha MotoGP	YAMAHA	45'22.266	30.769	RM/RM
8	Jack Miller	AUS	EG 0,0 Marc VDS	HONDA	45'26.735	35.238	RM/RM
9	Maverick Viñales	SPA	Movistar Yamaha MotoGP	YAMAHA	45'29.550	38.053	RM/RM
10	Pol Espargaro	SPA	Red Bull KTM Factory Racing	KTM	45'31.344	39.847	RM/RS
11	Alvaro Bautista	SPA	Pull&Bear Aspar Team	DUCATI	45'34.056	42.559	RM/RS
12	Bradley Smith	GBR	Red Bull KTM Factory Racing	KTM	45'36.099	44.602	RM/RS
13	Scott Redding	GBR	OCTO Pramac Racing	DUCATI	45'40.193	48.696	RM/RM
14	Hector Barbera	SPA	Reale Avintia Racing	DUCATI	45'41.555	50.058	RM/RM
15	Cal Crutchlow	GBR	LCR Honda	HONDA	45'42.202	50.705	RM/RM
16	Michael van der Mark	NED	Monster Yamaha Tech 3	YAMAHA	45'47.894	56.397	RM/RS
17	Andrea Iannone	ITA	Team SUZUKI ECSTAR	SUZUKI	45'49.888	58.391	RM/RM
18	Tito Rabat	SPA	EG 0,0 Marc VDS	HONDA	46'17.068	1'25.571	RM/RM
NC	Sam Lowes	GBR	Aprilia Racing Team Gresini	APRILIA	22'24.951	11 laps	RM/RM
NC	Karel Abraham	CZE	Pull&Bear Aspar Team	DUCATI	18'26.104	12 laps	RM/RM
NC	Loris Baz	FRA	Reale Avintia Racing	DUCATI	11'32.089	15 laps	RM/RS
DSQ	Alex Rins	SPA	Team SUZUKI ECSTAR	SUZUKI			RM/RM

*Michelin wet tyre options
FRONT : Rain Soft / Rain Medium   **REAR** : Rain Soft / Rain Medium

CHAMPIONSHIP STANDINGS

	RIDER	NAT	TEAM	POINTS
1	Marc Marquez	SPA	Repsol Honda Team	282
2	Andrea Dovizioso	ITA	Ducati Team	261
3	Maverick Viñales	SPA	Movistar Yamaha MotoGP	226
4	Valentino Rossi	ITA	Movistar Yamaha MotoGP	197
5	Dani Pedrosa	SPA	Repsol Honda Team	185
6	Johann Zarco	FRA	Monster Yamaha Tech 3	154
7	Jorge Lorenzo	SPA	Ducati Team	137
8	Danilo Petrucci	ITA	OCTO Pramac Racing	121
9	Cal Crutchlow	GBR	LCR Honda	104
10	Jonas Folger	GER	Monster Yamaha Tech 3	84
11	Alvaro Bautista	SPA	Pull&Bear Aspar Team	75
12	Jack Miller	AUS	EG 0,0 Marc VDS	73
13	Scott Redding	GBR	OCTO Pramac Racing	64
14	Aleix Espargaro	SPA	Aprilia Racing Team Gresini	62
15	Andrea Iannone	ITA	Team SUZUKI ECSTAR	60
16	Pol Espargaro	SPA	Red Bull KTM Factory Racing	55
17	Alex Rins	SPA	Team SUZUKI ECSTAR	46
18	Loris Baz	FRA	Reale Avintia Racing	45
19	Karel Abraham	CZE	Pull&Bear Aspar Team	30
20	Tito Rabat	SPA	EG 0,0 Marc VDS	29
21	Hector Barbera	SPA	Reale Avintia Racing	27
22	Bradley Smith	GBR	Red Bull KTM Factory Racing	24
23	Michele Pirro	ITA	Ducati Team	18
24	Mika Kallio	FIN	Red Bull KTM Factory Racing	11
25	Sam Lowes	GBR	Aprilia Racing Team Gresini	5
26	Katsuyuki Nakasuga	JPN	Yamalube Yamaha Factory Racing	4
27	Sylvain Guintoli	FRA	Team SUZUKI ECSTAR	1

12 | BRADLEY SMITH
Very fast with the soft rear in the first part of the race when he got up to sixth. After which he had to deal with the tyre not liking the drier - but not dry - track.

13 | SCOTT REDDING
Went with the soft tyre because, like others, he got no feeling from the medium on the sighting lap. It was fine until half-distance after which he dropped back from sixth place as the tyre suffered.

14 | HECTOR BARBERA
Used the harder tyre, as he did 12 months earlier to finish fourth, but had no feel. Also realised his bike was set way too stiff for the conditions so it was a case of survival rather than racing.

15 | CAL CRUTCHLOW
In survival mode for the whole race with what may well have been a misshapen rear tyre generating a major vibration right from the sighting lap. Not the way Cal wanted to celebrate his 32nd birthday.

16 | MICHAEL VAN DR MARK
Replaced Folger for his first taste of the M1 Yamaha and did a sound job.

17 | ANDREA IANNONE
A major disappointment after the last two races, especially Japan where the Suzukis were superb in the wet. Andrea had no grip front or rear from start to finish.

18 | TITO RABAT
Like several others never found any grip from either tyre. It was so bad for Tito that he considered pulling in but persevered to the finish.

DID NOT FINISH

SAM LOWES
Crashed after five laps, got back for his spare bike and crashed that after another five laps.

ALEX RINS
Disqualified for using a short cut back to the pits during the race after his second crash of the race.

KAREL ABRAHAM
Started well and had got past Vinales when he lost the front in a straight line.

LORIS BAZ
Change to the soft rear on the grid because he had no feeling with the medium. Knew it wouldn't last but took the risk and battled hard until he pushed the front and fell.

DID NOT RACE

JONAS FOLGER
Still out due to illness. Replaced by Van Der Mark

ALEIX ESPARGARO
Recovering from operation on the hand fracture sustained in Australia.

A TWIST IN THE TALE

Marc Marquez is champion again after finishing third behind Dani Pedrosa and Johann Zarco.

A difference of 21 points meant two things had to happen for Andrea Dovizioso to become World Champion. First, he had to win the race. Secondly, Marc Marquez had to finish lower than 11th. It was quite possible to see one of those things happening, but almost impossible to envisage both. It was even more difficult after qualifying. Marquez was on pole despite his daily crash with Dovi on the back of the third row. He was a second slower in qualifying and 0.7 seconds behind Marc in Free Practice. This would be a terminal deficit to Marquez on any circuit, at Valencia, a twisty track that multiplies gaps, it signaled that the deal was effectively done. Then there was the small matter of the front row: Marquez, Johann Zarco, Andrea Iannone, described by the Spaniard as "dangerous" and by the Italian as "the three worst riders" in MotoGP, he too meant dangerous. Surely there would be drama in the opening corners as Jorge Lorenzo piled through from the second row to join motorcycle racing's three top hooligans.

There wasn't. That came later.

Marquez got away first with his team mate Pedrosa riding shotgun in second before Zarco pushed through. Marc then took a long look over his shoulder and let the Yamaha through. He was also checking Dovi's position. And so the race settled down with Jorge Lorenzo in fourth pushing to try and tow Dovi

MAIN | The talking point of the race; should Lorenzo have let Dovizioso through?

BELOW, LEFT-RIGHT | Dani Pedrosa prepares to pounce; Andrea Dovizioso contemplates his task from the third row of the grid; The facory Yamahas reverted to last year's chassis for the race but it didn't transform Valentino Rossi's form

RIGHT | Zarco leads, Marquez juggles with the risk/reward conundrum

'A WIN IS A WIN, AND THIS WAS A VERY TOUGH AND HARD-FOUGHT ONE'

DANI PEDROSA

up to Pedrosa and within range of the leaders. And that's how it stayed for 22 of the 40 laps. The only question was when and how Lorenzo would let Dovizioso through. He didn't, so he got the now fabled SUGGEST MAPPING 8 message on his dash. When that didn't work a large downward-pointing Day-Glo arrow appeared on his pitboard. That didn't work either. The Ducati pit started to look a trifle fractious.

What was Jorge up to? Why didn't he let Dovi through to see if he could close the gap? The answer, according to both riders, was simple; they were going as quick as they could. Dovi said he felt more comfortable following Jorge, and Jorge said he would certainly have moved over if and when they got to the leaders. And here is the problem with all advice from pit lane, the best riders in the world know what is going on and Gigi Dall'Igna later said they didn't understand the true pace of their riders. The frustration on show was, however, understandable. With the clarity of hindsight it is fair to say that no-one did much wrong. And what happened in the next couple of laps bears out this analysis.

On Lap 23 Marc Marquez decides that Dovi's position means he cannot win the race and the championship, he can now attack and go for the win. He leads over the line and, anxious to keep out of range of a Zarco lunge, gets into Turn 1 far too quickly and loses the front at around 100mph. His left knee and elbow are on the ground, his right foot is a yard from the footpeg, the front is folded, he has crashed. And then the bike is back on its wheels and hammering through the gravel trap. Marc rejoins the track in fifth place. It's worth noting that the mistake was forced by fear of what Zarco would do, which is as eloquent a tribute to the rookie's season as you could hope to hear.

The Ducatis now see a chance, it might be infinitesimally small but they see it and try to up their pace. A lap later they are both on the floor; Jorge crashed first, Andrea three corners later. So they really were on the limit keeping up with the front three. Lorenzo made Dovi's life easier but it was obvious that Andrea was not his usual smooth self. As he later said, he had been over the limit all race and Jorge had helped, not hindered, him. As for

HISTORY BOYS

This was one of the greatest seasons of recent years, maybe
ever, thanks to the crescendo that was its second half. Right up
to the final race the two contenders exchanged wins with no
interference from the Yamahas, and this is what we remember.
We may say we want to see eight different winners but what we
remember are the great confrontations: Ago versus Hailwood;
Roberts versus Spencer; Rainey versus Schwantz; Rossi versus
all sorts of people. These are what we recall over the years,

these are the stories we tell our grandchildren. Who came third?
Be honest, you don't care and neither do they.

To make this year even more special, we had two contrasting
characters fighting it out. Andrea Dovizioso always a rider
with speed and precision, added steel to his game, and Marc
Marquez just carried on being Marc Marquez. As if this wasn't
enough, the two combatants maintained the highest standards
of sportsmanship. This is what Marc had to say about Dovi
straight after the race: "What an incredible opponent. What
an incredible person. I am disappointed that he didn't finish

Jorge, he defended his actions robustly, saying he would have moved over if they had managed to get to the leaders. As far as Jorge was concerned, he had done the best for Ducati and Dovi, but the bottom line was they did not have the pace at a track that the bike and Dovi have never liked. Gigi Dall'Igna later confirmed that Dovi never had better pace than Jorge and what happened on track gave Ducati the best chance.

That flurry of action left Zarco and Pedrosa to fight for victory at a pace the Ducatis could never have managed. Zarco said before the race that he could fight for the win and he meant it, but Dani Pedrosa put a move on him at the first corner of the final lap that brooked no answer it was clean, clinical and deprived Zarco of the space he needed to get on the throttle early. He had done everything for Honda that his old foe Lorenzo could not do for Ducati.

A delirious Marquez arrived just a few seconds later and celebrated his sixth world title with a giant dice – suitably weighted to roll a six every time. Marc then said it was a shame that Andrea wouldn't be on the podium with him, as HRC and Ducati management exchanged compliments in pitlane. It had been that sort of championship.

It was Marc's fourth MotoGP championship in the five years he has been in the class. He did it with what he calls 'Marquez Style' to the end, in other words crashing 27 times during the season and making impossible saves at crucial moments. He is only 24 years old and is now the youngest ever six-times World Champion (including his 125cc and Moto2 crowns) and the youngest ever four-times champion in the top class, younger than Rossi and younger than Hailwood, by common consent the two greatest ever. And he's not finished yet.

MAIN | *Please do not throw confetti - ah, too late...*

LEFT, TOP-BOTTOM | *Jack Miller spent most of the race annoying Valentino; This pair are going to meet on the podium a few more times next season; Alex Rins quietly slipped in the best result of his rookie year*

the race. I have a really good relationship with him and the Ducati guys. I saw them go to my box to congratulate the mechanics—full respect. I learned many things from Andrea, especially mental things. The way to approach the races, the way to approach the weekend. He showed me that you need to understand well and forget the others. Not many people can do it. He is one of the best or maybe the best. We have respect for each other, but when you are on the track, you are fighting for what you want. I understand this is racing."

ROUND 18 | VALENCIA

RACE RESULTS

WINNER | DANI PEDROSA

CIRCUIT LENGTH | 4.0 KM | 2.49 MILES

NO. OF LAPS | 30

RACE DISTANCE | 120.2 KM | 74.7 MILES

CIRCUIT RECORD LAP | 1'31.171, 158.1 KM/H, JORGE LORENZO (2016)

CIRCUIT BEST LAP | 1'29.401, 161.2 KM/H, JORGE LORENZO (2016)

RACE CONDITION | DRY

AIR | 25°C

HUMIDITY | 22%

GROUND | 26°C

Sectors
Speed Trap
Finish Line

i1
i2
AFICIÓN | 7
ANGEL NIETO | 6
2 | MICK DOOHAN
10
11
8   9
3
13
5
i3
4
12 | CHAMPI HERREROS
14 | ADRIAN CAMPOS
FL
S
1 | JORGE LORENZO

TISSOT
SWISS WATCHES SINCE 1853
MotoGP
OFFICIAL TIMEKEEPER

MICHELIN
MotoGP
OFFICIAL MotoGP™ CLASS TYRE

FRONT TYRES
L M R
SOFT
MEDIUM
HARD

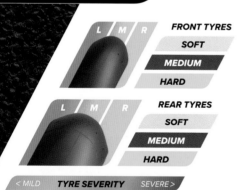

REAR TYRES
L M R
SOFT
MEDIUM
HARD

< MILD   **TYRE SEVERITY**   SEVERE >

QUALIFYING RESULTS

	RIDER	NAT	TEAM	MACHINE	QP/TIME	GAP 1ST/PREV	
1	Marc Marquez	SPA	Repsol Honda Team	HONDA	Q2	1'29.897	
2	Johann Zarco	FRA	Monster Yamaha Tech 3	YAMAHA	Q2	1'30.246	0.349	0.349
3	Andrea Iannone	ITA	Team SUZUKI ECSTAR	SUZUKI	Q2	1'30.399	0.502	0.153
4	Jorge Lorenzo	SPA	Ducati Team	DUCATI	Q2	1'30.460	0.563	0.061
5	Dani Pedrosa	SPA	Repsol Honda Team	HONDA	Q2	1'30.589	0.692	0.129
6	Michele Pirro	ITA	Ducati Team	DUCATI	Q2	1'30.764	0.867	0.175
7	Valentino Rossi	ITA	Movistar Yamaha MotoGP	YAMAHA	Q2	1'30.848	0.951	0.084
8	Aleix Espargaro	SPA	Aprilia Racing Team Gresini	APRILIA	Q2	1'30.857	0.960	0.009
9	Andrea Dovizioso	ITA	Ducati Team	DUCATI	Q2	1'30.961	1.064	0.104
10	Alex Rins	SPA	Team SUZUKI ECSTAR	SUZUKI	Q2	1'30.972	1.075	0.011
11	Pol Espargaro	SPA	Red Bull KTM Factory Racing	KTM	Q2	1'31.044	1.147	0.072
12	Jack Miller	AUS	EG 0,0 Marc VDS	HONDA	Q2	1'31.190	1.293	0.146
13	Maverick Viñales	SPA	Movistar Yamaha MotoGP	YAMAHA	Q1	1'31.030	*0.137	0.117
14	Tito Rabat	SPA	EG 0,0 Marc VDS	HONDA	Q1	1'31.197	*0.304	0.167
15	Danilo Petrucci	ITA	OCTO Pramac Racing	DUCATI	Q1	1'31.216	*0.323	0.019
16	Cal Crutchlow	GBR	LCR Honda	HONDA	Q1	1'31.297	*0.404	0.081
17	Bradley Smith	GBR	Red Bull KTM Factory Racing	KTM	Q1	1'31.300	*0.407	0.003
18	Karel Abraham	CZE	Pull&Bear Aspar Team	DUCATI	Q1	1'31.325	*0.432	0.025
19	Mika Kallio	FIN	Red Bull KTM Factory Racing	KTM	Q1	1'31.361	*0.468	0.036
20	Hector Barbera	SPA	Reale Avintia Racing	DUCATI	Q1	1'31.487	*0.594	0.126
21	Alvaro Bautista	SPA	Pull&Bear Aspar Team	DUCATI	Q1	1'31.578	*0.685	0.091
22	Scott Redding	GBR	OCTO Pramac Racing	DUCATI	Q1	1'31.625	*0.732	0.047
23	Loris Baz	FRA	Reale Avintia Racing	DUCATI	Q1	1'31.775	*0.882	0.150
24	Sam Lowes	GBR	Aprilia Racing Team Gresini	APRILIA	Q1	1'31.816	*0.923	0.041
25	Michael van der Mark	NED	Monster Yamaha Tech 3	YAMAHA	Q1	1'32.504	*1.611	0.688

* Gap to the fastest rider in the Q1 session
** Went forward from Q1 to Q2

1 DANI PEDROSA
A magnificent effort on one of his best tracks. Rode shotgun for Marquez in the early laps before being relegated by Zarco. Kept the Ducatis at a safe distance, and after Marquez had his moment, attacked the Yamaha and didn't let the Frenchman back within range.

2 JOHANN ZARCO
Top Yamaha by a distance all weekend. Said he could fight for the lead and did so on soft tyres front and rear. Led much of the race and when Marquez came past he nearly crashed trying to keep ahead.

The win was snatched away by a brilliantly precise move by Pedrosa on the first corner of the last lap.

3 MARC MARQUEZ
Didn't have to risk anything but to the surprise of no one went for the win in the final stages and nearly paid the price. Instead he made his best save of the year and finished on the podium as a four-time MotoGP champion, having helped Honda to the constructors' and teams' championships.

4 ALEX RINS
Lost places off the start and then ran

a superb race for his best result of the year, Suzuki's season suddenly didn't look so bad.

5 VALENTINO ROSSI
Used the 2016 chassis but Valentino had the type of race he was expecting and suffered lack of grip. A strange end to a very strange season.

6 ANDREA IANNONE
Great qualifying and good early pace but couldn't push to the maximum on the brakes. Nevertheless, clear reasons for optimism.

7 JACK MILLER
Aggressive in the first few laps which put him in a position to fight with Rossi for much of the race before a couple of warnings from the front tyre made him drop a couple of places. Nevertheless, rounded out the season with three top-ten finishes.

8 CAL CRUTCHLOW
A great result from 16th on the grid. Without the bad qualifying, Cal would probably have been in the fight for fourth place. As it was, he rode a very strong final third of the race.

9 MICHELE PIRRO
The Ducati factory tester had his third wild-card ride of the year and again finished in the top-ten. Used the soft front to try and race with the leaders at the start, but that limited his prospects later on. When he saw the two regular riders crash he knew he had to get to the flag for whatever points he could.

10 TITO RABAT
A gutsy ride after being pushed back to 18th on the first lap. Confirmed his good form at this track with an admirable comeback.

11 BRADLEY SMITH
Went after Espargaro and his Aprilia to ruffle his feathers and hopefully help KTM to beat the Italian factory in the constructors' championship. The plan worked and Bradley had a near perfect opening few laps then managed worn tyres in the concluding laps.

12 MAVERICK VIÑALES
The only cheerful note was good pace in Sunday morning warm-up. Other than that another weekend with too many questions and not enough answers. He used the 2016 chassis but it didn't appear to make much difference.

RACE LAP CHART

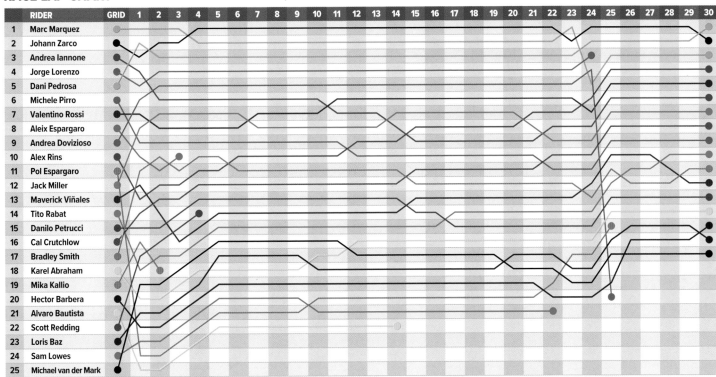

	RIDER	GRID	1	2	3	4	5	6	7	8	9	10	11	12	13	14	15	16	17	18	19	20	21	22	23	24	25	26	27	28	29	30
1	Marc Marquez																															
2	Johann Zarco																															
3	Andrea Iannone																															
4	Jorge Lorenzo																															
5	Dani Pedrosa																															
6	Michele Pirro																															
7	Valentino Rossi																															
8	Aleix Espargaro																															
9	Andrea Dovizioso																															
10	Alex Rins																															
11	Pol Espargaro																															
12	Jack Miller																															
13	Maverick Viñales																															
14	Tito Rabat																															
15	Danilo Petrucci																															
16	Cal Crutchlow																															
17	Bradley Smith																															
18	Karel Abraham																															
19	Mika Kallio																															
20	Hector Barbera																															
21	Alvaro Bautista																															
22	Scott Redding																															
23	Loris Baz																															
24	Sam Lowes																															
25	Michael van der Mark																															

RACE CLASSIFICATION AFTER 30 LAPS = 120.15 KM

	RIDER	NAT	TEAM	MACHINE	TIME	+ GAP	TYRES
1	Dani Pedrosa	SPA	Repsol Honda Team	HONDA	46'08.125		H/M
2	Johann Zarco	FRA	Monster Yamaha Tech 3	YAMAHA	46'08.462	0.337	S/S
3	Marc Marquez	SPA	Repsol Honda Team	HONDA	46'18.986	10.861	H/S
4	Alex Rins	SPA	Team SUZUKI ECSTAR	SUZUKI	46'21.692	13.567	M/S
5	Valentino Rossi	ITA	Movistar Yamaha MotoGP	YAMAHA	46'21.942	13.817	M/S
6	Andrea Iannone	ITA	Team SUZUKI ECSTAR	SUZUKI	46'22.641	14.516	H/M
7	Jack Miller	AUS	EG 0,0 Marc VDS	HONDA	46'25.212	17.087	M/S
8	Cal Crutchlow	GBR	LCR Honda	HONDA	46'25.355	17.230	H/S
9	Michele Pirro	ITA	Ducati Team	DUCATI	46'34.067	25.942	S/S
10	Tito Rabat	SPA	EG 0,0 Marc VDS	HONDA	46'35.145	27.020	M/S
11	Bradley Smith	GBR	Red Bull KTM Factory Racing	KTM	46'38.960	30.835	H/S
12	Maverick Viñales	SPA	Movistar Yamaha MotoGP	YAMAHA	46'43.137	35.012	M/S
13	Danilo Petrucci	ITA	OCTO Pramac Racing	DUCATI	46'46.201	38.076	H/S
14	Karel Abraham	CZE	Pull&Bear Aspar Team	DUCATI	46'50.113	41.988	H/S
15	Hector Barbera	SPA	Reale Avintia Racing	DUCATI	46'55.828	47.703	M/S
16	Loris Baz	FRA	Reale Avintia Racing	DUCATI	46'55.834	47.709	H/S
17	Michael van der Mark	NED	Monster Yamaha Tech 3	YAMAHA	47'00.259	52.134	M/S
NC	Pol Espargaro	SPA	Red Bull KTM Factory Racing	KTM	39'06.114	5 laps	H/S
NC	Andrea Dovizioso	ITA	Ducati Team	DUCATI	39'55.165	5 laps	H/S
NC	Jorge Lorenzo	SPA	Ducati Team	DUCATI	36'55.021	6 laps	H/S
NC	Sam Lowes	GBR	Aprilia Racing Team Gresini	APRILIA	34'54.863	8 laps	H/S
NC	Alvaro Bautista	SPA	Pull&Bear Aspar Team	DUCATI	22'28.282	16 laps	H/M
NC	Scott Redding	GBR	OCTO Pramac Racing	DUCATI	6'19.954	26 laps	H/S
NC	Aleix Espargaro	SPA	Aprilia Racing Team Gresini	APRILIA	4'44.941	27 laps	H/S
NC	Mika Kallio	FIN	Red Bull KTM Factory Racing	KTM	3'14.772	28 laps	H/S

CHAMPIONSHIP STANDINGS

	RIDER	NAT	TEAM	POINTS
1	Marc Marquez	SPA	Repsol Honda Team	298
2	Andrea Dovizioso	ITA	Ducati Team	261
3	Maverick Viñales	SPA	Movistar Yamaha MotoGP	230
4	Dani Pedrosa	SPA	Repsol Honda Team	210
5	Valentino Rossi	ITA	Movistar Yamaha MotoGP	208
6	Johann Zarco	FRA	Monster Yamaha Tech 3	174
7	Jorge Lorenzo	SPA	Ducati Team	137
8	Danilo Petrucci	ITA	OCTO Pramac Racing	124
9	Cal Crutchlow	GBR	LCR Honda	112
10	Jonas Folger	GER	Monster Yamaha Tech 3	84
11	Jack Miller	AUS	EG 0,0 Marc VDS	82
12	Alvaro Bautista	SPA	Pull&Bear Aspar Team	75
13	Andrea Iannone	ITA	Team SUZUKI ECSTAR	70
14	Scott Redding	GBR	OCTO Pramac Racing	64
15	Aleix Espargaro	SPA	Aprilia Racing Team Gresini	62
16	Alex Rins	SPA	Team SUZUKI ECSTAR	59
17	Pol Espargaro	SPA	Red Bull KTM Factory Racing	55
18	Loris Baz	FRA	Reale Avintia Racing	45
19	Tito Rabat	SPA	EG 0,0 Marc VDS	35
20	Karel Abraham	CZE	Pull&Bear Aspar Team	32
21	Bradley Smith	GBR	Red Bull KTM Factory Racing	29
22	Hector Barbera	SPA	Reale Avintia Racing	28
23	Michele Pirro	ITA	Ducati Team	25
24	Mika Kallio	FIN	Red Bull KTM Factory Racing	11
25	Sam Lowes	GBR	Aprilia Racing Team Gresini	5
26	Katsuyuki Nakasuga	JPN	Yamalube Yamaha Factory Racing	4
27	Sylvain Guintoli	FRA	Team SUZUKI ECSTAR	1

13 DANILO PETRUCCI
Not the 100th GP start he would have wished for. Like his teammate never found the feel he was looking for.

14 KAREL ABRAHAM
Had problems with the front brake early in the race but managed to adjust it enough to be useable. Couldn't close down Petrucci but pleased to earn a couple of points.

15 HECTOR BARBERA
Not the finishing place he wanted to end his MotoGP career, especially at his home track, but had a proper scrap with his teammate over the closing laps.

16 LORIS BAZ
Like all the Ducatis, he had problems. After bashing fairings with Van Der Mark he closed in on his teammate for a very entertaining last few laps in MotoGP.

17 MICHAEL VAN DER MARK
Enjoyed his second MotoGP race, qualified vey well and raced with some experienced men on Sunday. The team boss was impressed.

DID NOT FINISH

POL ESPARGARO
Started from pit lane because he had to take a tenth engine, not because they'd broken but because the four sealed motors from earlier in the year wouldn't fit the current chassis. Outbraked himself trying to make up ground.

ANDREA DOVIZIOSO
Started from the third row, followed his teammate for much of the race in fifth place until they crashed on the same lap just after Marquez's major

save. Never had the pace to win, when they pushed, they crashed.

JORGE LORENZO
Led his teammate in pursuit of the front three for much of the race. Ignored pitboard and dash messages to let him through and when Marquez dropped back after his big save the pair crashed within a lap of each other.

SAM LOWES
Running decent lap times but problems shifting down the box made him go deep a couple of times and that affected Sam's concentration.

ALVARO BAUTISTA
Crashed twice. The first time after his front wheel was knocked from under him, the second time at Turn 1 on his own. Used the hard front tyre and never liked the feeling.

SCOTT REDDING
Never felt good and ended his two years with the Pramac team by crashing at Turn 1.

ALEIX ESPARGARO
Back from the hand injury suffered in Australia but with a bout of bronchitis. Never clicked with the front-end feel,

especially with a full tank, and that's what caused the crash.

MIKA KALLIO
Crashed at Turn 2 on the third lap when he lost the front.

DID NOT RACE

JONAS FOLGER
Diagnosed with a liver condition that caused his exhaustion. Should be back in 2018.

THE RESULTS

Official MotoGP Timing by **TISSOT**
www.motogp.com

TISSOT SWISS WATCHES SINCE 1853 / motoGP
OFFICIAL TIMEKEEPER

MotoGP™ WORLD CHAMPIONSHIP CLASSIFICATION

	RIDER	NAT	POINTS	QAT	ARG	AME	ESP	FRA	ITA	CAT	NED	GER	CZE	AUT	GBR	RSM	ARA	JPN	AUS	MAL	VAL
1	Marc Marquez	SPA	298	13	-	25	20	-	10	20	16	25	25	20	-	25	25	20	25	13	16
2	Andrea Dovizioso	ITA	261	20	-	10	11	13	25	25	11	8	10	25	25	16	9	25	3	25	-
3	Maverick Viñales	SPA	230	25	25	-	10	25	20	6	-	13	16	10	20	13	13	7	16	7	4
4	Dani Pedrosa	SPA	210	11	-	16	25	16	-	16	3	16	20	16	9	2	20	-	4	11	25
5	Valentino Rossi	ITA	208	16	20	20	6	-	13	8	25	11	13	9	16	-	11	-	20	9	11
6	Johann Zarco	FRA	174	-	11	11	13	20	9	11	2	7	4	11	10	1	7	8	13	16	20
7	Jorge Lorenzo	SPA	137	5	-	7	16	10	8	13	1	5	1	13	11	-	16	10	1	20	-
8	Danilo Petrucci	ITA	124	-	9	8	9	-	16	-	20	4	9	-	-	20	0	16	0	10	3
9	Cal Crutchlow	GBR	112	-	16	13	-	11	-	5	13	6	11	1	13	3	-	-	11	1	8
10	Jonas Folger	GER	84	6	10	5	8	9	3	10	-	20	6	-	-	7	0	-	-	-	-
11	Jack Miller	AUS	82	8	7	6	-	8	1	-	10	1	2	-	0	10	3	-	9	8	9
12	Alvaro Bautista	SPA	75	-	13	1	-	-	11	9	-	10	-	8	6	4	8	-	0	5	-
13	Andrea Iannone	ITA	70	-	0	9	-	6	6	0	7	-	0	5	-	-	4	13	10	0	10
14	Scott Redding	GBR	64	9	8	4	5	-	4	3	-	0	0	4	8	9	2	0	5	3	-
15	Aleix Espargaro	SPA	62	10	-	0	7	-	-	-	6	9	8	3	-	-	10	9	---	-	-
16	Alex Rins	SPA	59	7	-	-	-	-	-	-	0	0	5	0	7	8	0	11	8	-	13
17	Pol Espargaro	SPA	55	0	2	-	-	4	-	0	5	3	7	-	5	5	6	5	7	6	-
18	Loris Baz	FRA	45	4	5	-	3	7	0	4	8	0	-	7	1	0	0	6	0	-	0
19	Tito Rabat	SPA	35	1	4	3	-	5	5	1	4	0	0	0	4	-	1	1	0	0	6
20	Karel Abraham	CZE	32	2	6	-	1	-	0	2	9	0	3	2	3	0	-	-	2	-	2
21	Bradley Smith	GBR	29	0	1	0	2	3	0	-	-	2	-	0	0	6	0	0	6	4	5
22	Hector Barbera	SPA	28	3	3	2	4	-	2	7	0	-	0	0	2	-	0	2	0	2	1
23	Michele Pirro	ITA	25	-	-	-	-	-	7	-	-	-	-	-	-	11	-	-	-	-	7
24	Mika Kallio	FIN	11	-	-	-	-	-	-	-	-	0	6	-	-	5	-	-	-	-	-
25	Sam Lowes	GBR	5	0	-	-	0	2	0	0	-	-	0	0	-	0	3	0	-	-	-
26	Katsuyuki Nakasuga	JPN	1	-	-	-	-	-	-	-	-	-	-	-	-	-	-	1	-	-	-
27	Sylvain Guintoli	FRA	1	-	-	-	-	1	0	0	-	-	-	-	-	-	-	-	-	-	-
28	Michael van der Mark	NED	0	-	-	-	-	-	-	-	-	-	-	-	-	-	-	-	-	0	0
29	Takuya Tsuda	JPN	0	-	-	-	0	-	-	-	-	-	-	-	-	-	-	-	-	-	-
30	Hiroshi Aoyama	JPN	0	-	-	-	-	-	-	-	-	-	-	-	-	-	-	0	-	-	-
31	Broc Parkes	AUS	0	-	-	-	-	-	-	-	-	-	-	-	-	-	-	-	0	-	-

CONSTRUCTORS

	RIDER	POINTS	QAT	ARG	AME	ESP	FRA	ITA	CAT	NED	GER	CZE	AUT	GBR	RSM	ARA	JPN	AUS	MAL	VAL
1	HONDA	357	13	16	25	25	16	10	20	16	25	25	20	13	25	25	20	25	13	25
2	YAMAHA	321	25	25	20	13	25	20	11	25	20	16	11	20	13	13	8	20	16	20
3	DUCATI	310	20	13	10	16	13	25	25	20	10	10	25	25	20	16	25	5	25	7
4	SUZUKI	100	7	-	9	-	6	6	-	7	-	5	5	7	8	4	13	10	-	13
5	KTM	69	-	2	-	2	4	-	-	5	3	7	6	5	6	6	5	7	6	5
6	APRILIA	64	10	-	-	7	2	-	-	6	9	8	3	-	-	10	9	-	-	-

TEAMS

	RIDER	POINTS	QAT	ARG	AME	ESP	FRA	ITA	CAT	NED	GER	CZE	AUT	GBR	RSM	ARA	JPN	AUS	MAL	VAL
1	Repsol Honda Team	508	24	-	41	45	16	10	36	19	41	45	36	9	27	45	20	29	24	41
2	Movistar Yamaha Motogp	438	41	45	20	16	25	33	14	25	24	29	19	36	13	24	7	36	16	15
3	Ducati Team	398	25	-	17	27	23	33	38	12	13	11	38	36	16	25	35	4	45	-
4	Monster Yamaha Tech 3	258	6	21	16	21	29	12	21	2	27	10	11	10	8	7	8	13	16	20
5	OCTO Pramac Racing	188	9	17	12	14	-	20	3	20	4	9	4	8	29	2	16	5	13	3
6	Team SUZUKI ECSTAR	130	7	-	9	-	7	6	-	7	-	5	5	7	8	4	24	18	-	23
7	EG 0,0 Marc VDS	117	9	11	9	-	13	6	1	14	1	2	-	4	10	4	1	9	8	15
8	LCR Honda	112	-	16	13	-	11	-	5	13	6	11	1	13	3	-	-	11	1	8
9	Pull&Bear Aspar Team	107	2	19	1	1	-	11	11	9	10	3	10	9	4	8	-	2	5	2
10	Red Bull KTM Factory Racing	84	-	3	-	2	7	-	-	5	5	7	-	5	11	6	5	13	10	5
11	Reale Avintia Racing	73	7	8	2	7	7	2	11	8	-	-	7	3	-	-	8	-	2	1
12	Aprilia Racing Team Gresini	67	10	-	-	7	2	-	-	6	9	8	3	-	-	10	12	-	-	-

SHARK MOTOGP REPLICA HELMETS'

PUT YOUR SKILLS TO THE TEST

THE 2-WHEEL DRIVING EXPERIENCES
AT THE RED BULL RING

**FOR MORE INFORMATION VISIT
PROJEKT-SPIELBERG.COM**

FRANKY SAYS RELAX

Franco Morbidelli was the inspiration behind an Italian renaissance in this year's Moto2 World Championship.

Eight wins and three additional podiums?? made him the first Italian World Champion at Grand Prix level since mentor Valentino Rossi's MotoGP triumph in 2009.

He is the first rider from Rossi's famed VR46 Academy to win a World Championship and he proved that you can negotiate an unconventional path to Grand Prix glory by being the first Moto2 World Champion not to pass through the 125cc or Moto3 category, having cut his teeth in the European Superstock arena.

Victories in Qatar, Argentina and Austin made him the first rider since the late Daijiro Kato in 2001 to win the opening three rounds of an intermediate class battle.

He may have made it four on the spin had it not been for a crash out of the lead under severe pressure from Estrella Galicia 0,0 Marc VDS teammate Alex Marquez. A recurring theme of the season was Morbidelli's ability to handle pressure and bounce back from a disappointing result.

His response to the Jerez tumble was an emphatic win in Le Mans before a fourth and fifth in Mugello and Circuit de Barcelona-Catalunya moved closest rival Tom Luthi to within four-points.

Morbidelli responded with back-to-back victories from pole position in Assen and Sachsenring but luck deserted him in Brno when the race was halted for rain while he led.

Luthi won a six-lap dash and the pendulum swung again when Morbidelli blew a three-second lead with a crash on a Misano track turned into an ice rink by torrential rain.

Extra spice was added to the Morbidelli and Luthi title fight because it was at Silverstone that it was confirmed they were to be comrades on Honda RC213V machinery for the Marc VDS squad in 2018.

When the pair headed off on the annual flyaway triple header there were just 16-points splitting them.

Luthi's form deserted him at the worst possible time when he limped home 11th with a misting visor in a rain-drenched Japanese round and two bruising pre-race crashes in Australia left him down in 10th.

Morbidelli had his first match point in Malaysia but he was crowned champion without turning a wheel in anger.

It was a cruel case of a broken left ankle and broken dreams for Luthi when he was sidelined by a ferocious qualifying high-side.

Morbidelli wasn't the only headline-grabbing act in Moto2 this year.

Technical interest and chassis competition was heightened by the arrival of KTM and the return of Suter.

The Austrian brand stuck rigidly to its tried and trusted steel trellis frame chassis and its impact was instant when Oliveira took pole position in just the second race in Argentina.

He followed that with a first podium and there was more top-three success in Jerez, Circuit de Barcelona-Catalunya, Sachsenring, Brno and Motorland Aragon before KTM reveled in a barnstorming finale.

Oliveira took KTM's first intermediate class triumph since Mika Kallio in the 250cc category in Donington Park in 2008 with a start-to-finish win over Red Bull Ajo teammate Brad Binder at Twin-Ring Motegi.

He repeated that dominance in Sepang and was again followed home by South African Binder, who had been a slow burner at the start of the year while he recovered from a serious left-arm injury suffered in a winter testing crash in Valencia.

Oliveira's late surge secured him third in the standings after a late capitulation from Marquez.

The Spaniard broke his Moto2 victory duck in Jerez and was unstoppable again on home soil in Circuit de Barcelona-Catalunya.

A crash out of the lead in Silverstone and a left hip injury from a heavy FP1 crash in Misano ruled him out of the San Marino round. The injury forced him to retire in Motorland Aragon and two crashes in the Sepang race ended his quest for an overall top three finish.

There were numerous feel good stories throughout the season.

Mattia Pasini rolled back the years with a daring last lap raid on Luthi and Marquez in Mugello to take his first victory since 2009. He thought he was back on the podium again just a week later in Barcelona but was disqualified after the Italtrans Racing Team was penalised for an illegal oil sample.

Xavi Vierge's second in Japan was the first podium for Tech 3 Racing since Bradley Smith in 2011. Hafizh Syahrin had not scored a podium in five years and then took two in three races with his renowned wet-weather skills coming to the fore in Misano and Motegi.

Pecco Bagnaia made a habit of finishing inside the top six in a stellar rookie campaign that included podium finishes in Jerez, Le Mans, Sachsenring and Misano.

CLOCKWISE FROM TOP LEFT | *KTM arrived in Moto2 and were competitive from the off; Taka Nakagami was intermittently brilliant and is off to MotoGP for 2018; Mattia Pasini was the story of the year and his last lap at Mugello was truly magnificent; Pecco Bagnaia was a stunning Rookie of the Year; Alex Marquez's championship challenge faded after an injury sustained at Misano; the Class of '17*

1 | QATAR

Italian Franco Morbidelli (Estrella Galicia Kalex) scored a stunning maiden GP win, constantly increasing his advantage over his pursuers, sometimes by as much as half a second a lap.

Thomas Luthi (CarXpert Kalex) finished second after briefly leading the second lap. He spent the latter stages resisting Takaaki Nakagami (Idemitsu Kalex).

Miguel Oliveira (Red Bull KTM) got the better of Morbidelli's teammate Alex Marquez (Estrella Kalex) for fourth place, well ahead of Rossi's half-brother Luca Marini (Forward Team Kalex) who took sixth, two tenths ahead of rookie Fabio Quartararo (HP 40 Kalex).

2 | ARGENTINA

Three laps in and we were set for another Moto2 snore-fest. Franco Morbidelli [Marc VDS Kalex] gapped Alex Marquez [Marc VDS Kalex] to the tune of 0.7 seconds after six laps, and the championship leader appeared to have the race won.

Not so. For Marquez now appears at ease in this class, and gradually reeled the Italian in. Lacking the frenetic overtaking of Moto3, but equally as tense, this cat-and-mouse game between the teammates was enhanced by the presence of pole-sitter Miguel Oliveira [Ajo KTM], who closed to within 1.3 seconds with three to go.

It was then that Marquez finally made his play for the lead, diving under at turn five. Morbidelli was not to be denied, responding, and brilliantly upping the pace. Marquez couldn't bear the sight of it, high-siding out of turn seven on the final lap as he gave chase. Thus Thomas Luthi [Interwetten Kalex] inherited a fortunate third.

3 | USA

Franco Morbidelli (Estrella Galicia Kalex) dominated Moto2 for the third successive race, resisting persistent pressure from Thomas Luthi (CarXpert Kalex). Takaaki Nakagami (Idemitsu Kalex) rode an excellent race, finally bettering Alex Marquez (Estrella Galicia Kalex).

Twenty-two-year-old Morbidelli led from pole, briefly relinquishing the lead to Marquez, then reasserting himself, despite Luthi closing on several occasions. In the final few laps the former European Superstock 600 champion had more pace than anyone, so he was able to open the gap to 2.6 seconds at the finish.

4 | SPAIN

Alex Marquez (Estrella Galicia Kalex) scored his first Moto2 win. In the early stages of the race Marquez and teammate Franco Morbidelli raced ahead to dispute the lead between themselves. Marquez led the first seven laps, putting Morbidelli ahead, but the very next lap the championship leader slid off.

That left Marquez four seconds clear of rookie Francesco Bagnaia (Sky VR46 Kalex) who had a superb ride to second, 3.4 seconds behind Marquez and just ahead of Miguel Oliveira (Red Bull KTM). Oliveira made sure of his second podium of the year when he got the better of Mattia Pasini (Italtrans Kalex) who had used up his rear grip.

5 | FRANCE

Italian Franco Morbidelli (Estrella Galicia Kalex) won a high-tension victory, beating off an early challenge from pole-starter Thomas Luthi (CarXpert Kalex), then resisting huge pressure from remarkable rookie Francesco Bagnaia (Sky VR46 Kalex).

The two Italians traded lap records, Bagnaia closing the gap, Morbidelli digging deeper to reopen the gap and so on, lap after lap. Finally Morbidelli took the chequered flag 1.7 seconds ahead of his younger compatriot. Morbidelli's fourth win from five races extended his championship lead over third-placed Luthi to 20 points.

6 | ITALY

The stretch of tarmac that begins at the swooping, downhill Casanova-Savelli right-left and precedes the fearsome Arrabbiata right is easily among the most spectacular on the calendar. It would be the scene of the day's standout manoeuvre.

Having led the majority of the 21-lap race, Mattia Pasini [Italtrans Kalex] was pushed back to third at turn one on the final lap, as both Thomas Luthi [Interwetten Kalex] and Alex Marquez [Marc VDS Kalex] pounced. But what followed was truly remarkable. First, Pasini lined up Marquez at Casanova, before diving under at Savelli. In a flash, the Italian was by Luthi too, moving past at Arrabbiata 1.

"He did the race that every Italian rider dreams about at night," said Rossi. A first grand prix win since this race nine years before was just reward for Pasini's remarkable last lap.

2017 FIM MotoGP™ WORLD CHAMPIONSHIP

10 | CZECH REPUBLIC

A championship can often turn in an instant. As the Moto2 race entered its eighth lap, another rain shower arrived. At that point, it had all been going rather well for title leader Franco Morbidelli (Marc VDS Kalex), who sat second, with main rival Thomas Luthi (Interwetten Kalex) seventh. But with the race red flagged, and a re-start scheduled for just six laps, Luthi sensed an opportunity.

Run in wet conditions, the Swiss rider fitted a rear tyre that he had previously run in similar conditions on Friday. It was an inspired choice, as he gained the hole-shot, easing clear of Alex Marquez [Marc VDS Kalex] to win his first race of the year by 4.9 seconds. Morbidelli endured a nightmare six laps, struggling to eighth place, 19 seconds back, his 34-point championship lead shrinking to 17 in the blink of an eye.

"I had a good feeling in warm-up in the wet," said Luthi. "The start was a key point. I tried to keep the rhythm. It's really cool to be on the top of the podium." Miguel Oliveira [Ajo KTM] was third.

11 | AUSTRIA

This was a thriller, with high-tension excitement fizzing throughout. The battle at the front was a three-way affair, with points leader Franco Morbidelli (Estrella Galicia Kalex) resisting huge pressure from title rivals Alex Marquez (Estrella Galicia Kalex) and Thomas Luthi (CarXpert Kalex). Both men took turns out front but only for a matter of moments before cool-headed Morbidelli moved back in front.

Morbidelli's resistance to pressure was remarkable – he never panicked or put a wheel wrong, always maintaining his composure while Marquez and Luthi did everything in their power to make their attacks stick. For much of the race Morbidelli was only a couple of tenths ahead, all three of the front-runners taking turns at riding the fastest lap. Finally the intense rivalry between Marquez and Luthi gave Morbidelli the break he needed, the 22-year-old Italian extending his advantage to a full second for the last three laps.

12 | GREAT BRITAIN

Takaaki Nakagami (Idemitsu Kalex) won his second Moto2 race, just days after it was announced that he will graduate to MotoGP in 2018. The 25-year-old Japanese ace dominated the race after taking the lead from championship leader Franco Morbidelli (Estrella Galicia Kalex).

Morbidelli spent the early stages chasing teammate Alex Marquez. The pair swapped the lead until Marquez slid off, then Morbidelli had Nakagami come past; the Japanese resisting serious late-race pressure from pole-starter Mattia Pasini (Italtrans Kalex).

Podium regular Thomas Luthi (Interwetten Kalex) didn't quite make the top three this time, taking fourth place. The battle for fifth was the most frantic of the race, with up to eight riders disputing the position, finally taken by rookie Francesco Bagnaia (Sky VR46 Kalex).

7 | CATALUNYA

Local hero Alex Marquez (Estrella Galicia Kalex) dominated the Moto2 race, leading all the way from pole position to chequered flag. Marc's 21-year-old younger brother set a stunning pace, building a one-second advantage on the first lap and extending his lead to over four seconds. He crossed the finish line 3.5 seconds ahead of Mugello winner Mattia Pasini (Italtrans Kalex), who beat podium-regular Thomas Luthi (Interwetten Kalex) by nine tenths.

World Championship leader Franco Morbidelli (Estrella Galicia Kalex) could only finish sixth, struggling with corner entry.

8 | NETHERLANDS

Starting the last 2.8-mile sprint of the 24 scheduled, Thomas Luthi [Interwetten Kalex] appeared to have timed a late attack on title rival Franco Morbidelli [Marc VDS Kalex] to perfection. But the wily Italian was back at turn nine, believing with total conviction he could hold Luthi at bay in the final sector. He did. But only just. 0.15 seconds was in it.

Takaaki Nakagami [IDEMITSU Honda Kalex] was third, but only after race direction judged Mattia Pasini's [Italtrans Kalex] cutting of the final chicane on the last two laps to be illegal. The Italian crossed the line third, but was soon demoted a place, much to his comical disdain. Miguel Oliveira [KTM Racing] and Alex Marquez [Marc VDS Kalex] also contributed to the best race in the intermediate category for years.

9 | GERMANY

Franco Morbidelli (Estrella Galicia 0,0 Kalex) scored a magnificent victory, beating Miguel Oliveira (Red Bull KTM) by six hundredths of a second. The Italian's sixth of the season increased his championship lead to 37 points over his title challengers – teammate Alex Marquez and Thomas Luthi (Interwetten Kalex) – crashed while challenging for the lead.

In the closing stages Morbidelli came under pressure from Oliveira, who was ahead on the penultimate lap. But Morbidelli wasn't prepared to take a safe second to protect his points lead, so he retook the lead on the last lap.

The battle for the final place on the podium was similarly exciting and ended in this order: Francesco Bagnaia (Sky VR46 Kalex), Simone Corsi (Speed Up) and Mattia Pasini (Italtrans Kalex).

Takaaki Nakagami had a week he'll never forget in August. First came the long-awaited announcement about a switch to partner Cal Crutchlow in the LCR Honda MotoGP squad. Seven days later he was victorious for only the second time in his career in Silverstone.

Sadly, with the triumph came tragedy too.

When Dominique Aegerter splashed his way to a universally popular win for Kiefer Racing in Misano, it felt like a triumph for the underdog.

It was a first win for a Suter chassis since Luthi had won in Valencia in 2014 and it was a first for Kiefer Racing since Stefan Bradl prevailed in Silverstone back in his title winning year in 2011. It was also a historic first 1-2 for Swiss talent.

Or so we thought. The euphoria sadly didn't last. News emerged in Japan that Aegerter had been disqualified from the Misano classification due to an illegal oil sample.

Immensely likeable team boss Stefan Kiefer put forward a strong and impassioned denial of any intentional wrongdoing.

The Misano disqualification quickly paled into insignificance when Kiefer passed away on the eve of practice for the Sepang round.

ABOVE | Tom Luthi's challenge was ended by two big crashes in Australia and another a week later in Malaysia

Moto2™ WORLD CHAMPIONSHIP STANDING

	RIDER	NAT	MANUFACTURER	POINTS
1	Franco Morbidelli	ITA	KALEX	308
2	Thomas Luthi	SWI	KALEX	243
3	Miguel Oliveira	POR	KTM	241
4	Alex Marquez	SPA	KALEX	201
5	Francesco Bagnaia	ITA	KALEX	174
6	Mattia Pasini	ITA	KALEX	148
7	Takaaki Nakagami	JPN	KALEX	137
8	Brad Binder	RSA	KTM	125
9	Simone Corsi	ITA	SPEED UP	117
10	Hafizh Syahrin	MAL	KALEX	106
11	Xavi Vierge	SPA	Tech 3	98
12	Dominique Aegerter	SWI	SUTER	88
13	Fabio Quartararo	FRA	KALEX	64
14	Jorge Navarro	SPA	KALEX	60
15	Luca Marini	ITA	KALEX	59
16	Lorenzo Baldassarri	ITA	KALEX	51
17	Marcel Schrotter	GER	SUTER	50
18	Sandro Cortese	GER	SUTER	43
19	Axel Pons	SPA	KALEX	27
20	Jesko Raffin	SWI	KALEX	26
21	Remy Gardner	AUS	Tech 3	23
22	Isaac Viñales	SPA	KALEX	18
23	Xavier Simeon	BEL	KALEX	16
24	Yonny Hernandez	COL	KALEX	16
25	Stefano Manzi	ITA	KALEX	14
26	Tetsuta Nagashima	JPN	KALEX	14
27	Khairul Idham Pawi	MAL	KALEX	10
28	Andrea Locatelli	ITA	KALEX	8
29	Ricard Cardus	SPA	KTM	7
30	Joe Roberts	USA	KALEX	6
31	Augusto Fernandez	SPA	SPEED UP	6
32	Alex de Angelis	RSM	KALEX	5
33	Danny Kent	GBR	SUTER	3
34	Edgar Pons	SPA	KALEX	2
35	Iker Lecuona	SPA	KALEX	2
36	Ikuhiro Enokido	JPN	KALEX	2
37	Tarran Mackenzie	GBR	SUTER	1
38	Federico Fuligni	ITA	KALEX	1
39	Eric Granado	BRA	KALEX	
40	Julian Simon	SPA	KALEX	
41	Ryo Mizuno	JPN	KALEX	
42	Karel Hanika	CZE	KALEX	
43	Axel Bassani	ITA	SPEED UP	
44	Steven Odendaal	RSA	NTS	
45	Jake Dixon	GBR	SUTER	

13 | SAN MARINO

For title leader Franco Morbidelli [Marc VDS Kalex], all was going well in the first three laps of his home race. He had built up a 2.4 second lead, pole-man Mattia Pasini [Italtrans Kalex] had already fallen, and title rival Thomas Luthi [Interwetten Kalex] was fifth, and struggling to find any feeling amid the murk.

But so often these episodes change in an instant. Braking for turn eight, Morbidelli tucked the front, leaving Dominique Aegerter [Kiefer Suter] free at the front. Soon Luthi was up to speed. The following 19 laps were a cat-and-mouse game between he and his countryman, with Hafizh Syahrin [Petronas Kalex] lurking in third. Ultimately Luthi had a championship to consider, and eased off on the final lap. Morbidelli's lead is cut from 29 to nine points as a result.

"I saw Tom was always behind and I didn't want to crash," said Aegerter, basking in his first win since Germany '14, and Suter's first since Valencia the same year. "It's amazing to win here."

14 | ARAGÓN

Franco Morbidelli (Estrella Galicia Kalex) scored a brilliant Moto2 victory, winning a red-hot duel with Mattia Pasini (Italtrans Kalex) on the final lap. It was a particularly impressive and hard-fought success, considering that Morbidelli could have settled for a risk-free second-place finish to extend his championship advantage over fourth-place finisher Thomas Luthi (Interwetten Kalex).

Morbidelli dominated the early stages, building a 1.5 second lead, until Pasini got up to full speed as his fuel load lightened. The Italians spent the second half of the race locked together, Pasini getting ahead on several occasions, only for Morbidelli to counter-attack. On the last lap Morbidelli made his final, decisive move at the downhill turn nine, holding his advantage to the finish to win by 0.145 seconds.

Pole-position man Miguel Oliveira (Red Bull KTM) was with the leaders in the first laps but couldn't quite go with Morbidelli as the pace increased.

15 | JAPAN

Alex Marquez (Estrella Galicia Kalex) fought his way through the spray to take an impressive win from Xavi Vierge (Tech 3). It was the 21-year-old former Moto3 Champion's third Moto2 victory, since his first at Jerez in May.

Vierge's excellent second-place finish, just 1.4 seconds behind Marquez was his first GP podium. Third place went to Hafizh Syahrin (Petronas Kalex) who enjoyed an impressive charge through the pack. An impressive Francesco Bagnaia (Sky Racing Team VR46 Kalex) took fourth place from Mattia Pasini (Italtrans Racing Team Kalex) and pole-starter and long-time leader Takaaki Nakagami (Idemitsu Asia Kalex), who lost speed in the closing stages as the rain eased.

The race was crucial for the outcome of the championship, with series leader Franco Morbidelli (Estrella Galicia Kalex) taking eighth, three places ahead of challenger Thomas Luthi (CarXpert Interwetten Kalex) who suffered vision problems in the spray.

16 | AUSTRALIA

From as early as the winter tests, it was more a case of 'when', not 'if' KTM's tubular steel chassis would win out in the intermediate category. After a season of high promise, Miguel Oliveira (Ajo KTM) finally delivered, dominating until a light shower arrived with three laps to go, making for a tense finale.

Mid-race charger Takaaki Nakagami overtook both Brad Binder (Ajo KTM) and Franco Morbidelli to sit a strong second. Sensing Oliveira's nerves with three laps to play, Nakagami pushed on, only for transmission issues to force a fast crash at Lukey Heights.

Oliveira never looked back thereafter, with Binder easing clear of Morbidelli [Marc VDS Kalex] for a safe second and KTM one-two. "It was the longest race of my life," said Oliveira. "When it started to rain I struggled a little but now I just feel happiness."

It was another disastrous day for Morbidelli's title rival Thomas Luthi [Interwetten Kalex]. A crash on Sunday morning left the Swiss rider battered and bruised. He could do no better than tenth.

17 | MALAYSIA

The drama arrived on qualifying day. Chasing title rival Franco Morbidelli's pole time [Marc VDS Kalex], Thomas Luthi high-sided his Interwetten Kalex on the exit of turn two. Upon landing the Swiss rider fractured his left ankle, and banged his head, forcing his withdrawal from Sunday's race. With Luthi unable to score points, Morbidelli – 29 points ahead in the title race – was automatically crowned champion.

It was no surprise then that the race that followed was something of a damp squib. Miguel Oliveira [Ajo KTM] was never headed in a dominant showing that resulted in a winning margin of 2.3 seconds. It was a second straight one-two for the ever-improving KTM chassis, with Brad Binder [Ajo KTM] breaking clear of Morbidelli in the closing laps to claim a second podium in as many weeks.

"My plan wasn't to break away," said Oliveira. "I was going to follow Brad and Franco but I went for it. The race was so long. I was able to keep my focus and continue to pull away."

18 | VALENCIA

Miguel Oliveira (Red Bull KTM) scored a superb third consecutive victory, hunting down recently crowned champion Franco Morbidelli (Estrella Galicia Kalex) during the final stages. Morbidelli tried everything but could not keep the Portuguese rider at bay, so he settled for second comfortably ahead of Oliveira's teammate Brad Binder, who achieved his third successive podium.

Twenty-two-year-old Oliveira came through from the second row of the grid, but took some time to get the better of pole-sitter Alex Marquez (Estrella Galicia Kalex) who contested the early lead with teammate Morbidelli. That tussle cost Oliveira a lot of time, so that when he finally made it into second place, he was more than two seconds behind the leader.

Oliveira applied himself to this task with typical precision. He made a strong pass at turn four on lap 22 of 27. Morbidelli eventually completing the race 2.154 seconds behind the winner and two seconds ahead of Binder.

Moto2™ World Champions 2017

Thanks to all our riders, teams, partners, suppliers, employees and fans

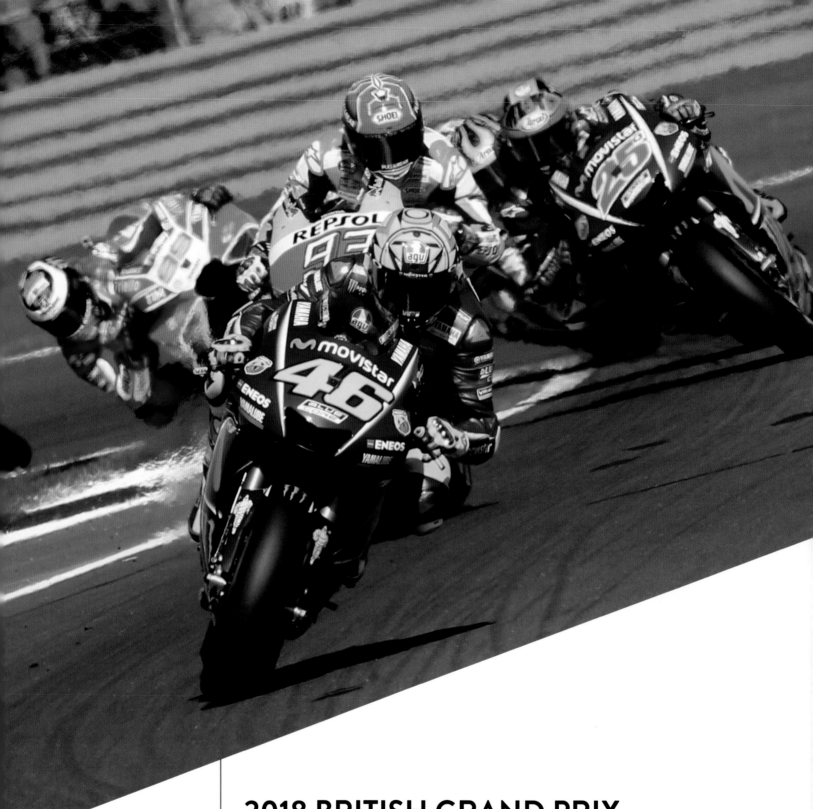

MIR THE MAGICIAN

The story of the 2017 Moto3 World Championship turned into a fairytale for one outstanding young Spanish talent.

Predicted to be the most open title race since Moto3 was introduced in 2012, Joan Mir blended master tactics, peerless speed and unerring consistency to transform the year into a record-breaking romp.

Before this year, only Valentino Rossi, Marc Marquez and Fausto Gresini were members of an exclusive club to have won ten or more races in a single season in the lightweight World Championship.

Mir added his name to that star-studded group in a season he and Honda enjoyed unrivalled domination.

Mir won seven of the first 11 races and only once in that purple patch - in Germany - did he win from the front row.

Wins from 16th in Argentina, eighth in France and tenth in Austria demonstrated flair and aggression but also composure and maturity way beyond his 20 years.

Those rampages through the field prompted his Leopard Racing squad to brand him 'Miracle Mir'. That seemed a wholly appropriate moniker, as his performances earned him rave reviews from the top talent in MotoGP and a contract to move to Moto2 with the high-profile Estrella Galicia 0,0 Marc VDS squad in 2018.

Winning the title became a Mir formality and he had his first chance to wrap it up in Japan's Twin Ring Motegi.

An uncharacteristic but entirely understandable nervy ride to 17th in a rain-lashed Japanese Grand Prix put the champagne on ice. But a return to winning ways in a typically frantic Phillip Island battle cut short by rain meant he became Spain's third Moto3 World Champion alongside Maverick Viñales and Alex Marquez.

Mir's dazzling form was the main contributing factor in Honda handing out a pummeling to rivals KTM.

Andrea Migno's debut win for SKY Racing Team VR46 in a memorable Mugello melee?? was the Austrian factory's solitary success. And Honda's superiority was so one-sided that its NSF250R machine locked out the podium in all but four races??

A third place and career first podium for Marcos Ramirez in Sachsenring, a first podium in two years for Philipp Oettl in Austria, and a rare top three for Niccolo Antonelli in Japan avoided further humiliation for KTM.

Honda's other victories were shared equally between Romano Fenati and Aron Canet???

Fiery Fenati was back to restore his reputation, which had been tarnished by his ruthless dismissal from Rossi's SKY Racing Team in Austria the previous summer.

A lifeline was thrown by the Marinelli Rivacold Snipers Honda project and Fenati was the rain master of Misano and Motegi with convincing wins in both.

Too often though he slipped off the radar with 13th place finishes in Mugello and Red Bull Ring, which seriously undermined his title aspirations.

Canet broke his victory duck in front of a delirious home crowd in Jerez and there were further wins in Assen and Silverstone.

But his title challenge was dented by costly crashes in Austin, Sachsenring and Misano.

Jorge Martin was the undisputed qualifying king of 2017 on the Del Conca Gresini Honda. But a pole position count that nearly hit double figures wasn't converted into an elusive first win?? Martin had speed to burn over one lap but his title hopes were vanquished by a vicious practice high-side in Sachsenring, which left him with a broken right tibia, ankle and heel.

Scotsman John McPhee started the season in sparkling form with back-to-back second places behind Mir in Qatar and Argentina. Only one other podium followed in Assen as inconsistency crept in and by the end of the year the ambitious British Talent Team announced it was going into temporary self-imposed exile at World Championship level.

The Dorna-supported initiative to unearth and nurture British prospects will instead concentrate on a two-rider project with Tom Booth-Amos and Charlie Nesbitt in the Spanish-based FIM CEV Repsol Moto3 Junior World Championship.

LEFT | *Andrea Migno's win at Mugello was a rare victory for KTM against the Honda armada*

RIGHT, CLOCKWISE FROM TOP LEFT | *Romano Fenati was fast but infuriatingly inconsistent; Hondas lead the way at Catalunya; Joan Mir leads a typically frantic Moto3 pack; Jorge Martin was the pole-position king but his maiden win proved elusive; the Class of '17; the Estrella Galicia duo of Aaron Canet and Enea Bastianini did not have the impact expected*

1 | QATAR

Honda riders monopolised a Moto3 podium for the first time since the 2015 German GP, 19-year-old Spaniard Joan Mir (Leopard Honda) beating Scotsman John McPhee (British Team Honda) by 0.135 seconds and pole-starter Jorge Martin (Del Conca Honda) by a further 0.083 seconds.

Aron Canet (Estrella Honda) and Romano Fenati (Marinelli Honda) completed the top five, with Andrea Migno (Sky VR46 KTM) the first non-Honda finisher.

2 | ARGENTINA

2016's principal lesson in Moto3 was a cool head goes a long way in the frantic junior class. And as Sunday's 21-lap brawl showed us, 19-year old Spaniard Joan Mir [Leopard Honda] possesses an ice-cool temperament that matches an unquestionable speed.

Caught out by a late shower in qualifying, Mir was all-but-stranded by the session's end. Not to worry, however, as he ascended the order from 16th on the grid with ease, joining fellow front runners John McPhee (British Team Honda), Jorge Martin (Gresini Honda), Philipp Oettl (Schedl Racing KTM) and Andrea Migno (Sky VR46 KTM) as early as lap six.

Ultimately, he maintained his calm in the face of McPhee's attentions all the way to the flag, braking almost to the point of no return at turn 13 to defiantly defend his position. McPhee was second, 0.26 seconds back, Martin third.

3 | USA

Disgraced Moto3 star Romano Fenati (Marinelli Honda) scored his comeback win at COTA, eight months after he had been sacked by Rossi's Sky VR46 team for bad behaviour.

Ironically, Fenati won the race after launching a Rossi/Laguna 2008 style on pole-starter Aron Canet (Estrella Galicia Honda), who had been way faster than anyone on practice. Finally Canet lost his cool and crashed, just as Casey Stoner did at Laguna in 2008.

The podium was monopolised by Honda riders for the third consecutive race, with Gresini team-mates Jorge Martin and Fabio Di Giannantonio.

4 | SPAIN

Seventeen-year-old Aron Canet (Estrella Galicia Honda) won a thrilling Moto3 race at the very last corner, passing Romano Fenati (Snipers Honda) and Joan Mir (Leopard Honda) to score his first GP victory and head a fourth-consecutive all-Honda podium.

The race was a typical Moto3 encounter, with a dozen riders fighting in the lead group. In the final laps the contest for victory was reduced to four, with Canet, Fenati and Mir battling with Marcos Ramirez (Platinum Bay KTM), who crossed the line in fourth, just two tenths behind the winner.

5 | FRANCE

Teenager Joan Mir (Leopard Honda) won a dominant victory to increase his points lead after closest title challengers Romano Fenati (Marinelli Honda) and Jorge Martin (Del Conca Honda) crashed out.

The race was restarted after a mass pile-up, triggered by a rider who had fallen on lap one, then picked up his machine and leaked oil onto the asphalt.

Fenati took charge of the restart, chased by Martin and Mir. Martin was the first to fall, then Fenati. Mir was joined on the podium by Aron Canet (Estrella Galicia Honda) and Martin's teammate Fabio Di Giannantonio.

6 | ITALY

It's official. This was the closest grand prix of them all. A wild, hair-raising 20-rider dash along Mugello's front straight was as stupefying as it sounds. The form book was suitably thrown out the window, as 22 men were covered by 1.5 seconds with three laps remaining.

In the end, home hero Andrea Migno [Sky VR46 KTM] held his nerve on the last lap to hold off the ever-present Fabio Di Giannantonio [Gresini Honda] to clinch his maiden GP win by three hundredths of a second, and KTM's first of the year. By the race's standards, Juanfran Guevara [RBA Racing KTM] was a long way off (0.166 seconds) in third.

2017 FIM MotoGP™ WORLD CHAMPIONSHIP

7 | CATALUNYA

Joan Mir (Leopard Honda) won a brilliant, last-gasp Moto3 victory, snatching the lead from Jorge Martin (Del Conca Honda) four corners before the chequered flag. Mir's move pushed Martin wide, which allowed Romano Fenati (Marinelli Honda) to dive past at the chicane, demoting Martin to third.

The top three were separated by less than three tenths of a second. Mir's fourth victory of 2017 extends his championship lead to 45 points over Fenati.

8 | NETHERLANDS

Judging by showings in Qatar, Argentina and Barcelona, few can match the mettle of championship leader Joan Mir (Leopard Honda) in a last lap shootout. But Moto3 is rarely straightforward. Here, the Majorcan led a dramatic eleven-rider gaggle into the circuit's final sector for the final time.

It was here that he came undone. Running wide at turn ten was enough to allow one, two, three bikes and more through. Taking advantage of his countryman's error, Aron Canet [Estrella Galicia Honda] resisted Romano Fenati's [Snipers Honda] advances at the final chicane for a second win of the year, with John McPhee [British Talent Honda] a tight third. Mir was ninth, 0.98 seconds back from the winner.

9 | GERMANY

Nineteen-year-old Spaniard Joan Mir (Leopard Honda) won a thrilling three-way contest, banishing memories of his last-lap mistake at Assen. Mir's fifth success of the season increased his title lead to 37 points.

Mir spent most of the race fighting with COTA winner Romano Fenati (Snipers Honda) and first-time podium finisher Marco Ramirez (KTM). Positions changed constantly, Mir timing his final attack to perfection, diving past Fenati at the penultimate corner. The trio was just two tenths of a second apart at the flag.

Assen winner Aron Canet (Estrella Galicia Honda), crashed out while in the middle of a frantic 14-rider skirmish for sixth place.

10 | CZECH REPUBLIC

As the season lurches into its second half, Joan Mir [Leopard Honda] still can do no wrong. Starting a damp Moto3 race, the Spaniard took his time to assess the conditions as Bo Bendsneyder [Ajo KTM] and Juanfran Guevara [RBA KTM] made the early running. As Mir edged closer, title contender Romano Fenati [Snipers Racing Honda] joined the fray, and ultimately it was the championship's leading two men who forged ahead in the final three laps.

Despite Fenati's best efforts, Mir couldn't resist a hairy out-braking attempt on the final lap to claim his sixth win from ten outings this year. Not since 1997, when a certain Valentino Rossi was on his way to a maiden world crown, has a rider in the junior class been as greedy in the opening ten run outs - quite an omen.

Aron Canet [Estrella Galicia Honda] completed a remarkable comeback from 22nd on lap two to overhaul Bendsneyder and Guevara on the final lap for third.

11 | AUSTRIA

Joan Mir (Leopard Honda) performed another fabulous disappearing act, fighting through from tenth on the grid to leave the pack way behind. While a gang of up to 14 riders disputed second place Mir maintained an astonishingly fast pace, at one point stretching his lead to more than four seconds.

Finally the 19-year-old Spaniard crossed the finish line three tenths ahead of Philipp Oettl (KTM), who was three seconds in front of Jorge Martin (Del Conca Honda), contesting his first race since returning to injury. Just 1.6 seconds covering second place to 14th, with seven Hondas in the top ten.

Mir's amazing record of seven victories puts him 64 points ahead in the championship chase.

12 | GREAT BRITAIN

Aron Canet (Estrella Galicia Honda) won a breath-taking and shortened Moto3 race, fighting his way through from 16th on the grid, the result of a strategic error in qualifying. The 17-year-old Spaniard led an all-Honda top three, from teammate Enea Bastianini and Jorge Martin (Del Conca Honda).

The race was typical harum-scarum stuff, with positions changing constantly. At half-distance the top 17 were covered by 1.9 seconds and when the red flag came out the top 11 were separated by 1.7 seconds. The race was stopped, after Juanfran Guevara (KTM) and Bo Bendsneyder (KTM) crashed. Neither was badly hurt.

Numerous riders led, including championship leader Joan Mir (Leopard Honda), who finally placed fifth, teammate Livio Loi who came in sixth, and pole-starter Romano Fenati (Snipers Honda), who was seventh.

The intention is to revive the British Talent Team in the future and McPhee was not completely cut adrift. Dorna found him a seat on a KTM in the CIP squad for 2018.

Another high-profile project will also be missing from the 2018 Moto3 World Championship grid.

Indian manufacturer Mahindra first entered the World Championship back in 2011 and it enjoyed a breakthrough 2016 when Pecco Bagnaia won twice in Assen and Sepang. McPhee also won on board a Peugeot-branded Mahindra in Brno, but an alarming slump in results in 2017 was fundamental to Mahindra's decision to depart and focus exclusively on Formula E and electric mobility.

There was a happy swansong when Marco Bezzecchi, who is another product of the seemingly endless production line of talent rolling out of Rossi's VR46 Academy, took his first podium and Mahindra's last in treacherously wet conditions in Japan for the CIP Team.

It's worthy of mention too that while Nakarin Atiratphuvapat's 13th place in Le Mans didn't grab many global headlines, it did give him the honour of being the first Thai rider ever to score points in the lightweight World Championship.

ABOVE | Joan Mir dominated the year and moves up to Moto2 for 2108 with the Marc VDS team

Moto3™ WORLD CHAMPIONSHIP STANDING

	RIDER	NAT	MANUFACTURER	POINTS
1	Joan Mir	SPA	HONDA	341
2	Romano Fenati	ITA	HONDA	248
3	Aron Canet	SPA	HONDA	199
4	Jorge Martin	SPA	HONDA	196
5	Fabio di Giannantonio	ITA	HONDA	153
6	Enea Bastianini	ITA	HONDA	141
7	John McPhee	GBR	HONDA	131
8	Marcos Ramirez	SPA	KTM	123
9	Andrea Migno	ITA	KTM	118
10	Philipp Oettl	GER	KTM	105
11	Juanfran Guevara	SPA	KTM	88
12	Nicolo Bulega	ITA	KTM	81
13	Livio Loi	BEL	HONDA	80
14	Tatsuki Suzuki	JPN	HONDA	71
15	Bo Bendsneyder	NED	KTM	65
16	Gabriel Rodrigo	ARG	KTM	54
17	Adam Norrodin	MAL	HONDA	42
18	Niccolò Antonelli	ITA	KTM	38
19	Darryn Binder	RSA	KTM	35
20	Ayumu SASAKI	JPN	HONDA	32
21	Jules Danilo	FRA	HONDA	29
22	Jakub Kornfeil	CZE	PEUGEOT	26
23	Marco Bezzecchi	ITA	MAHINDRA	20
24	Dennis Foggia	ITA	KTM	19
25	Nakarin Atiratphuvapat	THA	HONDA	16
26	Albert Arenas	SPA	MAHINDRA	14
27	Jaume Masia	SPA	KTM	13
28	Lorenzo dalla Porta	ITA	MAHINDRA	9
29	Manuel Pagliani	ITA	MAHINDRA	8
30	Kaito Toba	JPN	HONDA	7
31	Kazuki Masaki	JPN	HONDA	6
32	Danny Kent	GBR	KTM	6
33	Alex Fabbri	RSM	MAHINDRA	3
34	Tony Arbolino	ITA	HONDA	2
35	Maria Herrera	SPA	KTM	1
36	Tim Georgi	GER	KTM	
37	Tom Booth-Amos	GBR	KTM	
38	Patrik Pulkkinen	FIN	PEUGEOT	
39	Tom Toparis	AUS	KTM	
40	Raul Fernandez	SPA	MAHINDRA	
41	Maximilian Kofler	AUT	KTM	
42	Aaron Polanco	SPA	HONDA	
43	Gabriel Martinez-Abrego	MEX	KTM	
44	Aleix Viu	SPA	KTM	

13 | SAN MARINO

For what Moto3 lacked in fighting toward the front, it more than made up for in the drama of seeing which rider could stay up. Just 15 of the 31 starters made it to the chequered flag, with four of those 15 falling and remounting.

There would be no stopping Romano Fenati [Rivacold Snipers Honda] once he took command on lap three. Regularly a second faster than his pursuers per lap, the Italian came home 28 seconds clear - the third biggest winning margin in Moto3 history - of title rival Joan Mir [Leopard Honda]. Fabio Di Giannantonio [Gresini Honda] took a distant third after Aron Canet [Estrella Galicia Honda] fell disputing the final podium place.

"The water changed lap by lap," Fenati explained. "In the middle of the race there was less water then it rained again. I'm happy because this is not my perfect condition. I push from the start, kept the gap and managed the race to the end."

14 | ARAGÓN

The brilliant Joan Mir (Leopard Honda) scored his eighth Moto3 victory of the year in nerve-jangling style, pouncing on the final lap to beat Fabio Di Giannantonio (Gresini Honda) by 0.043 seconds, with Enea Bastianini (Estrella Galicia Honda) a further 0.008 seconds behind.

'Miracle Mir', as he is known by his team, Di Giannantonio and Bastianini were closely followed over the line by Jorge Martin (Gresini Honda), Aron Canet (Estrella Galicia Honda) and John McPhee (British Team Honda), who finished half a second behind the winner and made it an all-Honda top six.

After the race Mir was sanctioned for overly-aggressive weaving on the final lap: a penalty of six grid positions at the next race.

The first non-Honda rider was Marcos Ramirez (Platinum Bay Real Estate KTM), who finished just seven tenths behind Mir.

15 | JAPAN

Romano Fenati (Marinelli Rivacold Snipers Honda NSF250RW) once again proved his brilliance in wet, slippery conditions by taking a dominant victory, just weeks after he won in similar soaking conditions at Misano.

Fenati's third victory of the year kept the championship alive. Series leader Joan Mir (Leopard Honda) went into the race holding a mammoth 80-point lead, but finished outside the points in 17th position. The young Spaniard had started from 20th on the grid – the result of a sanction imposed at the last race – and the atrocious visibility prevented him from moving forward.

16 | AUSTRALIA

The rain may have arrived to prematurely end this eight-rider thriller, but for the laps before the brief storm it was hard to envision this result going any other way. Joan Mir [Leopard Honda] put his Honda NSF250RW at the front of the pack, showing just why he has been a champion-in-waiting for several months.

Having repeatedly tried to break clear through the twisty section, Mir's advantage would be decimated by slipstream along the front straight. Still, he led when it really mattered – crossing the line first on lap 15 when the heavy rain arrived. 25 points was sufficient in wrapping up a first world title for the Majorcan after that brief wobble in Japan. "It's incredible when you follow something with all your strength for a lot of years, and then you achieve it, it's an amazing feeling," said Mir with a now insurmountable lead.

Teammate Livio Loi [Leopard Honda] was second, with pole sitter Jorge Martin [Gresini Honda] a frustrating third, 1.2 seconds covering the top eight at the flag.

17 | MALAYSIA

For the second weekend running, recently crowned champion Joan Mir [Leopard Honda] batted away comparisons to Valentino Rossi. It wasn't just the manner of the 20-year old's tenth win of the season at Sepang, achieved in his now trademark style – watching over his rivals before a well-timed and thought out late push - that had reporters mentioning him in the same breath as the GOAT. One more win in '17 and Mir will equal Rossi's 20-year old record of eleven wins in the junior category across a calendar year.

This latest triumph was no less impressive than the nine that came before. Chasing down early leader Jorge Martin [Gresini Honda], Mir timed his late attack to perfection, breaking clear of his countryman and late charger Enea Bastianini [Estrella Galicia Honda] with three laps to go to come home 0.7 seconds ahead.

"It was difficult to manage with the heat but it's the best way to celebrate a World Championship," he said. "At the end, we've done a fantastic season." Another plan that came to fruition.

18 | VALENCIA

Jorge Martin (Del Conca Honda) finally achieved his first Grand Prix victory, at the end of his 50th World Championship race. The 19-year-old started from pole for the eighth time in 2017, led from the start, then broke clear of the pack when Gabriel Rodrigo (RBA KTM) crashed just behind him, sending world champ Joan Mir (Leopard Honda) off the track and down to 19th.

By half-distance Martin was five seconds ahead of the dozen riders fighting for second place. Mir was the star of this battle, fighting his way back into podium contention to secure second place, which gave him the record for the most points scored in one season in the junior class.

Marcos Ramirez (Platinum Bay KTM) took the final place on the podium, crossing the line 0.117 seconds behind Mir and 0.076 seconds ahead of Romano Fenati (Snipers Honda), the championship runner-up. The group from second place to ninth crossed the line covered by 1.458 seconds, led by Enea Bastianini (Estrella Galicia Honda) in fifth place.

MASAKI LETS THE RESULTS DO THE TALKING

Kazuki Masaki's quiet nature is typical 'old school' Japanese, there is no self promotion, no overt arrogance, not even a surfeit of confidence. The 17-year-old does have a big smile and a huge amount of talent and with a perfect blend of consistency, determination backing up two race wins he took the Red Bull MotoGP Rookies Cup for 2017.

It was the eleventh Cup season with thirteen wonderful races on the superb KTM RC 250 Rs and enough drama to satisfy anyone. The enormously colourful Öncü twins from Turkey, who started the season just 13-years-old, set the series alight. Can looked an odds-on favourite for overall victory mid season after taking four wins in five races, including an Assen double.

Diminutive twin Deniz took the victory that Can missed in the middle of that quartet, Race 1 at the Sachsenring, then won again in Brno Race 2 making it a solid six race run of Öncü victories and Turkish national anthems.

Just when one nation seemed to have taken a grip on Rookies Cup the Japanese swamped the podium at the Red Bull Ring, taking all three places in Race 1. Ai Ogura, the 16-year-old won with Masaki second and 15-year-old Ryusei Yamanaka third.

Masaki won Race 2 and having already a solid six podiums to his name, he closed in on points leader Can Öncü who's season had started to show a few cracks when he slid off in Race 1 at Brno the previous weekend.

It was Can Öncü's fall at Misano though that really set up the Motorland Aragon finale as far as points were concerned. Masaki clinched the Cup with a perfect Race 1 win in Spain after an incredibly exciting race. Can Öncü was fifth, just not close enough to keep his hopes alive.

Aleix Viu, the 16-year-old Spaniard, had, with Can Öncü and Masaki, come to Aragon with a chance to take the Cup, just as he did twelve months previously. He crossed the line third in Race 1 and that was also not close enough to maintain his chances into Race 2.

Viu won the final race though in great style to overtake Can Öncü for second in the points, the same place he took in the 2016 Cup. Both Can Öncü and Masaki fell, showing just easily the fate of the Cup might have been different.

Demonstrating great class, Masaki, who had been unable to avoid the machine of Ogura crashing in front of him, managed to remount after some difficulty. He regained the track a lap behind but still then set the fastest lap of the race.

Both Masaki and Viu finished all their races through the season and apart from that final unlucky outing by Masaki, they were all in the points. Can Öncü had three race ending falls and losing those points cost him dear.

Otherwise Can Öncü was incredibly impressive as well as a lot of fun, those four wins were backed up by a second place, two thirds and a fifth. His season hadn't started that well, being involved in a multi bike first corner drama in Jerez. He remounted to finish 18th.

That first race was won by Rory Skinner, the 15-year-old Scot starting his third Rookies Cup season as one of the favourites. It was a well deserved victory but if you are an Ogura fan you might claim it was lucky as the pair were locked in an intense battle for the lead when the race was red flagged.

Ogura was actually in front at the time but with the result counted back to the last full lap, Skinner got the verdict. If there was any luck in that it was the last that Skinner saw all season. In the second race Skinner ran off track as he chased the lead and regained the circuit in an unsafe manner, colliding with Sean Kelly, the pair fell. Kelly was hurt enough to be taken for hospital for checks while Skinner got a grid penalty for Race 1 in Assen.

Skinner's fifth in Assen was a good result but after that the edge went off things and he couldn't finish in the top six. He ended the season very much back on the pace in Aragon where he had taken pole at the end of his first season but in the last lap wrestling match he came out seventh.

Deniz Öncü had, like his brother, been caught up in that first corner Jerez mess,

he took ninth in Race 2 while his brother grabbed third. The winner was Viu, very much pre-season favourite after two wins, six seconds and a third took him to overall second in the Cup the year before.

The intense fight at the head of the field in Race 1 at Jerez left Viu fifth and under no illusion that he would have an easy run to overall Cup victory. He took an excellent win in Race 2 though and left Jerez with the points lead.

He only had a three point advantage over Ogura and 15-year-old Czech Filip Salač but when both were injured in non Rookies Cup races and forced to miss the next four races Viu was effectively granted a nine point lead with Masaki the next man in the table.

Deniz Öncü's third in Race 2 at Jerez had been a warning. Hardly fair warning though for he obliterated the opposition in Assen. He won Race 1 from pole, no one got close after the first few laps and for Race 2 he was determined that they wouldn't even manage that.

Rain showers hung in the air as start time approached so a wet race was called and the distance shortened from 16 to 14 laps with the certainty that the Dunlop wet tyres would go the distance even if the rain stayed away.

Can Öncü looked at the sky, felt the sprinkle of rain and made a plan. "I knew that it really might rain heavily and I am not so good in the wet so I thought I would push as much as possible while the track was dry. So I went for it from the start and built as much of a lead as I could."

Though a misty drizzle hung around it was only right at the end that a heavier shower really wetted he track. "Suddenly it was slippery at a couple of corners, I was a bit lucky, had a big slide but stayed on the bike," admitted Öncü.

"I am so happy for these two wins and I know that next weekend in Germany my brother can continue to improve and I think we can both be on the podium there," enthused Can, doubly happy to see his twin brother Deniz take an excellent 5th after a race long battle in the huge chasing group.

It sounded a bit like sibling support but when Race 1 at the Sachsenring was soaking wet, Deniz was unbeatable. Can finished third behind 17-year-old local hero Kevin Orgis and the rest of the field were 20 seconds back.

Viu had taken a double podium in Assen as had Masaki but both suffered in the wet in Germany, Viu 15th and Masaki 10th. They bounced back to join Can Öncü on the podium in Race 2 while Deniz retired with loss of engine coolant.

Winning Race 1 in Brno seemingly put Can Öncü on course for the title, he was making it look easy. Then he crashed out of a wet Race 2 with a comfortable lead leaving his brother to again show his skill in such conditions, six races in a row to the Öncüs.

First lap collisions at the Red Bull ring left Can Öncü and Viu recovering to 14th and 10th respectively well behind the podium dominating Japanese. Öncü bounced back with second in Race 2 but Viu again had an off track excursion when he got too close to the Turk on the brakes and had to take avoiding action. He finished 11th and the weekend saw seen him slip to third in the points table.

Masaki cursed himself early in the year for being too cautious in the early laps. It was probably his only weak point and he certainly had that sorted by the end of the year to become a very worthy Rookies Cup champion.

The Japanese has the talent and experience to swell the ex-Rookie contingent that makes up half the Moto3 grid. Joan Mir is the third ex-Rookie Moto3 World Champion in a row. Masaki remains quiet, clearly very happy with his deserved success and hopefully his results will speak loudly for themselves, because he will not.

LEFT | *Kazuki Masaki with a happy grin, Cup winner at Motorland Aragon*

MIDDLE | *Kazuki Masaki (39) leads the pack off the line*

RIGHT | *The top three: Aleix Viu (81), Kazuki Masaki (39) and Can Öncü (65)*

TWO WHEELS FOR LIFE

PHOTOGRAPHERS | Tom Oldham (main) and Simon Devine

WHO WE ARE AND WHAT WE DO

Two Wheels for Life in 2017

Transport management is one of the most neglected yet most important aspects of the healthcare supply chain.

We know that one health worker on a motorcycle can reach almost 6 times the number of people and cover 6 times the distance in the same time when compared with health workers who have to walk. And most health workers in Africa have to walk - very long distances.

We are working to change this woeful situation and with your support we are on the road to success.

Our mission is to see resources focussed on the management of transport for predictable and reliable healthcare delivery and access for communities - however remote they may be.

THE WORK WE SUPPORT

Ensuring healthcare reaches even the most remote communities

Ensuring healthcare reaches even the most remote communities, Two Wheels for Life supports local development partner Riders for Health, delivering programmes in Sub-Saharan Africa.

Programmes in Lesotho, Liberia, Malawi, Kenya, Nigeria, Gambia and Zimbabwe

ensure that no matter how remote communities are, how poor or inaccessible the roads, healthcare can reach those who need it.

Vehicles are chosen to be suitable to the local terrain and serviced regularly, so they will always be ready and up to the job.

They are used by health workers to reach women in threatening labour and to transport critical diagnosis of HIV, AIDS and TB.

The programmes we support consistently reduce maternal and child mortality and cut in half the turnaround time for diagnosis of HIV, AIDS, TB and epidemics like Ebola.

A TALE OF TWO VILLAGES

By Barry Coleman, co-founder or Riders for Health

On a recent, sunlit Thursday morning, Maria Gonzalez, board member of Two Wheels for Life, stood beneath a tough old tree and looked at the insides of Lesotho.

What she saw was a landscape that is unlike any other, anywhere. Visitors sometimes draw comparisons. It's a bit like the Yorkshire moors, say the British ones. Very much like Wyoming, say the well-travelled Americans. Very much like the highlands of Aragon, or of Almeria, say the Spanish ones.

As they climb higher, as the truck struggles more, as the roads give up and the goats take over, the truth dawns. There's nowhere quite like this.

Not like this in a number of ways. 'Stunning' is a popular word these days. You hear or see it everywhere, from cookery shows to travel brochures. Of course the scenery of Lesotho is stunning. But even more stunning is the experience of the people who live in it.

In the first village that Maria and the visitors visited there is beautiful singing, stitched and refined into three and four part harmonies polished over hundreds of years. They are singing because for an hour or so, their isolation is over. Visitors have come, to say hello and to understand. Under another tree stands a motorcycle, a Suzuki. Among the visitors is the rider, who is actually a frequent visitor to the village.

She is Mahali Hlasa, the Riders for Health programme director for Lesotho. One of the programmes that Two Wheels for Life supports with money raised at Day of Champions and elsewhere. She speaks for a while (in one of the languages of Lesotho, 'Sesotho'), the headman replies and someone translates. There is laughter. They are pleased, they say, with the care and attention that the ministry of health and Riders give them. If there is HIV/AIDS it is dealt with. Blood samples are collected, the results are returned and treatment is close at hand.

In another village, higher yet, and far poorer, far smaller and with a still more 'stunning' view, there was no singing. In a small, uncomfortable hut, a woman was dying. Awful, stunning. But what was she dying of? We don't know and it matters. If it was AIDS or its buddy everyday tuberculosis, we could lift her, touch her, take her to hospital. But if it were the other TB, the multi-drug-resistant one, we could not. No-one could. There are very strict rules. She would die at a distance, untouchable. MDR TB is so, so much worse than Ebola, so much worse than any plague.

It's a beautiful country. Nowhere like it. Stunning.

Maria Gonzalez came down from the mountains somewhat changed. She could see that what Lesotho needs is more health workers reaching more people, more often. It needs more support, particularly more motorcycles and more ambulances that reach these remote places.

What now? Well, we'll see you at Day of Champions next year. Maria and Mahali will be there and so will all the MotoGP riders. And some of us, who have been going to those mountains as well as Day of Champions for many years, will hear, to the tune of one of Bob Marley's most famous songs...

WE'LL ALL GET TOGETHER; GONNA BE ALRIGHT.

MAIN | *Health care arrives by motorcycle at a clinic in Liberia*

LEFT | *Maria Gonzalez, board member of Two Wheels for Life, with school children in Lesotho*

MIDDLE | *Nnena and Makhata, child monitors for World Vision in Lesotho being trained to ride motorcycles by Riders for Health*

RIGHT | *Motorcycle couriers in Lesotho play a vital role in rapid diagnosis and treatment of disease*

FIND OUT MORE AT | TWOWHEELSFORLIFE.ORG.UK

FUNDRAISING

Raising money with our partners in MotoGP™

Two Wheels for Life are proud to be the official charity of MotoGP™ and the FIM. With their support we are able to run unique events and offer exclusive experiences to motor racing fans throughout the world, including our annual flagship event, Day of Champions.

Whether it's an exclusive Paddock Experience in Spain, a family day out before the British MotoGP™ or a weekend in the paddock at a top race circuit, racing fans can be part of the movement that shows two wheels save lives.

On Thursday 24th August, 4000 dedicated racing fans joined together with the MotoGP™ family at Silverstone, once again kick-starting the Octo British Grand Prix, raising an incredible £237,000.

With the support and dedication of the racing family Two Wheels for Life raised over £321,000 in 2017.

BELOW | *Photos from Day of Champions, 2017*

500cc

YEAR	RIDER	NAT	MANUFACTURER
1949	Leslie Graham	GBR	AJS
1950	Umberto Masetti	ITA	GILERA
1951	Geoff Duke	GBR	NORTON
1952	Umberto Masetti	ITA	GILERA
1953	Geoff Duke	GBR	GILERA
1954	Geoff Duke	GBR	GILERA
1955	Geoff Duke	GBR	GILERA
1956	John Surtees	GBR	MV AGUSTA
1957	Libero Liberati	ITA	GILERA
1958	John Surtees	GBR	MV AGUSTA
1959	John Surtees	GBR	MV AGUSTA
1960	John Surtees	GBR	MV AGUSTA
1961	Gary Hocking	CAF	MV AGUSTA
1962	Mike Hailwood	GBR	MV AGUSTA
1963	Mike Hailwood	GBR	MV AGUSTA
1964	Mike Hailwood	GBR	MV AGUSTA
1965	Mike Hailwood	GBR	MV AGUSTA
1966	Giacomo Agostini	ITA	MV AGUSTA
1967	Giacomo Agostini	ITA	MV AGUSTA
1968	Giacomo Agostini	ITA	MV AGUSTA
1969	Giacomo Agostini	ITA	MV AGUSTA
1970	Giacomo Agostini	ITA	MV AGUSTA
1971	Giacomo Agostini	ITA	MV AGUSTA
1972	Giacomo Agostini	ITA	MV AGUSTA
1973	Phil Read	GBR	MV AGUSTA
1974	Phil Read	GBR	MV AGUSTA
1975	Giacomo Agostini	ITA	YAMAHA
1976	Barry Sheene	GBR	SUZUKI
1977	Barry Sheene	GBR	SUZUKI
1978	Kenny Roberts	USA	YAMAHA
1979	Kenny Roberts	USA	YAMAHA
1980	Kenny Roberts	USA	YAMAHA
1981	Marco Lucchinelli	ITA	SUZUKI
1982	Franco Uncini	ITA	SUZUKI
1983	Freddie Spencer	USA	HONDA
1984	Eddie Lawson	USA	YAMAHA
1985	Freddie Spencer	USA	HONDA
1986	Eddie Lawson	USA	YAMAHA
1987	Wayne Gardner	AUS	HONDA
1988	Eddie Lawson	USA	YAMAHA
1989	Eddie Lawson	USA	HONDA
1990	Wayne Rainey	USA	YAMAHA
1991	Wayne Rainey	USA	YAMAHA
1992	Wayne Rainey	USA	YAMAHA
1993	Kevin Schwantz	USA	SUZUKI
1994	Mick Doohan	AUS	HONDA
1995	Mick Doohan	AUS	HONDA
1996	Mick Doohan	AUS	HONDA
1997	Mick Doohan	AUS	HONDA
1998	Mick Doohan	AUS	HONDA
1999	Àlex Crivillé	ESP	HONDA
2000	Kenny Roberts, Jr.	USA	SUZUKI
2001	Valentino Rossi	ITA	HONDA

MotoGP™

	RIDER	NAT	MANUFACTURER
2002	Valentino Rossi	ITA	HONDA
2003	Valentino Rossi	ITA	HONDA
2004	Valentino Rossi	ITA	YAMAHA
2005	Valentino Rossi	ITA	YAMAHA
2006	Nicky Hayden	USA	HONDA
2007	Casey Stoner	AUS	DUCATI
2008	Valentino Rossi	ITA	YAMAHA
2009	Valentino Rossi	ITA	YAMAHA

MotoGP™

	RIDER	NAT	MANUFACTURER
2010	Jorge Lorenzo	ESP	YAMAHA
2011	Casey Stoner	AUS	HONDA

MotoGP™

	RIDER	NAT	MANUFACTURER
2012	Jorge Lorenzo	ESP	YAMAHA
2013	Marc Marquez	ESP	HONDA
2014	Marc Marquez	ESP	HONDA
2015	Jorge Lorenzo	ESP	YAMAHA
2016	Marc Marquez	ESP	HONDA
2017	Marc Marquez	ESP	HONDA

250cc

	RIDER	NAT	MANUFACTURER
1949	Bruno Ruffo	ITA	MOTO GUZZI
1950	Dario Ambrosini	ITA	BENELLI
1951	Bruno Ruffo	ITA	MOTO GUZZI
1952	Enrico Lorenzetti	ITA	MOTO GUZZI
1953	Werner Haas	GER	NSU
1954	Werner Haas	GER	NSU
1955	Hermann Paul Müller	GER	NSU
1956	Carlo Ubbiali	ITA	MV AGUSTA
1957	Cecil Sandford	GBR	MONDIAL
1958	Tarquinio Provini	ITA	MV AGUSTA
1959	Carlo Ubbiali	ITA	MV AGUSTA
1960	Carlo Ubbiali	ITA	MV AGUSTA
1961	Mike Hailwood	GBR	HONDA
1962	Jim Redman	CAF	HONDA
1963	Jim Redman	CAF	HONDA
1964	Phil Read	GBR	YAMAHA
1965	Phil Read	GBR	YAMAHA
1966	Mike Hailwood	GBR	HONDA
1967	Mike Hailwood	GBR	HONDA
1968	Phil Read	GBR	YAMAHA
1969	Kel Carruthers	AUS	BENELLI
1970	Rodney Gould	GBR	YAMAHA
1971	Phil Read	GBR	YAMAHA
1972	Jarno Saarinen	FIN	YAMAHA
1973	Dieter Braun	GER	YAMAHA
1974	Walter Villa	ITA	HARLEY DAVIDSON
1975	Walter Villa	ITA	HARLEY DAVIDSON
1976	Walter Villa	ITA	HARLEY DAVIDSON
1977	Mario Lega	ITA	MORBIDELLI
1978	Kork Ballington	ZAF	Kawasaki
1979	Kork Ballington	ZAF	Kawasaki
1980	Anton Mang	GER	Kawasaki
1981	Anton Mang	GER	Kawasaki
1982	Jean-Louis Tournadre	FRA	YAMAHA
1983	Carlos Lavado	VEN	YAMAHA
1984	Christian Sarron	FRA	YAMAHA
1985	Freddie Spencer	USA	HONDA
1986	Carlos Lavado	VEN	YAMAHA
1987	Anton Mang	GER	HONDA
1988	Sito Pons	ESP	HONDA
1989	Sito Pons	ESP	HONDA
1990	John Kocinski	USA	YAMAHA
1991	Luca Cadalora	ITA	HONDA
1992	Luca Cadalora	ITA	HONDA
1993	Tetsuya Harada	JPN	YAMAHA
1994	Max Biaggi	ITA	APRILIA
1995	Max Biaggi	ITA	APRILIA
1996	Max Biaggi	ITA	APRILIA
1997	Max Biaggi	ITA	HONDA
1998	Loris Capirossi	ITA	APRILIA
1999	Valentino Rossi	ITA	APRILIA
2000	Olivier Jacque	FRA	YAMAHA
2001	Daijiro Kato	JPN	HONDA

250cc

	RIDER	NAT	MANUFACTURER
2002	Marco Melandri	ITA	APRILIA
2003	Manuel Poggiali	SMR	APRILIA
2004	Dani Pedrosa	ESP	HONDA
2005	Dani Pedrosa	ESP	HONDA
2006	Jorge Lorenzo	ESP	APRILIA
2007	Jorge Lorenzo	ESP	APRILIA
2008	Marco Simoncelli	ITA	GILERA
2009	Hiroshi Aoyama	JPN	HONDA

Moto2™

	RIDER	NAT	MANUFACTURER
2010	Toni Elías	ESP	MORIWAKI
2011	Stefan Bradl	GER	KALEX

Moto2™

	RIDER	NAT	MANUFACTURER
2012	Marc Marquez	ESP	SUTER
2013	Pol Espargaró	ESP	KALEX
2014	Esteve Rabat	ESP	KALEX
2015	Johann Zarco	FRA	KALEX
2016	Johann Zarco	FRA	KALEX
2017	Franco Morbidelli	ITA	KALEX

125cc

	RIDER	NAT	MANUFACTURER
1949	Nello Pagani	ITA	MONDIAL
1950	Bruno Ruffo	ITA	MONDIAL
1951	Carlo Ubbiali	ITA	MONDIAL
1952	Cecil Sandford	GBR	MV AGUSTA
1953	Werner Haas	GER	NSU
1954	Rupert Hollaus	AUT	NSU
1955	Carlo Ubbiali	ITA	MV AGUSTA
1956	Carlo Ubbiali	ITA	MV AGUSTA
1957	Tarquinio Provini	ITA	MONDIAL
1958	Carlo Ubbiali	ITA	MV AGUSTA
1959	Carlo Ubbiali	ITA	MV AGUSTA
1960	Carlo Ubbiali	ITA	MV AGUSTA
1961	Tom Phillis	AUS	HONDA
1962	Luigi Taveri	CHE	HONDA
1963	Hugh Anderson	AUS	SUZUKI
1964	Luigi Taveri	CHE	HONDA
1965	Hugh Anderson	AUS	SUZUKI
1966	Luigi Taveri	CHE	HONDA)
1967	Bill Ivy	GBR	YAMAHA
1968	Phil Read	GBR	YAMAHA
1969	Dave Simmonds	GBR	Kawasaki
1970	Dieter Braun	GER	SUZUKI
1971	Ángel Nieto	ESP	DERBI
1972	Ángel Nieto	ESP	DERBI
1973	Kent Andersson	SWE	YAMAHA
1974	Kent Andersson	SWE	YAMAHA
1975	Paolo Pileri	ITA	MORBIDELLI
1976	Pier Paolo Bianchi	ITA	MORBIDELLI
1977	Pier Paolo Bianchi	ITA	MORBIDELLI
1978	Eugenio Lazzarini	ITA	MBA
1979	Ángel Nieto	ESP	MINARELLI
1980	Pier Paolo Bianchi	ITA	MBA
1981	Ángel Nieto	ESP	MINARELLI
1982	Ángel Nieto	ESP	GARELLI
1983	Ángel Nieto	ESP	GARELLI
1984	Ángel Nieto	ESP	GARELLI
1985	Fausto Gresini	ITA	GARELLI
1986	Luca Cadalora	ITA	GARELLI
1987	Fausto Gresini	ITA	GARELLI
1988	Jorge Martínez	ESP	DERBI
1989	Àlex Crivillé	ESP	JJ COBAS
1990	Loris Capirossi	ITA	HONDA
1991	Loris Capirossi	ITA	HONDA
1992	Alessandro Gramigni	ITA	APRILIA
1993	Dirk Raudies	GER	HONDA
1994	Kazuto Sakata	JPN	APRILIA
1995	Haruchika Aoki	JPN	HONDA
1996	Haruchika Aoki	JPN	HONDA
1997	Valentino Rossi	ITA	APRILIA
1998	Kazuto Sakata	JPN	APRILIA
1999	Emilio Alzamora	ESP	HONDA
2000	Roberto Locatelli	ITA	APRILIA
2001	Manuel Poggiali	RSM	GILERA

125cc

	RIDER	NAT	MANUFACTURER
2002	Arnaud Vincent	FRA	APRILIA
2003	Dani Pedrosa	ESP	HONDA
2004	Andrea Dovizioso	ITA	HONDA
2005	Thomas Lüthi	CHE	HONDA
2006	Álvaro Bautista	ESP	APRILIA
2007	Gábor Talmácsi	ITA	APRILIA
2008	Mike di Meglio	FRA	DERBI
2009	Julián Simón	ESP	APRILIA

125cc

	RIDER	NAT	MANUFACTURER
2010	Marc Marquez	ESP	DERBI
2011	Nicolás Terol	ESP	APRILIA

Moto3™

	RIDER	NAT	MANUFACTURER
2012	Sandro Cortese	GER	KTM
2013	Maverick Viñales	ESP	KTM
2014	Alex Márquez	ESP	HONDA
2015	Danny Kent	GBR	HONDA
2016	Brad Binder	ZAF	KTM
2017	Joan Mir	SPA	HONDA